Archival Irruptions

RELIGIOUS CULTURES OF AFRICAN AND AFRICAN DIASPORA PEOPLE
Series editors:
Jacob K. Olupona, Harvard University
Dianne M. Stewart, Emory University
and Terrence L. Johnson, Georgetown University

The book series examines the religious, cultural, and political expressions of African, African American, and African Caribbean traditions. Through transnational, cross-cultural, and multidisciplinary approaches to the study of religion, the series investigates the epistemic boundaries of continental and diasporic religious practices and thought and explores the diverse and distinct ways African-derived religions inform culture and politics. The series aims to establish a forum for imagining the centrality of Black religions in the formation of the "New World."

Archival Irruptions

Constructing Religion and Criminalizing Obeah in Eighteenth-Century Jamaica

KATHARINE GERBNER

Duke University Press *Durham and London* 2025

© 2025 DUKE UNIVERSITY PRESS.
This work is licensed under a Creative Commons Attribution-Noncommercial 4.0 International License, available at https://creativecommons.org/licenses/by-nc/4.0/.

Project Editor: Bird Williams
Typeset in Garamond Premier Pro by Westchester Publishing Services

Library of Congress Cataloging-in-Publication Data
Names: Gerbner, Katharine, [date]– author.
Title: Archival irruptions : constructing religion and criminalizing Obeah in eighteenth-century Jamaica / Katharine Reid Gerbner.
Other titles: Constructing religion and criminalizing Obeah in eighteenth-century Jamaica | Religious cultures of African and African diaspora people.
Description: Durham : Duke University Press, 2025. | Series: Religious cultures of African and African diaspora people | Includes bibliographical references and index.
Identifiers: LCCN 2024060613 (print)
LCCN 2024060614 (ebook)
ISBN 9781478032403 (paperback)
ISBN 9781478029038 (hardcover)
ISBN 9781478061250 (ebook)
ISBN 9781478094364 (ebook other)
Subjects: LCSH: Obeah (Cult)—Jamaica—History—18th century. | Religion and sociology—Jamaica—History. | Black people—Jamaica—Religion—History. | Cults—Jamaica—History. | Witchcraft—Jamaica—History. | Religions—African influences.
Classification: LCC BL2532.O23 G47 2025 (print)
LCC BL2532.O23 (ebook)
DDC 299.6/7—dc23/eng/20250319
LC record available at https://lccn.loc.gov/2024060613
LC ebook record available at https://lccn.loc.gov/2024060614

Cover art: Moravian church register from Jamaica, 1759. Unitätsarchiv der Evangelischen Brüder-Unität, Herrnhut, Germany, R.15.C.a.02.05.02.

This book is freely available in an open access edition thanks to TOME (Toward an Open Monograph Ecosystem)—a collaboration of the Association of American Universities, the Association of University Presses, and the Association of Research Libraries—and the generous support of the University of Minnesota. Learn more at the TOME website, available at openmonographs.org.

For my parents, Anne and John Gerbner

Contents

Acknowledgments
ix

INTRODUCTION
1

PART I:
OBEAH

PART I INTRODUCTION
15

1
AFRICANA IRRUPTIONS
Baptism, Obeah, and Spaces of Correlation
17

2
RELIGIO-NATIONS IN THE ARCHIVES
Re/formations of Sacred Communities
37

3
MAROONS, BLOOD OATHS, AND
GENDERED IRRUPTIONS
Accompong and Margery
61

PART II:
HEUCHELEI

PART II INTRODUCTION
81

4
ARCHIVAL SILENCE, SEXUAL VIOLENCE
Reading for Re/membrance
83

5
POLICING BODIES, SAVING SOULS
Dissimulation in the Archives
101

6
CONSTRUCTING RELIGION, DEFINING CRIME
Assembling, Congregating, Binding
121

EPILOGUE
Land and Archive: Identifying and Interpreting Irruptions
141

Appendix 1
147
Appendix 2
149

Notes   Bibliography   Index
153   183   211

Acknowledgments

Let me begin by thanking the archivists who organize, preserve, and provide access to the sources I used to write this book. I could not have completed this research without the guidance of Paul Peucker at the Moravian Archives in Bethlehem, Pennsylvania. I learned how to read German Script from Paul and Lanie Graf in 2009, while Tom McCullough has tracked down several documents for me over the years. Learning German Script was a transformative experience that opened the world of the German Moravian records to me. Over the years, I have visited the Moravian Church House archives in London, where Lorraine Parsons welcomed me warmly; and I spent several months in Herrnhut, Germany, at the Unitätsarchiv der Evangelischen Brüder-Unität, where Rüdiger Kröger and Olaf Nippe helped me discover and discern the archival records from Jamaica and the Danish West Indies. I am grateful to them and to Claudia Mai, the current archives director, as well as the staff at the Unity Archives, for their help. I am also grateful to the Pietsch-Jentsch family, who opened their home to me during my stay in Berthelsdorf and Herrnhut.

While most archival sources for this project are held in Pennsylvania, Germany, and London—a legacy of mission history and colonialism—research in Jamaica was essential for writing this book. I am indebted to Craig Atwood and Bishop Hopeton Clennon for connecting me with several Moravians in Jamaica. Rev. Dr. Paul Gardner helped me find the Bogue plantation and the Carmel estate in St. Elizabeth Parish, and I am grateful to him and to Wilton Burton, who accompanied us to the Bogue and showed us the monument to the first missionaries at New Eden. In Accompong Town, Chief Richard Currie offered a kind welcome, and helped connect me with local Maroons. In Kingston, James Robertson and Linda Sturtz were fantastic hosts. They have also offered excellent feedback on many chapter drafts over the years. At the University of the West Indies–Mona, I am grateful to the archivists in the West Indies and Special Collections: Bernadette Worrell-Johnson, Paulette Kerr, Yulande Lindsay, and Frances Salmon. I also benefited from my conversation with Stanley Griffin about archives and archiving. Thank you.

Several mentors, colleagues, and friends offered support and encouragement during the earliest stages of research. Vincent Brown helped me navigate my first foray into these archives, and he remains a trusted mentor. His research has long been an inspiration for me, and I have been grateful for his incisive advice over the years. The late Richard Dunn gave me access to his primary research on Mesopotamia plantation, and I shared my early translations of the Moravian missionary records with him, which he used for his 2014 publication, *A Tale of Two Plantations*. I remain grateful to him and the late Mary Dunn for inviting me into their scholarly community with such generosity. David D. Hall has been a steadfast supporter, and I am grateful for his kindness and insight over many years.

Early in my research, I had the good fortune of meeting Kelly Wisecup, who invited me to participate in a special issue about Obeah in *Atlantic Studies*, where I published an early version of my findings. In 2015, soon after my *Atlantic Studies* article was published, I received an email from Dianne Stewart—a scholar I had never met, but whose work I had read and admired. This email was a turning point for me. At the time, I was a junior scholar, anxious about my research and my future. This gesture of unsolicited support from a senior scholar helped give me the confidence to expand my research on Obeah and the Moravian missionary archive into a full-length book. It is an honor to have this manuscript published as part of Dr. Stewart's co-edited series, Religious Cultures of African and African Diaspora People, at Duke University Press.

Acts of generosity from colleagues and friends continued to fuel my research as I imagined the full book project. Conversations with and/or feedback from Craig Atwood, Ken Bilby, Randy Browne, the late Trevor Burnard, Bradley Craig, Brent Crosson, Mitch Fraas, Marisa Fuentes, Aisha Ghani, Pablo Gómez, Glenda Goodman, Jerome Handler, Kelly Kaelin, Hillary Kaell, Terence Keel, Kathryn Lofton, Mona Oraby, Diana Paton, Paul Peucker, Shari Rabin, Shavagne Scott, Jon Sensbach, Dianne Stewart, Sasha Turner, and Tisa Wenger have helped me articulate key arguments in these pages. Alexis Wells-Oghoghomeh gave excellent feedback on the full manuscript, for which I am profoundly thankful. I am also grateful to my Am Civ cohort, especially Caitlin DeAngelis, Maggie Gates, Caitlin Rosenthal, Stephen Vider, and Tom Wickman, and for their enduring friendship. Thanks especially to Tom, Cate, and Stephen for their excellent feedback over the years.

I presented a draft of my book prospectus to my 2018–19 cohort of Young Scholars in American Religion (YSAR) where I received both heartening enthusiasm and helpful feedback that helped me hone the vision for this book. Sylvester Johnson and Sally Promey, the mentors of my YSAR cohort, have been steadfast supporters and scholarly role models for me. Joe Blankholm, Melissa Borja, Chris Cantwell, Matt Cressler, Sarah Dees, Jamil Drake, Samira Mehta, Alexis Wells-Oghoghomeh, and Shari Rabin have become close friends as well as trusted colleagues.

I have presented chapters of this book at several venues over the years, and the feedback I received has been immensely helpful. Many thanks, especially, to members of the following workshops and institutions: the North American Religions Colloquium at Harvard, especially Catherine Brekus, David Hempton, Steven Harris, and Ryan Tobler; the Cultures of Freedom seminar at NYU and CUNY Graduate Center, led by Herman Bennett and Jennifer Morgan; the Johns Hopkins History Seminar, organized by Sasha Turner; the Temple Early Atlantic Seminar, especially Jessica Chopin Roney and Jeremy Schipper; the Department of History and Archaeology's Faculty/Graduate Seminar at the University of the West Indies–Mona; the participants in the Centre for Global History Seminar at the University of Edinburgh, organized by Diana Paton and Nuala Zahadieh; the University of York Research Seminar, especially Simon Ditchfield and Laura Stewart; the Reformation Studies Seminar at the University of St. Andrews, especially Arthur Der Weduwen, Emma Hart, and Andrew Pettegree; the McNeil Center's Brown Bag Seminar at the University of Pennsylvania; Lauren Kassell and the History of Science and Medicine working group at the European University Institute; the Oberseminar in Early Modernity at the University of Giessen; the Religion and US Empire workshop in Minneapolis, organized by Sylvester Johnson and Tisa Wenger; the POLY Seminar at the Goethe-Universität Frankfurt; the Sixteenth-Century Conference, where I received helpful feedback from Becky Goetz and Hal Parker; the Moravians and Race Conference in Bethlehem, Pennsylvania; the Sensory Cultures Research Group at Yale, organized by Sally Promey; the Different Archives, Different Histories conference at the University of Illinois–Chicago, especially Mark Canuel and Marisa Fuentes; Kathryn Gin Lum and the American Religions workshop at Stanford; the Princeton Space and Time Symposium organized by Seth Perry; and the Princeton Religions of the Americas Colloquium.

At the University of Minnesota, my thinking about archives and archival production has been profoundly influenced by my colleagues and my students. In 2017, I began teaching a graduate seminar on "The Early Modern Archive," which

I cotaught with Margaret Carlyle and then Sinem Casale. Teaching this course has helped me think through the many meanings of the archive and examine the innovative methods modern scholars have used to examine archival sources. The Early Modern Archive course also gave me the opportunity to invite scholars to Minnesota to discuss their work. These conversations—with Herman Bennett, Vincent Brown, Cécile Fromont, Glenda Goodman, Zeb Tortorici, Kelly Wisecup, and many others—have been transformative, and I am grateful to Lydia Garver and the Center for Premodern Studies (formerly CSPW) at the University of Minnesota for supporting this class. I am also indebted to my wonderful graduate students over the years, who have made this class a joy to teach.

In the History department at the University of Minnesota, I have benefited from the generosity and friendship of my colleagues. Jeani O'Brien and Zozan Pehlivan were especially supportive as I went through the peer review process, and I am grateful to them both. David Chang and MJ Maynes offered excellent feedback on an early draft of chapter 4, while Barbara Welke helped me hone my vision for this book. I want to thank the members of the Atlantic World workshop at UMN—especially Sarah Chambers, Kirsten Fischer, Lisa Norling, Sarah Pawlicki, James Robertson, Hannah Smith, Colleen Stockman, Linda Sturtz, Marie Balsey Taylor, and Joanne Jancke Wegner—for reading numerous chapters over the past several years. I am also grateful to members of the WCHWGS workshop and the Political Theory workshop at Minnesota for offering feedback on chapters 4 and 6, respectively.

As I got closer to completing this manuscript, I discovered the Writing Hunkers at the University of Minnesota. The Writing Hunkers in May and August 2022 gave me the determination to complete a full draft of this manuscript, while the hunker in January 2025 gave me the space to work through copyedits. I am especially grateful to Dan Emery and Lee Fisher, who gave excellent feedback on my introduction and epilogue. Nathanael Homewood offered helpful suggestions in the last stages of writing. Thanks also to my weekly hunker group, Gillian Flynn, Laura Kalba, and Kate Paesani; and to my writing group, Susannah Drake, Penny Geng, Amna Khalid, Pamela Klasova, and Ahoo Najafian. Your feedback and support have helped me through many difficult moments in the writing process.

Funding from the NEH and the University of Minnesota helped to make this book possible. A Grant-in-Aid and a Talle fellowship from the University of Minnesota allowed me to hire research assistants and conduct archival visits. A Faculty Development Leave meant that I could take a full year's research leave with my NEH fellowship. The Institute of Advanced Study at the University of Minnesota provided me with a semester free of teaching and a vibrant community of scholars—thanks especially to Bianet Castellanos, Dwight Lewis, and Dan Greenberg. A TOME grant from the University of Minnesota Libraries made it possible for this manuscript to be published open access.

The process of transcribing and translating the Moravian records from Jamaica was incredibly time consuming. I am grateful to my graduate research assistants, Adam Blackler, Tanner Deeds, and Stephan Knott, who helped me with this process by double-checking my transcriptions and helping with translations. This book is far stronger due to your care and attention to detail. Thanks also to Hannah Smith for her help in the final stages of preparation, and to Catherine Jampel, whose incisive feedback transformed this book.

At Duke University Press, I am grateful to Miriam Angress for shepherding my manuscript through the process of submission and revision. I would also like to thank Bird Williams for helping with copyedits and the production process. The two peer reviewers for Duke offered immensely generous and thoughtful feedback that has made this a much stronger book. Portions of this book have appeared in previous publications. An early version of my findings was published in *Atlantic Studies* under the title "They Call Me Obea," while parts of chapters 3 and 6 appeared in two different articles: "Maroon Science," published in the edited volume *Critical Approaches to Science and Religion*; and "Religion and Rebellion," in the coedited volume *Religion and US Empire*. Additionally, there are a few lines in chapter 4 that appeared in my *William & Mary Quarterly* article, "Archival Violence, Archival Capital." I am grateful to these publishers for allowing me to reprint portions of these articles.

Finally, to my family: I am fortunate that my sisters, Erzsi and Emily, as well as my aunts, uncles, cousins, and in-laws, all support my research and writing. My sister-in-law, Amy Hordes, helped with copyediting, as did my parents. My husband, Sean Blanchet, read every chapter of this book and his feedback has sharpened my writing. More importantly, he encouraged me when I felt demoralized, and—crucially—made writing a possibility by taking care of our children. During the last stages of writing, Sean's support was especially important as I juggled new administrative responsibilities with book edits. I could not have finished this book without him. Thank you. And thank you to my sweet children, Lolo, Issa, and Laz, who presented me with notes of encouragement that I found on my desk and on my bedside table. I love you so much.

I dedicate this book to my parents, Anne and John Gerbner, who have always supported my intellectual endeavors. I am increasingly grateful for the way that you raised me to feel confident enough to ask and investigate the questions I have about history and religion: You instilled a trust in me that has made it possible for me to become a scholar and a teacher. I don't always know where my research will take me, but I thank you for believing that wherever it is, it will be worthwhile.

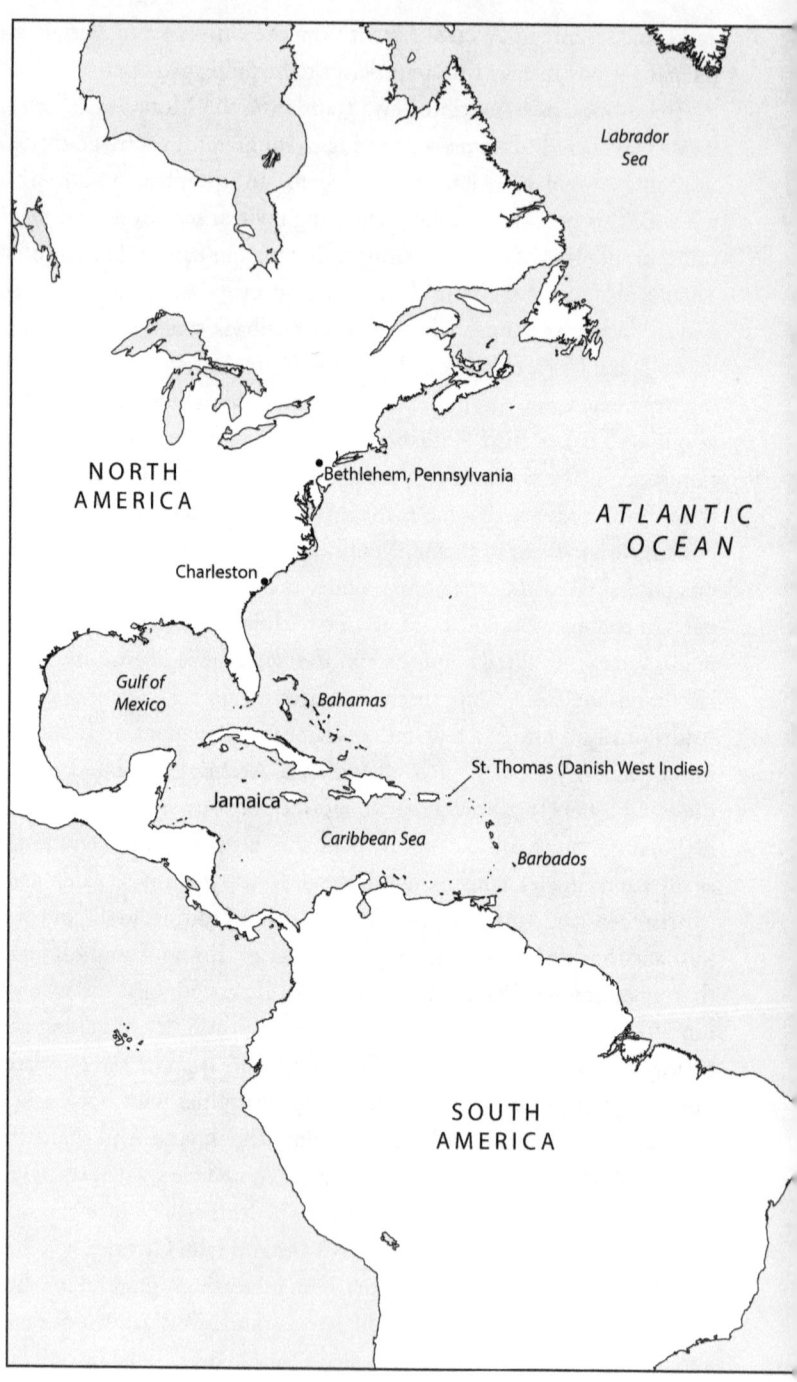

MAP FM.1. Map of the Atlantic World. Drawn by Bill Nelson for *Archival Irruptions*.

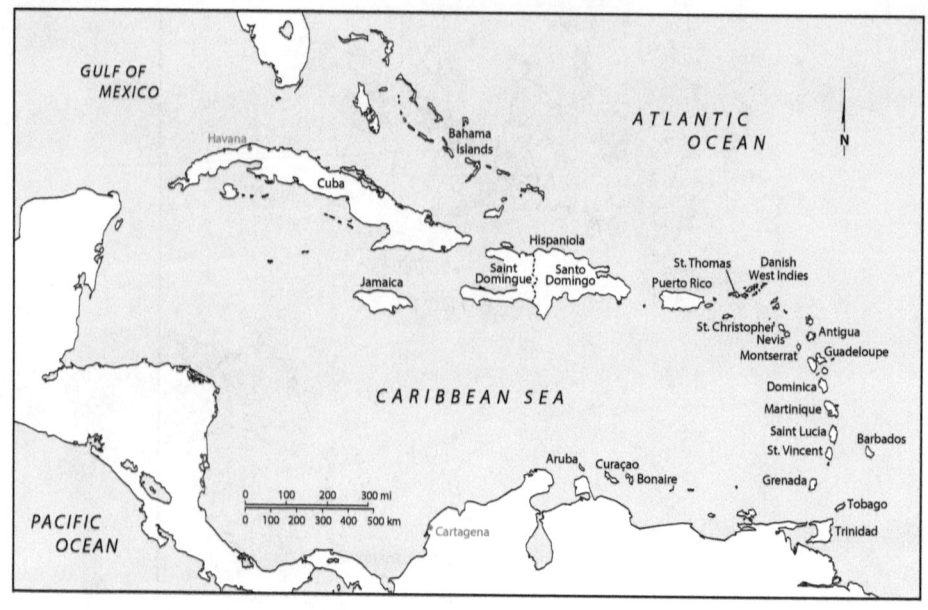

MAP FM.2. Map of the Caribbean. Drawn by Bill Nelson for *Archival Irruptions*.

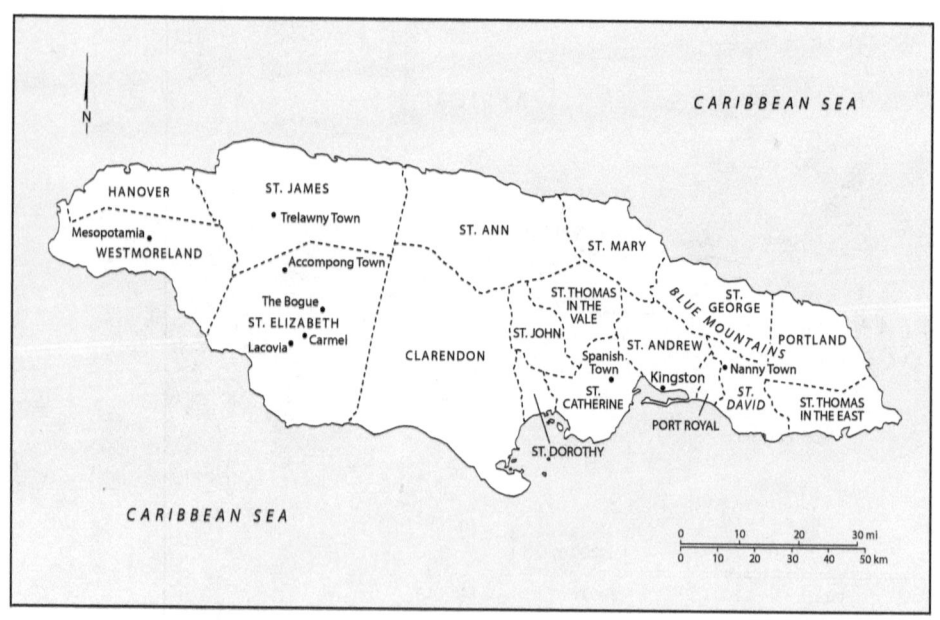

MAP FM.3. Map of Jamaica. Drawn by Bill Nelson for *Archival Irruptions*.

MAP FM.4. Map of western Jamaica. Drawn by Bill Nelson for *Archival Irruptions*.

Introduction

In December 1760, Obeah became a crime. Obeah, an Afro-Caribbean word that defies definition, has been called an Africana religion, a science, a healing practice, a form of black magic—and much more. While the meaning of Obeah remains a topic of debate, colonial lawmakers defined—and criminalized—Obeah as a "wicked Art" in the wake of Tacky's Revolt, the largest uprising of enslaved people in the eighteenth-century British Empire. The rebellion brought together Africans of diverse origins who waged a months-long attack on their enslavers. In response, lawmakers passed "The Act to Remedy the Evils arising from irregular Assemblies of Slaves," which was intended to prevent future uprisings. It was the first law to name Obeah, which was associated with "the Devil and other evil spirits."[1] The criminalization of Obeah has had long-lasting effects, and the practice remains a crime today in Jamaica.

Five years before Tacky's Revolt, Obeah entered the archives of slavery in very different terms. On March 17, 1755, a German Moravian missionary named

Zacharias George Caries wrote a letter to Johannes Watteville, a Moravian church leader. In his letter, Caries wrote, "they call me Obea[h], which supposedly means a Seer, or one who knows things that will happen in the future."[2] Caries's letter, which now sits in the Unitätsarchiv der Evangelischen Brüder-Unität in Herrnhut, Germany, is one of just a handful of archival references to Obeah before the practice was criminalized in 1760. Of those, it is the only source to describe Obeah outside the conceptual frameworks of witchcraft, superstition, or conjuring. Instead, it recounts how Afro-Jamaicans used the term. Most strikingly, it suggests that Obeah was not only an Afro-Caribbean practice: It was also the framework that Afro-Jamaicans used to interpret Moravian Christianity.

Archival Irruptions examines the chasm between Caries's description of Obeah as a prophetic tradition in 1755 and its criminalization in 1760. Chronologically, it uses these two events as bookends for a microhistorical study about the formation of religion as a category—a category that developed in the crucible of colonialism, missionization, and slavery. While missionaries policed the boundaries of Christianity, slave-owning legislators waged war on Africana sources of power. In their legal codes, they criminalized religio-political practices like Obeah and denigrated them as superstitious, antimodern, and evil. Their attacks were effective, and the oppression of Africana traditions such as Obeah has been formative for the modern category of religion.[3]

The state-sanctioned repression of Africana religions has made it difficult for scholars to write about the traditions that were targeted for criminalization, particularly during the colonial period. I address this problem by reading the archive for "irruptions," which I define as disruptions in the narrative field of an archival producer. There are many different types of irruptions, and I argue that Caries's reference to Obeah was an Africana irruption that creates an opportunity to write an alternative narration about Obeah in the Atlantic World.

The idea of an archival irruption—the methodological concept that underpins this book—builds on scholarship that interrogates the archive, especially in critical archival studies, Africana religious studies, and Native American and Indigenous studies.[4] I take inspiration from Lisa Brooks's metaphorical description of the "narrative field" of colonial archives, in which indigenous "weeds" can unsettle colonial narratives in unexpected ways.[5] I use the term *irruption* because it conveys a sense of rupture in the archive. *To irrupt* means to "to break into," often suddenly, while the noun *irruption* refers to the "act of bursting or breaking in."[6] By "bursting" into the narrative field of colonial and missionary archives, irruptions can be violent, but they also create narrative possibilities. I draw on both senses of the word in this book. Some irruptions I examine refer to unsettling themes and violent acts. Others, like Caries's reference to Obeah, offer a glimpse into a way of knowing that has been otherwise "silenced."

The Moravian archives from eighteenth-century Jamaica are an especially rich source of archival irruptions, but they have largely been ignored because they were written in *Kurrent*, an archaic form of handwritten German that requires specialized training to decipher.[7] Through a microhistory of the Moravian mission, alongside an analysis of British colonial and legal sources, I explore a series of irruptions in the archives. In doing so, I offer strategies for reading European archives through an Africana lens. While the current study focuses on Africana irruptions, the methods outlined here are applicable to studies of all colonial and missionary archives, and they can be utilized fruitfully alongside other archival strategies, such as reading "against the grain," reading "along the bias grain," or examining the "silences" in the archive.[8]

Reading for irruptions reveals a new story about Obeah, Christianity, and criminalization. For the Afro-Jamaicans who joined the Moravian church in the mid-1750s, there was initially a "space of correlation" between Obeah and Christianity.[9] This space of correlation was short-lived: in 1759, only four years after his arrival, Zacharias George Caries was expelled from the Jamaican mission, and the Moravian missionaries who replaced him eschewed any overlap between Obeah and Christianity. One story that this book tells is how the categories of Obeah and Christianity became incompatible through the twin processes of policing (chapter 5) and criminalization (chapter 6). This was not inevitable, and *Archival Irruptions* insists that we must reckon with the legacies of slavery to understand how and why some religious practices have been excluded from the lexicon of religion and criminalized.

The boundaries of religion have always been—and continue to be—policed, both within religious congregations and by colonial and postcolonial states. Still, it is not enough to say that Obeah belongs in the protected legal category of religion. Obeah was—and is—much more than that. While it is not possible to recover the full epistemic meaning of Obeah for its adherents in the eighteenth century, reading for Africana irruptions suggests that Obeah was a prophetic practice tied to healing modalities and death rites, and—crucially—formed a core component of what I call a religio-nation, a framework I describe at length in chapter 2. The term *religio-nation* is intended to draw attention to the fact that religious power was—and is—always political, and that political power is built on religious and sacred authority. This is true both for the Afro-Caribbean tradition of Obeah and for the British colonial state, which drew on notions of the sacred in its performance of lawmaking and policing (chapter 6). In criminalizing Obeah, Euro-Jamaican lawmakers sought to eradicate Obeah because it was a source of Africana religio-political power that threatened slavery and colonialism.

Re/formations

The examination of terms and categories is central to the methodology in this book. By reading for irruptions, we can see how modern categories were being re/formed under colonialism and slavery. I use the term *re/formations* to describe this process because it has multiple semantic fields of reference. When capitalized and written without a slash, the most common adjective to join *Reformation* is *Protestant*. One objective of *Archival Irruptions* is to center Africana theologies and Caribbean history within the long Reformation, including the transatlantic Protestant movements that followed it, such as the Great Awakening. The Moravian Church, which was founded in 1727 in eastern Germany, has played a central role in historical narratives about the transatlantic Great Awakening.[10] Beginning in the 1730s, the Moravian Church became a global missionary church, and Moravian missionaries focused their evangelism on non-Europeans.[11] George Whitefield and John Wesley, key figures in the Great Awakening, had close ties with the Moravian Church, and Moravians pioneered key revivalist strategies that were later replicated by the Methodist Church and many other Protestant denominations.[12] While the dominant story of the Great Awakening regarding Africans and their descendants has focused on the rise of Black Protestantism, *Archival Irruptions* tells a different kind of story, one that shows how Africana epistemologies are crucial for understanding the evolving meaning of Protestantism in the Atlantic world.[13]

Within the context of the African diaspora, the word *reformation* (not capitalized) takes on different contours, recalling classic debates about African cultures, societies, and religions as they moved across the Atlantic. Scholars have long debated how to theorize the consequences of enslavement and the Middle Passage on the myriad religious traditions of Africa, including Islam and Christianity. The core debate animating the field has pitted the survival and resilience of African religious traditions (retentions) against the creative development and adaptation of new religious and cultural traditions (creolization).[14] More recently, scholars have offered new metaphors and interpretive lenses to describe and analyze Black Atlantic histories, cultures, and religions through terms such as *re/membrance, religio-racial, dialogue, Africana nations,* or *assemblage*—to name just a few.[15] *Archival Irruptions* enters this conversation through a microhistory of one Afro-Moravian community in Jamaica. In this context, the term *reformation* underlines that religious traditions, whether European or African, were always in formation. I do this by arguing that the Moravian congregation in Jamaica should be understood as an Africana religio-nation, a concept I describe in chapter 2.

Finally, the idea of *re/formations* (lowercase, with a slash) connects with scholarship on the development of modern categories. *Archival Irruptions* argues that ideas about religion, crime, nation, and race were being formulated from the top down and the bottom up. Accordingly, this study is focused on the interplay between intimate relationships and legal codes, healing practices and state-sanctioned repression, parental caretaking and rebellion, sacred histories and sexual violence, the memory of ancestors, and missionary policies. It argues that we cannot understand the history of Christianity, the construction of crime, or the categories of religion and race without examining both intimate encounters and colonial statecraft within the context of slavery.

Re/formations of Religion

Historians of religion have long recognized that the modern category of religion developed, in part, out of the dynamics of imperialism.[16] *Archival Irruptions* places the construction of religion within the history of eighteenth-century Atlantic slavery and decenters colonial perspectives on religion by examining Africana epistemologies. I argue that scholars must examine the formation of religion under colonial slavery by reading for irruptions and analyzing the development of taxonomies. My method has three components: First, I read colonial and missionary archives for Africana irruptions to offer, in this case, an epistemological framework of Obeah before it was criminalized and excluded from the category of religion. Second, I attend to the ways that Europeans described the religio-political practices of others using freighted terms such as *fetish*, *superstition*, and *witchcraft*. Third, I examine the terms that scholars have used over the past century to denote practices that could fall under the category of "religious" or "religions." This method demonstrates that European archival sources rarely used the term *religion* to describe Africana religious practices, and modern scholars too often replicate these colonial sources.

Studying the intentional exclusion of Africana religio-political practices like Obeah from the category of religion is just as important as studying the construction of religion—if not more so. Scholars must be as attuned to the *absence* of religion as a category as to its presence. My methodological approach is inspired by Londa Schiebinger's concept of agnotology—the study of things that have been intentionally forgotten—and by studies of the African diaspora that counter epistemic violence and read colonial archives with an eye toward histories that have been suppressed.[17] I am especially influenced by studies of slavery and the archive, although these are rarely included in scholarship on the construction of religion. I argue that it is essential to attend to Africana scholarship and to read colonial and missionary archives for irruptions in order to identify epistemological formations outside the colonial construction of religion.

Ultimately, Africana traditions such as Obeah were both religions and sources of political power. In this way, Obeah can be compared to colonial political formations, which also sought to harness the power of the sacred to bind people together, a theme I explore in chapter 6. In keeping with this analysis, a larger argument of *Archival Irruptions* builds on the field of political theology, which emphasizes the interconnection between religion and politics. As a result, I often use the word *religio-political* to describe Obeah, and I argue that Obeah is a component of Africana religio-nation formation.

Re/formations of Crime

Many anti-colonial religious traditions—particularly those that were practiced under slavery—continue to be excluded from histories of religion because European authorities refused to recognize them as religions, and our archival documents bear that legacy. That refusal—a form of epistemic violence—was, I argue, the product of white colonials' and slaveholders' fear of slave rebellion and anti-colonial protest. Slave-owning lawmakers regarded Africana religious practices as dangerous, blamed Black religious leaders for slave rebellions, and categorized their practices as criminal. In thinking through the co-construction of religion and crime, my project builds on recent scholarship that has shown how policing the boundaries of religion has played—and continues to play—a central role in colonial and postcolonial governance.[18] By comparing slave law with missionary records that trace everyday life, it is possible to examine the dynamic creation of new ideas about "legitimate" religion and "criminal" worship practices. In doing so, *Archival Irruptions* argues that no study of religion can ignore the history of criminalization that has delegitimized and sought to eradicate sources of religious power that were used to protest against the colonial state.

Material objects were central to the way that missionaries and Protestant colonists defined and policed African religious and political practice. In fact, it is essential to stress that colonial lawmakers utilized a terminology in their lawbooks that limited most descriptions of African religious practice to a description of *objects*. Take, for example, the aforementioned 1760 Jamaican law. It specified that anyone who should make use of "any Blood, Feathers, Parrots Beaks, Dogs Teeth, Alligators Teeth, Broken Bottles, Grave Dirt, Rum, Egg-shells or any other Materials relative to the Practice of Obeah or Witchcraft" shall be convicted of "death or Transportation."[19] The word *religion* was rarely used in conjunction with African practices. This tactic, I argue, was intentional—an attempt to delegitimize African diasporic religious and intellectual history by materializing it. Within the context of Protestant theology and political theory, the emphasis on the material operated to exclude Africans from the sphere of the legitimately religious.

Re/formations of Race

The category of religion was constituted alongside evolving ideas about race and the creation of racial slavery. In my first book, *Christian Slavery: Conversion and Race in the Protestant Atlantic World*, I showed how British, Dutch, and Danish slave owners initially justified the enslavement of Africans and indigenous people through religious difference—what I call Protestant Supremacy. Protestant slave owners forbade enslaved people from accessing Christian rites, since Christianity—and especially Protestantism—was associated with freedom and political power. Over time, however, as enslaved and free Blacks fought their way into Protestant churches, slave-owning legislators inserted the term *white* into their law books to replace *Christian*. As they did so, White Supremacy overtook Protestant Supremacy as the dominant ideology of slavery.

Even as whiteness became more established and racial hierarchies formed the core of social ordering, religion played a fundamental role in codifying forms of belonging, power, and authority.[20] In eighteenth-century Jamaica, Protestant Christianity—and especially Anglicanism—was primarily coded as white. Meanwhile, most white Europeans coded Obeah as Black and African. Despite this, the Moravian records suggest that Africans and Afro-Jamaicans did not categorize Obeah solely as African or Black. By associating Obeah with a European Moravian missionary and interpreting Christian rituals through the lens of Obeah, we gain insight into African epistemological formations surrounding both Obeah and Christianity that did not have the same racial implications as they did for white colonials.

While *Obeah* and *Christianity* eventually became oppositional terms, this was a consequence of colonial oppression: lawmakers made a concerted effort to criminalize and racialize religio-political practices such as Obeah as Black. By the end of the eighteenth century, Moravian missionaries—like other white colonials—were explicitly positioning Obeah as antithetical to Christianity.[21] The complicated relationship between Obeah, Christianity, whiteness, and Africanness shows how race and religion can be understood through what Aisha Khan calls a "parallax view," in which the nexus of race and religion is continually evolving.[22]

Archival Irruptions: Metaphor and Epistemology

While writing this book, I became invested in the metalanguage of history—in the metaphors that I noticed myself using to understand the past: Was I unearthing, recovering, or uncovering documents and stories?[23] I observed that archivally trained historians often use ocular, aural, or wood-based metaphors to discuss the relationship between themselves and their objects of study. Interpretations offer a lens, while the archive has grains that one can go with or against.[24] Silences refer to the gaps—intentional or unintentional—that led to the exclusion of specific forms of knowledge within archival sources.[25] As I thought more about archives and metaphor, I turned to the insights offered by Native American and Indigenous studies (NAIS) scholarship to guide my own interpretations.[26] The historian Lisa Brooks describes writing history as "an inquiry into *pildowi ôjmowôgan*, the cyclical, spiraling process through which we (inclusive or exclusive) collectively participate in recovering and narrating 'a new history.'"[27] In *Our Beloved Kin*, Brooks elaborates on her approach to archives, colonialism, and metaphor: "Among the goals of this book is to provide, reveal, and restore alternative 'narrative fields,' which have sometimes arisen quite unexpectedly from the archive of colonial documents, like 'weeds' breaking through soil into that well-established 'field.'"[28]

Brooks's metaphor about the "narrative field" of colonialism offered a guide for me as I thought about the narratives that emerged from the Moravian missionaries' diaries. The missionaries' narrative field was unavoidable: Their desire to carry the gospel to the "heathen," their conception of Christian baptism, their ideas about the true conversion of the heart, their beliefs about what constitutes Christian behavior, and their convictions about sin form the dominant narrative of their documents. At the same time, there were alternative narrative fields that emerged from the missionaries' writing, like the "weeds" that Brooks describes, "breaking through soil into that well-established 'field.'"[29]

Archival Irruptions takes a twofold approach to the Moravian archives. First, I do not ignore the landscape of the missionaries' narrative field—instead, I aim to describe and analyze it carefully, examining both the missionaries' efforts to create a coherent narrative about their experiences as well as the disjunctures that appear in their sources—especially in the discordant diaries of different missionaries. Second, I use my analysis of the missionary field of narration to identify and examine the "weeds" that break through their narratives—what I call archival irruptions. These irruptions offer, as Brooks puts it, opportunities for "alternative narrations."

To draw out these alternative narrations, I take inspiration from Africana religious studies. As Dianne Stewart and Tracey Hucks explain, Africana peoples have been forced to "(1) endure tangible encounters with Catholic and Protestant missiology; (2) withstand the demonization of African religious cosmologies; (3) contest the infantilization of African rituals; and (4) subvert the criminalization of African practices while protecting the integrity of their inner cosmologies and meanings."[30] In their vision for Africana religious studies, Stewart and Hucks argue that multiple methods are needed to counter the "epistemic racism" that has marked African diasporic history. *Archival Irruptions* is intended as a contribution to the field of Africana religious studies by reading archival sources for irruptions that can be interpreted by drawing upon the rich fields of African and African diasporic scholarship. In doing so, I aim to recenter the lives, experiences, and perspectives of men and women who were targeted by systemic repression and criminalization.

Methodologically, reading for irruptions requires three steps: (1) analyzing the narrative field of the archival producer, (2) identifying irruptions in the archive's narrative field, and (3) immersing oneself in scholarship that can help to interpret the irruptions. The final step is essential, since the narrative fields of archival producers often suppress, misunderstand, or censor the epistemological frameworks and intellectual histories of enslaved and colonized peoples.

There are two additional layers of analysis that are important for interpreting irruptions: first, scholars must attend to the *process* of archiving by considering why their sources were preserved. This inquiry aligns with Michel-Rolph Trouillot's "moment of fact assembly (the making of archives)" and with Ann Stoler's conceptualization of archiving-as-process rather than archives-as-things.[31] Second, as scholars examine irruptions in the archive, they should play close attention to their own reactions. Drawing on Zeb Tortorici's concept of "visceral archives," I argue that recognizing how we feel when we do archival research is important for two reasons: first, it can attune us to the toll that archival research can have on our own bodies; and second, our visceral reactions are themselves important indicators that can help us as we search for irruptions.[32] Over the course of my research for this book, there were several moments when I felt myself become surprised or turn away in revulsion. As I thought about my own visceral reactions and why they were produced, I used this somatic knowledge to deepen my analysis of archival irruptions.

Microhistory and the Moravian Archives

Archival Irruptions is primarily focused on an analysis of the Moravian missionary archive, most of which is written in German Script, an archaic form of handwritten German also known as *Kurrent* or *Sütterlin*.[33] The Moravian sources include letters, diaries, and church membership records written by white missionaries and—in some cases—Black Christians who were members of the Moravian Church. These records have been largely ignored by Atlantic and Caribbean historians because most are written in an archaic form of handwritten German.[34] Over the past fifteen years, I have transcribed hundreds of pages of *Kurrent* into modern German, and then translated them into English.[35] *Archival Irruptions* is the first book-length academic study based on the Moravian archives from eighteenth-century Jamaica, and I include excerpts and translations from archival sources in appendix 2 and an accompanying website in the hopes that more scholars can easily access and use these materials.[36]

Archival Irruptions utilizes a microhistorical methodology for three reasons. First, through a sustained investigation of a specific community, it is possible to see how everyday concerns—such as creating and sustaining sacred bonds, avoiding violence and illness, and caring for intimate relationships—were vital and consequential in determining the boundaries of religion, Christianity, and Obeah. Second, microhistories are an important methodological tool for telling African diasporic histories and remembering the individual human lives caught up in the overwhelming horror of the transatlantic slave trade and Caribbean slavery. A microhistorical scope also reveals important patterns in Africana history: Using the Moravian records, for example, we can see how the community of Afro-Caribbeans that came together to worship in the mid-1750s was transnational and dynamic.[37] By closely reading baptismal registers and Moravian diaries, we can identify how first- and second-generation Africans were re/forming families and communities, and we can chart the emergence of new Africana religio-nations, as I describe in chapter 2.

Finally, a microhistorical approach allows me to read for archival irruptions with care and specificity. Over the course of my research, I examined and compared the production of archival manuscripts by multiple individuals, showing how missionaries described the same events in different ways. I identified and analyzed cases of censorship, showing how knowledge about religion and violence was contoured and erased. I also compared Moravian missionary sources to accounts written by white English colonials, showing how they overlap and diverge. Over the years, I compiled scattered references to dozens of enslaved and free Black men and women, connecting them to reveal kinship bonds and surprising stories.

It is worth noting that this type of archival analysis is time-consuming. This book is a microhistory for many reasons, but one is practical: it is laborious to do archival research with an eye toward irruptions. This is especially true when the archival sources are handwritten in archaic scripts and/or languages that are non-native to the scholar. While these methodological strategies take time, they are important: by identifying the "weeds," as Brooks calls them, that break through the narrative field of colonial archives, we can utilize European sources to tell Africana stories.

Chapter Outline

The first half of this book is titled "Obeah," because Obeah is one such "weed" that emerges—not systematically, but unexpectedly—from a missionary letter. It is discordant with the narrative the missionaries are trying to write, and through the disjuncture, I seek to write an alternative narrative about the mission that reframes Christianity through the lens of Obeah. Part 1 begins in 1755 on the Bogue plantation in St. Elizabeth Parish, Jamaica, where the Moravian missionary Zacharias George Caries arrived with two other European missionaries, Gottlieb Haberecht and Thomas Shallecross, to evangelize to Africans and African-descended people. The following year, Caries founded the nearby mission station known as Carmel (formerly Risbys), which served as headquarters for the mission. The first three chapters focus on records that Caries and Haberecht produced in 1755 and 1756—before the arrival of the Moravian missionary Christian Heinrich Rauch in 1757.[38] While these chapters use Caries's handwritten manuscripts as their primary source, they reframe them: Instead of a narrative about missionary encounter, these chapters identify and examine a series of Africana irruptions in missionary diaries and letters.

Chapter 1, "Africana Irruptions" uses an offhand comment by Caries to reconsider how Afro-Jamaicans perceived the presence of a Moravian missionary. Building on scholarship about Obeah and Afro-Caribbean linguistic, religious, political, and medical history, it argues that scholars should interpret Moravian Christianity through the epistemology of Obeah. It then rereads Caries's diaries for evidence of what Caries did to become known as an Obeah man, offering a framework for understanding Obeah before its criminalization.

The second chapter, "Religio-Nations in the Archives," takes a different methodological approach to the missionary records. It is a close study of the first Afro-Jamaican members of the Moravian church, based on church registers and diaries. Caries's baptismal records include references to each individual's African nation and, in some cases, the nations of their parents and grandparents. This chapter argues that the nation designators can be interpreted as archival irruptions and posits that Afro-Moravians were forming a new religio-nation within the Moravian congregation. The concept of a religio-nation, furthermore, should be understood as part of the semantic field of Obeah.

Enslaved people were not the only people of African descent to interact with the missionaries. Beginning in 1755, just a few months after his arrival, Caries met Accompong, a Maroon leader who governed a town in the interior of Jamaica. Maroons were free Blacks who founded separate communities in the mountainous region of the island. After decades of warfare with colonial forces, Maroon leaders—including Accompong—signed a peace treaty with the British in 1739. Chapter 3, "Maroons, Blood Oaths, and Gendered Irruptions," reads the missionary archives to reveal the central role that one Maroon woman named Margery played in sustaining Maroon sovereignty and cultivating bonds between the Maroons and enslaved people.

Part II begins in January 1757, when the Moravian missionary Christian Heinrich Rauch arrived at the Bogue with his wife, Anna Rauch, and another missionary couple, Charles and Maria Schulz. Anna Rauch's presence had a profound impact on the type of information that her husband recorded. Moreover, the simultaneous production of three daily diaries—from Christian Rauch, Caries, and Schulz—offers opportunities for historians. The second half of this book is titled "*Heuchelei*," a German word meaning "dissimulation" or "hypocrisy," and it explores why the Moravians lost their status as Obeah men in the years after Rauch's arrival. Caries used the word *Heuchelei* to describe his devolving relationship with Afro-Moravians, but the word also characterized the relationship between Caries and Rauch, as the two missionaries disputed narratives and disagreed about the plan for the mission. I use the term *Heuchelei* to signal the breakdown of coherent mission narratives after Rauch's arrival, and I argue that dissimulation in the archives offers an opportunity to tease out Africana narratives and to reveal censored stories from the disrupted narrative field of the Moravian missionary sources. Part II shows how scholars can gain insight into Africana diasporic histories by making these fault lines in our archival sources visible.

Chapter 4, "Archival Silence, Sexual Violence" interrogates a horrific rape that Christian Heinrich Rauch recorded in his diary. Rauch sent copies of his diaries to Moravian church leaders in Bethlehem and Herrnhut, where his words were copied, extracted, and circulated farther around the globe. In the process, the story of the young girl attacked by white colonials was censored and deleted. This chapter does three things: First, it interrogates the intentional erasure of sexual violence from the Moravian records. Second, it compares the production of knowledge about sexual violence in the Moravian missionary diaries to the better-known diary of Thomas Thistlewood to show the extent of silences in the missionary records. Finally, it asks what religion meant within the context of widespread sexual violence and draws on Alexis Wells-Oghoghomeh's framework of "re/membrance" to recenter the ethical and moral priorities of enslaved women.[39] I argue that the missionaries' inability to protect their congregants from sexual violence was one reason that Afro-Moravians stopped viewing them as Obeah practitioners.

The arrival of new missionaries presented grave challenges to the day-to-day functioning of the Moravian mission. Chapter 5, "Policing Bodies, Saving Souls," examines the feud between Caries and Rauch and argues that Rauch's orientation toward policing and colonial law meant that there was no longer a "space of correlation" between Obeah and Moravian Christianity. In 1759, Caries was expelled from the mission while Rauch severed ties with the Accompong Town Maroons and sought to align the mission with the colonial government. During this time, many Afro-Caribbeans stopped attending worship meetings. While the missionaries interpreted their behavior through the framework of "sin," chapter 5 argues that from an Africana perspective, the missionaries had failed as Obeah men.

In 1760, the largest slave rebellion in the eighteenth-century British Empire broke out in Jamaica. The missionaries recorded the movements of rebels and the white militia in their diaries and letters. Tacky's Revolt, as the rebellion came to be called, led to a major shift in the policing of the enslaved population. Most notably, as described earlier, it led colonial lawmakers to criminalize Obeah. Chapter 6, "Constructing Religion, Defining Crime," assesses the meaning of "lived religion" during the rebellion. It then examines the criminalization of Obeah in the context of a broader, global shift in the construction of religion as a category. It argues that lawmakers used the category of religion as a tool to police enslaved people. In order to counter this epistemic violence, scholars need to change the way they identify religion in their sources by attending to processes of assembling, congregating, and binding.

The construction of religion was an ongoing and contentious process, particularly under slavery. Even as missionaries and colonial authorities sought to police the boundaries of religion to exclude Afro-Caribbean practices, enslaved and free Blacks were participating in the re/formation of religion. The epilogue argues that historians and religious studies scholars must attend to archival irruptions in their research to counter the legacies of slavery and colonization that marked the formation of religion in the early modern world. Without reading for irruptions, we risk repeating the epistemic violence of our archives.

PART I

Obeah

On Christmas Eve 1756, the Moravian meeting house in Jamaica was packed. Roughly four hundred congregants "fell to their knees and prayed."[1] Reflecting on the event, the Moravian missionary Zacharias George Caries wrote that "there were at least 28 different types of people ... proclaiming the gospel with grace and conviction." Africans from diverse nations had attended their meetings, as had Creoles, including "6 [single] brothers, 2 widowers, and 35 married men."[2] In the two years since his arrival, Caries had baptized sixty-nine Afro-Jamaicans at the Bogue plantation in Jamaica.[3] By contrast, in Saint Thomas, the first Moravian mission in the Caribbean, the first baptism was not performed until four years after the mission's founding.[4] In Barbados, at the Anglican-run Codrington Plantation, the first missionary failed to baptize a single person.[5]

I argue that the initial success of the Moravian mission should be interpreted through an Africana lens and that Moravian baptism should be understood within the framework of Obeah. Soon after the worship service on Christmas

Eve, for example, one Afro-Moravian told a story about how he "had been summoned" by a white couple to answer questions about whether he was a Christian. In explaining the Moravian baptismal ceremony, he pointed to the baptismal water in the Moravian meeting house. "There stands also a Pele [*sic*] of water w[hi]ch our Saviour has mingled with him own Blood," he stated. "Our Sav[io]r mixes the water with his Blood," he repeated.[6] The reference to mixing water and blood, while inclusive of Christian connotations, resonated strongly with one of the core practices of Obeah practitioners, which was to perform blood oaths to strengthen community bonds.

Part 1, "Obeah," analyzes a series of irruptions in the Moravian missionary archives in 1755–56 to argue that there was initially a space of correlation between Obeah and Christianity. Afro-Moravians interpreted the sacrament of baptism, as well as Caries's healing work and his prophetic power, as evidence of Obeah. While I center Obeah in the framework of the mission, this does not imply that Afro-Moravians were not Christian. Instead, I place the authority for terminology in the hands of Afro-Moravians and reject a politics of authenticity that seeks to police the boundaries of religion.

I

Africana Irruptions

BAPTISM, OBEAH, AND SPACES OF CORRELATION

Just before dawn on April 27, 1755, a Black Creole man named Cuffy was dressed in a long white shirt with large sleeves, a white cap with red ribbons resting on the top of his head. Surrounding him were thirteen other Black men, some African born, others born in Jamaica or elsewhere in the Caribbean. All were dressed in a similar fashion, with long white shirts kept meticulously clean and white caps adorning their heads.[1] Cuffy's five-year-old son, also named Cuffy, would join the gathering later that morning. Cuffy's brother, Simon, and his father, Zebedei, were in attendance as well. The younger Cuffy sat quietly with his "hands folded all the time & hearing with great attention." That evening, his father walked to the front of the meeting house. A dozen men, dressed in white, surrounded him in a semicircle while nearly one hundred others looked on as Cuffy was "overstream'd with Blood and water." The symbolic and literal power of blood, water, and wounds formed the core of the ceremony.[2]

The written description of the event comes to us through Zacharias George Caries, the first Moravian missionary stationed in Jamaica. Caries took care creating the manuscript that is now held in London at the Moravian Church House. Unlike his typical diary entries, written in small print and solely in black ink, Caries wrote in large print and interspersed red ink with black.[3] Caries's ceremonial font indicates that this baptism was a pivotal moment for his mission. But what did the event represent for Cuffy and the other individuals who took part in the Moravian baptism? This chapter reads the events of April 27 and missionary sources from 1755–56 for archival irruptions: moments when Africana epistemologies break through the narrative field of a missionary archive, as detailed in the introduction. Using this methodological strategy, I argue that Cuffy's baptism must be understood within the framework of Obeah.

On March 17, six weeks before Cuffy's baptism and only three months after Caries's arrival, Caries wrote that Afro-Caribbeans called him "Obea[h]." In the same letter, he described how these congregants were "longing for [baptism]" and "they can hardly wait."[4] The link between Obeah and baptism offers new insight into the meaning of Obeah before it was criminalized.[5] Significantly, Caries's definition of Obeah differed from that of other European commentators. Rather than comparing Obeah to witchcraft or conjuring, as most British observers had, Caries wrote that Obeah "supposedly means a Seer, or one who knows things that will happen in the future."[6] This chapter asks why Afro-Jamaicans called Caries Obeah by examining how Caries's activities during his first months in Jamaica contributed to his reputation as an Obeah man. It then draws on Africana scholarship to interpret the missionary records.

By reinterpreting the meaning of Christianity through an Africana lens—which the idea of Caries as an Obeah man suggests we do—we can move away from the European conceptual landscape of conversion and into a framework defined by spaces of correlation. "Spaces of correlation," as described by Cécile Fromont, are "cultural creations such as narratives, artworks, or performances that offer a yet unspecified domain in which their creators can bring together ideas and forms belonging to radically different realms, confront them, and eventually turn them into interrelated parts of a new system of thought and expression."[7] I argue that Cuffy's baptism—which centered "blood and wounds" theology—was a space of correlation that Cuffy interpreted through the framework of Obeah.

The first two sections of this chapter review scholarly literature on Obeah to establish that Caries's diary offers a singular opportunity to examine Obeah before its criminalization. This is followed by an overview of Caries's mission and the overall Moravian missionary strategy. Caries intentionally set himself apart from other whites in Jamaica: he presented himself as an individual who was skilled in both medical and spiritual matters, and he emphasized the theological power of blood and wounds. Through healing practices, baptisms, and prophetic practice, Afro-Caribbeans found spaces of correlation between Moravian Christianity and Obeah, which, as Dianne Stewart has argued, was "an institution entailing much more than expert knowledge of botanic therapeutic properties."[8] The third section details four key spaces of correlation between Obeah and Moravian Christianity: (1) blood and wounds, (2) baptismal rites, (3) the creation of a Moravian religio-nation based on Black leadership, and (4) death rituals and eschatology.

Investigating these spaces of correlation requires three steps: first, analyzing the narrative field of the missionary archives; second, identifying irruptions; and third, interpreting those irruptions alongside scholarship about Africana religions, politics, and epistemology. This final step is essential because archival irruptions, by definition, do not fit into the frameworks and narrative structures of Christian missions or European colonialism. Recognizing and interpreting their significance requires an attention to what Jacob Olupona calls "indigenous hermeneutics": the practice of "exploring paradigms and modes of interpretation that are explicitly embedded in the traditions we study."[9] In the case of Obeah, our interpretation must be embedded in scholarship that centers Africana terms, epistemologies, and experiences.

Overall, this chapter argues that Obeah was not just an Afro-Caribbean practice; it was the framework through which Afro-Jamaicans interpreted European religious, medical, and political practices. Several scholars have argued that Obeah conflicts with European methods of categorization that divide religion from medicine, science, and politics.[10] In order to more fully imagine the role of Obeah in mid-eighteenth-century Jamaica, scholars must eschew these categories and view Christian practice as being part of the Afro-Caribbean category of Obeah. Only by flipping the hierarchy of categories—and searching for spaces of correlation—can the breadth, ubiquity, and significance of Obeah be more fully understood.

Defining Obeah: The Challenges of the Archives

Studying the references to Obeah that have survived in the written record is a case study in the problematic nature of the archive—especially the archives of slavery and colonialism. Scholars continue to debate the etymology of Obeah, which was also spelled "obia," "oby," "obey," or "obi," but all agree that it has an African origin and that it first appears in the written record in the early eighteenth-century Caribbean.[11] Aside from Caries's letter, there are just a small number of known references to Obeah in the pre-1760 archival sources. In Barbados, the English army officer Thomas Walduck referred to Obeah in several letters written from Barbados between 1710 and 1712, categorizing it as a form of witchcraft.[12] In 1729, the Anglican minister of Christ Church in Barbados referred to "Oby Negroes, or conjurers," and their "bad practices," while Griffith Hughes, the minister of St. Lucy's Parish during the late 1730s and 1740s, referred to "Obeah Negroes ... [as] sort of physicians and conjurers" or "Obeah Doctors."[13]

Some early sources connect Obeah to rebellious activity. After a suspected conspiracy in Antigua in 1736, for example, a man named Quawcoo was accused of being an "Obiaman or Wizard" who had administered a blood oath to the gathered rebels. In his subsequent trial, Quawcoo was described as an "Old Oby Man and Physition and Cormantee," and the trial records connect Obeah to medical work, Africanness, superstition, rebellion, and wizardry.[14] Diana Paton has argued that Quawcoo was also involved in divination, which aligns with Caries's definition of an Obeah practitioner as a "Seer."[15]

In Jamaica, the earliest references to Obeah refer to the Maroons, sovereign nations of African-descended people who lived in the interior of the island. As detailed in chapter 3, Maroons followed the leadership of Obeah men and women, and British colonial sources refer to the Maroon leader Nanny as the "rebels old obeah woman."[16] Sources from the First Maroon War indicate that Obeah was used in battle and that Obeah practitioners who failed to protect combatants could lose their status.[17] Otherwise, the best-known reference to Obeah before 1760 is from Thomas Thistlewood's diary. In 1753, Thistlewood, an English overseer and enslaver in Westmoreland Parish, observed as Guy, an enslaved man, "acted ... his Obia, &c. with singing, dancing &c," commenting that it was "odd enough."[18]

These early archival references, which were recorded by British colonists and travelers, fit Afro-Caribbean practices into an epistemological framework based in British culture and belief. For some, "conjurer" was the most relevant counterpart to Obeah, while for others, Obeah men and women were "physicians." Walduck, the army officer, compared the practice of Obeah to folk belief in England, identifying it as a form of superstition, while Thistlewood was reminded of an English conjurer when he witnessed enslaved Africans interacting with an Obeah man.[19] References related to rebellion, like the trial records about Quawcoo, offer additional insight, even as they denigrate Obeah as superstitious and dangerous. While these archival documents were recorded for the purpose of punishment and surveillance, they confirm the role of Obeah in building community (albeit in a negative sense) as well as the significance of oaths, both of which I describe at length in subsequent parts of this chapter and in chapter 6.

In 1760, British colonists identified Obeah practitioners as principal conspirators of Tacky's Revolt. The rebellion, which extended through several parishes, threatened British control of the island. During the rebellion (see chapter 6), Obeah men and women protected rebels from bullets and encouraged loyalty to the uprising through binding oaths. In response, as noted previously, the Jamaican Assembly passed the "Act to Remedy the Evils Arising from Irregular Assemblies of Slaves," which sought to place greater controls on the enslaved population. For the first time in the history of the British West Indies, the act also criminalized Obeah, defining it as a "wicked Art." Obeah was deemed a capital offense, punishable by execution or transportation, suggesting that it was seen as a major threat to the colonial order.[20]

After Obeah was criminalized, references to it became increasingly common in colonial histories, newspapers, official reports, novels, and plays. In his multivolume *History of Jamaica*, the enslaver-historian Edward Long depicted Obeah men as "pretended conjurers," while Bryan Edwards, a proslavery planter-politician, wrote that Obeah was "a term of African origin, signifying sorcery or witchcraft."[21] The legend of Three-Fingered Jack, an Obeah practitioner, was retold in two novels as well as numerous theatrical performances and articles.[22] As Kelly Wisecup has shown, although these authors sought to control Obeah in their texts, they struggled to fully account for the supernatural powers invoked by Obeah practitioners.[23] Indeed, even as they rejected and mocked Obeah as barbaric and ridiculous, colonial writers remained fascinated by the practice. Vincent Brown has argued that "whites both believed in and doubted the efficacy of black supernatural power" and that after Tacky's Revolt, colonial authorities betrayed their own fear of its power by making sure to execute Obeah men with "more awesome displays than they normally projected."[24]

Anti-Obeah legislation in the late eighteenth-century connected Obeah with poisoning—a departure from previous laws.[25] In the postemancipation period, Diana Paton has shown how Obeah became part of a "Mighty Experiment" to see whether African-descended people were "ready" for freedom, and it was frequently compared to voodoo in the "black republic" of Haiti.[26] During this period, the legal definition of Obeah shifted away from the more serious crime of witchcraft to the more banal accusation of fraud. Rather than being considered a capital offense, postemancipation Obeah regulations mimicked the English vagrancy law of 1824, which sought to police fraudulent activity. Even as Obeah was downgraded to a noncapital crime, however, it became more widely prosecuted.[27] As a result, most archival sources about Obeah during this period are court cases concerning Obeah accusations.

Obeah remains a crime in Jamaica today, despite efforts to decriminalize the practice. As a result, it is excluded from the legal category of religion.[28] Still, recent studies have suggested that Obeah continues to operate in unexpected ways in Caribbean societies well into the twenty-first century. J. Brent Crosson has argued that Obeah acts as a "technology of justice-making." Based on his fieldwork in Trinidad, Crosson conceptualizes Obeah not only as a religion but also as a method to "afflict wrongdoers and force confessions when a racist and classist criminal justice system fail[s] to take action."[29] Aisha Khan, meanwhile, has shown how Obeah operates as a "complex vehicle" for "racialized religion and religionized race."[30]

The meaning of Obeah today has been indelibly marked by the conjoined histories of enslavement, colonialism, and criminalization, a legacy that makes it difficult to know what Obeah meant before the term became part of the legal apparatus of colonial oppression. Moreover, the archival record related to Obeah is a product of this racist colonial history: Every reference to Obeah before 1760 is written by a European who—whether an enslaver, a minister, a member of the military, or a politician—was invested in the system of slavery and believed that Africans were inferior to Europeans. As a result, their archival traces are marked with the lens of White Christian Supremacy and waver between fear, dismissal, and repulsion in their description of Obeah and its power. The frustrating nature of the colonial archive of Obeah has led the scholars Tracey Hucks and Dianne Stewart to argue that the "colonial cult of obeah fixation" was, itself a "lived religion" for whites who oriented their world "through imaginations and persecutions of Obeah/African religions."[31]

While Caries's reference to "Obea" cannot reveal the full epistemological scope of Obeah as it operated for Africans and their descendants in the mid-eighteenth century, it does offer a methodological opportunity. While Moravian missionaries, like British commentators, assumed the superiority of Christianity and European culture over African and Afro-Caribbean practices, the volume of their records and the existence of Africana irruptions in the missionary archive offer an opportunity to gain a different perspective on Obeah. This is, in part, because Moravian missionaries—particularly in the early years of their mission—had a unique position within Jamaican society as outsiders whose primary objective was to develop a Christian community of enslaved and free Blacks on the island. The following section outlines the historical circumstances surrounding the creation of the Moravian archive in Jamaica, demonstrating why Caries's reference to Obeah was an Africana irruption.

An Outsider in the "Devil's Nest": Moravian Global Missions

Zacharias George Caries was an unusual figure in Jamaica. As a Moravian, he was a religious minority in a colony dominated by the Anglican Church.[32] As a native German speaker, he was a linguistic foreigner in an English colony.[33] And as a missionary whose primary goal was to convert enslaved Africans to Christianity, his objectives diverged from those of the majority of Europeans who arrived in the British Caribbean. Yet, while his background and intentions set him apart from other Euro-Jamaicans, Caries held a uniquely protected position as the emissary of two wealthy planters.

Caries's patrons, William Foster and Joseph Foster Barham, were absentee slave owners living in London. In the mid-eighteenth century, the brothers met the Moravian preacher John Cennick and experienced a religious awakening that prompted them to rethink their relationship with their enslaved laborers. In the wake of their conversion, Foster and Barham began to communicate with Cennick about their moral qualms about employing "heathen" slaves.[34] Their discomfort translated into a proposal for a Moravian mission station. William Foster promised to provide the missionaries with a house and one hundred acres of land, while Joseph Foster Barham offered the brethren three hundred acres of land and a house.[35] Caries, who had toured the British Isles with John Cennick and was acquainted with Foster and Barham, was chosen as the leader of the new mission, alongside Thomas Shallecross and Gottlieb Haberecht. For their first mission location, they chose William Foster's plantation, the Bogue, located in St. Elizabeth Parish, just south of the mountainous region known as "Cockpit Country."

Despite the support of wealthy slave owners, Moravian leaders were skeptical about the mission. They described Jamaica as "a devil's nest, which is worse than all the other islands," and warned Caries not to baptize anyone too quickly; not to preach to whites unless specifically invited; and never to baptize a white child.[36] "Your principal purpose," they wrote, "are the poor black nations that have until now heard nothing healthy about the Savior and his wounds."[37] Church leaders based their instructions on the first Moravian mission in the Caribbean, founded in Saint Thomas in 1732. In the Danish West Indies, missionaries and Black Moravians had been physically and verbally abused by white colonists on the island.[38] Seeking to avoid a similar conflict, Caries was advised to keep a low profile and not to socialize with whites.

Caries, Haberecht, and Shallecross departed from London on October 6, 1754, after meeting with Foster and Barham. On their journey across the

Atlantic, Caries kept a daily diary, in which he commented on the activities of the missionaries. From these entries, we learn that the three missionaries set themselves apart from other white people. A week into their transatlantic journey, Caries wrote, "The People ask'd Br Sh[alle]cross if we were Jews, since we observ'd the Sabbath."[39] Shallecross replied, "You may think of us what you please, but I can tell you our Religion is the crucified Savior."[40] The missionaries' cautious and evasive response reflected the Moravians' precarious political situation in the 1750s. Due to their radical theology, which emphasized the blood and wounds of Christ, the Moravians had gained a controversial reputation in Europe and the Americas. Anti-Moravian pamphlets were circulated throughout the Atlantic world and the Moravians were banished from some regions.[41] Despite their marginalized position, the Moravians achieved official sanction from the British government in 1749 when Parliament, with support from Anglican bishops, recognized the Moravian Church as "an Antient [sic] Protestant Episcopal Church."[42] While the act did not counter the antipathy Moravians continued to face, it did give Moravian missionaries access to the British colonies.

The missionaries arrived in Jamaica on December 6, 1754, less than a year after Foster and Barham's official proposal. Despite their official recognition by the Crown and the support of two wealthy absentee slave owners, Moravians remained outsiders in Jamaica, and many British colonials were wary of the brethren. The Anglican clergy were particularly suspicious of the new arrivals. When Dr. Harris, the minister of St. Elizabeth Parish, heard of Caries's arrival, he was "alarmed" and planned to complain to the local vestry.[43] When Caries heard this news, he sent word to the minister that his "intention was not to infringe on any of his Rights, nor to marry or baptize any of the white People."[44] Again, in September 1755, Caries made a great effort to publicize the fact that he would not evangelize to whites.[45]

Caries's interest in converting only enslaved Africans was part of the broader Moravian mission strategy. The Moravian Church, unlike other Protestant denominations at the time, specifically targeted non-Europeans for evangelization in the Caribbean. This policy was due to both idealism and pragmatism. Moravians were a controversial Protestant denomination, so evangelizing to non-Europeans allowed them to claim that they were not seeking to "steal" converts from other Protestant churches. Instead, their goal was to bring the gospel to "heathen" who would otherwise remain ignorant of Christianity. Theologically, the Moravians developed an identity as a *Pilgergemeine*, a "pilgrim congregation" founded on the principle of spreading the gospel to all nations.

In sharp contrast to the Moravians' emphasis on evangelism and itinerancy, the Anglican Church in Jamaica had long since established itself as a planters' stronghold. Although small numbers of Afro-Caribbeans were baptized in the Anglican Church, it remained a predominantly white institution that catered to the needs of the white elite, and Anglican ministers rarely concerned themselves with the Black population.[46] As a result, Moravians would have appeared to enslaved and free Afro-Caribbeans as unusual and distinct Europeans who did not conform to the expected norms for white colonials or Anglican ministers.

When Caries arrived in Jamaica, his physical appearance set him apart from other whites. He was likely donning the typical dress for a Moravian man: a "simple, knee-length coat" of "plain cloth" that was either "brown, dark blue, grey, or green."[47] While Moravian men were not dressed as distinctively as Moravian women, who wore caps covering their hair and ribbons representing their age and marital status, their plain style would have been notable. It is possible that Caries may have worn a distinctive colored ribbon around his neck to represent his unmarried status.[48] The Moravian leader Count Zinzendorf compared this practice to military dress. Just as "one divides armies into corps, regiments and battalions and fleets into squadrons," the Moravian congregation was divided into "choirs and classes" based on age and rank. Each rank was signified by a different colored ribbon.[49]

Afro-Jamaicans recognized that Caries's appearance set him apart from both white settlers and other Protestant ministers. Unlike ministers in the Lutheran and Reformed churches, Moravian preachers did not wear official gowns.[50] Instead, Caries wore sober colors and plain cloth to denote his theological belief that he was a poor sinner. Black men and women occasionally asked the missionaries about their clothing. When the missionaries founded a new mission station at Mesopotamia plantation, for example, an enslaved man named Mathew asked why they did not wear "priests' clothing."[51] The comment suggests that Afro-Jamaicans recognized that the Moravian missionaries were different from the other white people they had encountered.

The archive that Caries produced reflects his position as a white outsider who was oriented toward the lives of Afro-Caribbeans, both enslaved and free. His daily entries focus on his interactions with enslaved and free Blacks at the Bogue, including notes about whom he spoke to, what they discussed, and the worship services he officiated. While his perspective retains basic assumptions about the supremacy of Christianity, Caries also demonstrated flexibility in his interpretation of African religions, occasionally integrating African traditions into Moravian rituals—often unknowingly.

Spaces of Correlation

The Moravians' distinctive theology and worship practices made it possible to create spaces of correlation between Obeah and Moravian Christianity. By reading Caries's diaries with an Africana lens, it is possible to identify four spaces of correlation that emerged in the Moravian congregation at the Bogue during 1755–56: (1) the healing powers of blood and wounds, (2) the ritual of baptism, (3) the creation of a religio-nation based on Black leadership and support for Black kinship networks, and (4) prophetic power, especially related to death and the afterlife. By identifying these spaces of correlation, we can glimpse an epistemological formation of Obeah outside of the registers of European witchcraft, conjuring, or superstition.

Blood and Wounds

Caries presented himself to the Black men and women at the Bogue as a practitioner skilled in dealing with blood and wounds—both physically and theologically. Soon after his arrival, he began visiting the dwellings of the enslaved, making sure to attend to the needs of the ill. On December 23, Caries wrote that he visited a sick Black man at a nearby plantation and soon thereafter, he reported regular visits to enslaved men and women in which he tended to their physical ailments.[52] In recognition of his medical expertise, enslaved people began to give Caries gifts. On January 21, after Caries "visited the sick," he received "a Plate of Candi[e]d Sugar in the Name of all the Boilers of the Sugar."[53] In the following weeks, Caries reported frequent visits to the sick as well as increasingly large worship meetings. On January 26, he reported that after he "visited the sick" in the afternoon, a "large number" came to the meeting.[54]

By tending to the ill, Caries demonstrated healing powers typical of Obeah men in the eighteenth century. As Jerome Handler and Kenneth Bilby have argued, early references suggest that Obeah was part of the Afro-Caribbean "medicinal complex." Griffith Hughes, the rector of St. Lucy Parish on Barbados, for example, referred to Obeah practitioners as "a sort of physicians and conjurers, or Obeah Doctors."[55] And in modern Maroon communities such as the Aluku (Boni) of French Guiana, "obia" most commonly refers to "medicine, remedy or healing power."[56]

Caries's approach to healing connected the physical body to the blood and wounds of Christ. On January 17, 1755, he described Jesus as "the great Ph[y]sician of the Soul" whose "Blood would heal all Damage."[57] In doing so, he rejected a clear divide between body and spirit, a perspective that was also evident in his worship meetings where he emphasized the wounds of

Christ. A week after his arrival in Jamaica, Caries wrote that he "held a long conversation with my dear Lord, desired him to anoint me afresh, to plunge me deep into his dear Wounds, & bless me with his thro[ugh] pierced Hands."[58] A few months later, on March 9, Caries spoke about Jesus's "bleeding wounds, his bloody sweat, pain, agony & the great love to sinners."[59] Caries's theological focus on pain, rather than sin, was likely appealing to enslaved men and women who were forced to endure immense physical and psychological suffering within the brutal Jamaican slave system. It also offered a space of correlation with West African religious traditions, which did not highlight the concept sin, a divergence I describe at length in chapter 5.

When Cuffy and other Afro-Moravians narrated their decision to join the Moravian congregation, the image of the suffering and bleeding Christ played a central role. In July 1755, Caries asked baptized Afro-Moravians to dictate letters to William Foster, their absentee enslaver. While the letters were often formulaic, a careful reading reveals important information about how Africans and Afro-Jamaicans described Moravian Christianity.[60] In the letters, the image of the suffering and bleeding Jesus emerges as a central theme. Cuffy, for example, combined the language of the heart with the Moravian theological focus on the wounds of Christ when he stated that he was "glad to have . . . my Heart dip[ped] in our Saviours wounds."[61] Titus, the third person baptized, had been sick with dysentery earlier in the year, and he wrote that Caries had tended to him during his illness. Titus's message also included a long reference to death and the suffering Jesus. "He suffered on the cross & died for us," he wrote.[62]

During the early to mid-eighteenth century, Moravians focused their blood and wounds theology on Jesus's "side wound," which they referred to as the *Seitenhölchen*, or "little side hole." Accordingly, Moravians often displayed images of the bleeding Jesus on the cross featuring the side hole and, occasionally, devotional images of the side hole itself.[63] While we do not know which physical depictions were on display at the Moravian mission house at the Bogue, there was likely a crucifix depicting the suffering Jesus. Cécile Fromont has written about how crucifixes offered a "space of correlation" within Kongo Christianity. As she has described, "the cross formed the nexus through which central African and Christian discourses of power and cosmological thought entered into dialogue. . . . A Kongo *nkisi* became a Christian sign, and a Christian cross, a Kongo power object."[64]

Similar transformations were happening in the Moravian mission, as the image of Jesus's bloody body on the cross resonated with African notions of the sacredness of blood and its central role in religious rituals. While most Afro-Moravians would not have shared the framework of Kongo Christianity, we do know that some Black congregants were from the Kingdom of Kongo. As I describe in chapter 2, Coal (baptized Sadook) was identified as a member of the Kongo nation and may have viewed the Moravian image of the crucified Jesus as a Kongo *nkisi*. For others, the sacred quality of Jesus's blood may have connected with blood rites. The historian Walter Rucker, for example, has argued that Obeah practice was connected to Akan blood oaths, a topic explored more fully in chapter 3.[65]

Aside from crucifixes, printed images of Jesus's blood and wounds played an important role in the mission. In April 1755, Caries noted that it "came in [his] Mind to show... some Prints," all of Jesus. The first depicted Jesus at age twelve, the second at his crucifixion, and the third in his grave. In his description of the subsequent conversation about the printed images, Caries wrote that one Afro-Moravian commented on Jesus's great suffering, while another stared at the images for an extended period. "He could not sufficiently look at them," Caries wrote, and it was "late before they went away."[66] As these references suggest, for Afro-Moravians, blood and wounds offered a powerful space of correlation. On the one hand, Caries's healing practice was evidence of his role as an Obeah man who was expected to have medicinal knowledge. But the theological significance of blood and wounds within Moravian worship services also connected with African traditions that featured blood as a crucial component of sacred practice and religio-political community formation.

Baptism

A few weeks after he was identified as an Obeah man, Caries reported that the first baptisms would soon take place. "Their names," he wrote, "are 1) [Cuffy], who will be named Ludwig after our dear Papa and 2) John, after our dear Johannes" (the Moravian leaders Count Ludwig von Zinzendorf and Johannes von Watteville, respectively).[67] Caries added that they had twelve candidates for baptism and, perhaps most surprisingly, Maroons from Accompong Town had expressed interest in the Moravian congregation, a topic detailed in chapter 3.[68] By June, Caries was more desperate for Moravian reinforcements. "The number of our dear black audience is always increasing, and our new chapel that was just enlarged will soon be completely full."[69] By the end of 1756, Caries had baptized sixty-nine men at the Bogue, nearly half of the enslaved male population on the estate.[70] Considering that infants and boys were included in the tally of 154, the percentage of enslaved male converts at the Bogue was probably more than 50 percent.[71]

While Caries viewed the high rate of baptism as a sign of his success, an Africana reading of Caries's journal demonstrates that it was the Black men and women at the Bogue—not Caries—who provided the impetus for baptism. In fact, Caries disobeyed orders from the Moravian leadership by performing baptisms after just four months in Jamaica. Moravian leaders Count Zinzendorf and Johannes von Watteville had instructed Caries to be sparing and to wait a long time before baptizing anyone. Caries, who was aware of these guidelines, tried to justify his baptisms in his diary and letters, but it is clear he knew he had acted against orders.[72] Eventually, as detailed in chapter 5, he was expelled from the mission for performing baptisms too quickly.

Caries wrote regularly about the pressure he received from enslaved and free Blacks to offer the sacrament of baptism. On March 17, 1755, in the same letter where he noted that he was called "Obea," he wrote extensively about the demand for baptism. Initially, "two of them professed a deep desire to be baptized." Gottlieb Haberecht, Caries's fellow missionary, supported them and urged Caries to move forward with baptism. Caries, however, worried that it was still too soon. By March, there were twelve candidates, "and their longing for it has been growing so much that they can hardly wait." Caries decided to consult the lot, the Moravians' method of determining God's will. In response, wrote Caries, "the Lord instructed us to wait until April 27 for the first baptism."[73] The demand for baptism did not abate after April 27. Over a year later, in July 1756, Caries complained, "We already have 57 baptized, [and] we also have just as many candidates for baptism, many of whom overrun us, begging for baptism, and we have no reason to object to this, but we are still very sparing with baptism because there are already too many baptized."[74] By reading Caries's diary with an Africana lens, we can see that it was the men and women at the Bogue who demanded baptism from Caries. Crucially, they did so *after* Caries had been identified as an Obeah man. While Caries viewed his baptismal rates as a sign of Christian conversion, the Afro-Caribbeans who requested baptism did not interpret the rite in the same way as Caries did.

Baptism, like blood and wounds, was a space of correlation between Obeah and Moravian Christianity. In the Danish West Indies, the Moravian missionary and historian C. G. A. Oldendorp interviewed several Africans who compared Christian and African baptism.[75] Based on his interview with enslaved men and women from what Oldendorp called the Watje nation, he concluded, "They have some form of baptism everywhere. It happens usually with children who are already rather big, but sometimes with little kids. They make a circle under the open sky. The black priest stirs water and salt together in a jug, and the mother brings the child to him. He puts the water in a calabash and pours it three times over the head of the child and prays that God will help him and protect him from his enemies."[76] Oldendorp's interviews offer insight into how Afro-Moravians may have interpreted Christian rituals through the lens of African religious experiences. The water ritual described by Oldendorp, for example, was intended to "protect" the baptized "from his [or her] enemies" and to request help from God. It is likely that Afro-Caribbeans had similar expectations for Christian baptism—they believed that it would protect them from harm and improve their relationship with the divine.

Afro-Caribbeans at the Bogue also recognized similarities between the Moravian God and the gods of their homelands. In June 1756, Caries wrote about a conversation he had with several baptized Afro-Moravians. In it, they described their homelands and told Caries that they "always believed there was a God." In "Coromantee," they called god "Jamconpon, in Ibo, Gicoquowi & in Congo, Simiapumgo."[77] Jancómpon was the Akan sky god who was distinct from the "personal, local, and lesser deities, ancestral spirits" known as *bossum* (or *obosum*).[78] "Simiapumgo" may be an alternate spelling of Nzambi a Mpungu, the supreme god in Kongo religion, while "Gicoquowi" may refer to the Ibo god Chukwu.[79] If so, all three were considered supreme gods within West African and West Central African cosmology. Within these religious traditions, supreme gods did not negate the existence of other gods, power objects, or shrines; instead, they were all part of a complex theological system. As a result, it is significant that Afro-Moravians connected the Moravian god with the supreme beings in African religions, since they could do so without rejecting other aspects of their cosmologies.

While many Protestant missionaries would have rejected the comparison to African gods as a sign of heathenism, Caries exhibited more flexibility. He and the newly baptized members of the congregation all agreed that they believed in the same god, and that god could have different names. Caries then presented the Christian theological belief that "God became a Man, suffer[e]d & d[ie]d for us" as compatible with Ibo, Coromantee, and Kongo religious thought. As a result, the baptism that Caries understood to represent "conversion"—a new birth and a departure from the past in Protestant theology—is better understood through the framework of correlations, as Afro-Moravians brought their religious experiences to bear on Christian theology.

Religio-Nation Formation: Black Leadership and Kinship Networks

Aside from offering spiritual protection through baptism, the institutional structure of the Moravian Church provided leadership roles for Afro-Moravians and support for kinship networks. While these roles are not always associated with Obeah men and women, Dianne Stewart has sought to "reframe Obeah as a protean institutional structure" with "religious offices such as mediums, diviners, and other gifted or trained spiritualists."[80] Meanwhile, Diana Paton has suggested that Obeah practitioners in the early colonial period were "at the heart of the community."[81] Building on these perspectives, I argue that institution- and community-building were key components of Obeah, and they help to explain the initial appeal of the Moravian congregation. Afro-Moravians saw Caries's mission as an opportunity to bolster their preexisting leadership roles, to support their families, and to foster community by drawing on the power of blood and wounds theology and baptism. Through their efforts, the Moravian congregation became a religio-nation, a theoretical framework I describe in chapter 2.

For Cuffy, the first Afro-Caribbean baptized in Jamaica, the Moravian congregation offered a way to advocate for his family. Tracing references to Cuffy's family in the archival records demonstrates this trend. On May 13, 1755, just two weeks after Cuffy's baptism, Caries noted that "[Cuffy's] Father, Mother & 2 brothers are pretty people. One of his Br[others] is a Candidate for Baptism."[82] In August, Cuffy's brother Simon [John] was baptized. The following November, Caries reported, "I returned home & spoke with our [Cuffy] ... who told me a great deal of his old father's & his wife's desire to be baptized."[83] As the wording of this passage makes clear, it was Cuffy, not Caries, who labored to bring his family into the Moravian fold. When Cuffy's father Zebedei [Cyrus] was baptized, Caries credited his sons: "none were more Delighted than [Cuffy] & Simon to see their aged Father baptiz[e]d." After his father's baptism, Cuffy saw more opportunities for his family. He told Caries that his other brother was "indentur'd ... 12 or 14 miles from hence" and while he "has 2 years to serve, [he] is really a dear man who loves our Savr & comes as often as he can to the Meeting."[84] Implicit in Cuffy's comment was his hope that Caries could decrease the length of his brother's indenture or arrange for him to be able to come home more frequently.

Afro-Jamaicans used the Moravian church to bolster their preexisting leadership roles. Many preached themselves, gaining a following among the enslaved population. Titus, the third person baptized at the Bogue, was already a preacher before he was baptized. As Caries noted in his diary, "after dinner I spoke with Titus, a Candidate, who ... does already labour among his People."[85] As this quotation demonstrates, Titus, who was married to a Maroon woman named Margery (see chapter 3), was already a recognized spiritual practitioner before he became a Moravian.

Titus and Cuffy were given official titles of leadership called "Helpers." Within the structure of the Moravian church, Helpers played a role similar to that of a deacon or an elder. They were responsible for leading small worship services, or "bands," which were divided by age and gender, and for fostering community. Helpers tended to the sick, spoke at funerals and other services, and taught new congregants how to participate in worship services.[86] In this way, the Moravian church institutionalized Black leadership and supported Black-led community formation, since worship bands often met outside the purview of white missionaries.[87]

Caries did not baptize women during the first two years of the mission because he was not accompanied by a female missionary. However, the important role of Black women in the Moravian congregation emerges throughout the pages of the Moravian sources. In 1756, Caries recorded a list of all "Female Candidates for Baptism," in which he wrote the names of thirty women at the Bogue who had been regularly participating in Moravian worship services. On another page, he created a list of women who were "recommended" to become baptismal candidates, where he included forty-one additional names. Caries added each woman's "husband" to the left of her name, a patriarchal decision that nevertheless offers an opportunity to identify kinship formations and family relationships within the Moravian congregation.[88]

By comparing Caries's lists of female baptismal candidates with his diary entries, it is possible to see how Black women spread the word about the Moravian congregation, as they did in other Moravian missions.[89] In chapter 3, I highlight the role of Margery, a Maroon woman, showing how she facilitated Maroon involvement in the Moravian church. In chapter 4, I focus on Elizabeth (formerly Coco), who was one of the first women to be baptized after the arrival of Anna Rauch, the first female missionary. Other women who played an important role in the congregation included Silva, Cuffy's wife, who was listed among the baptismal candidates in 1756; and Barbara (Salome), the first woman baptized at the Bogue in 1757.[90]

Recognizing the importance of Black leadership and community formation in the Moravian congregation suggests that joining the Moravian church was not a break with the past; instead, Afro-Moravians saw the church as an opportunity to expand their leadership roles and advocate for their family members. For them, the formation of a sacred community was a key component of Obeah, alongside blood and wounds theology and baptism.

"Blessed Are the Dead": Death Rites and Prophetic Power

Death rituals were central to the meaning of Obeah and to the cultivation of power and influence in eighteenth-century Jamaica. As Walter Rucker has argued, "*obeah* was the quintessential marker of a radical mortuary and political sphere."[91] Meanwhile, Vincent Brown has shown that funerals and death rites were a vital social activity for all Jamaicans, Black and white.[92] Caries took part in the struggle to gain authority over the meanings of death. In doing so, he acted as a mediator between the worlds of the living and the dead and claimed prophetic powers regarding the afterlife—all important features of Obeah.

The most striking moment of Caries's consolidation of power occurred on the death of Sampson, a leader within the enslaved community and a baptized Moravian. Using eight full pages of his diary, Caries recounted every step in the process of Sampson's death and burial. On the morning of October 4, Sampson "sat down on a chair, where he spoke at length to the Savior by himself" and then "slept until midday."[93] At noon, Caries was called to Sampson's side just in time to see him "go home."[94] Caries's description of death as "going home" may have been a powerful space of correlation for West Africans. Many Africans believed that they would return home to their ancestral lands after death, where they would be "reunited as spirits and ancestors with lost kin and friends."[95] While Caries would not have recognized this space of correlation, Afro-Moravians may have seen his comments as confirmation in their belief in the afterlife.

Sampson's moment of death was of utmost importance. Caries took it as a sign from God that Sampson had died exactly two years after Count Zinzendorf and Joseph Spangenberg had sent him to Jamaica during a conference in the Moravian community of Herrnhut, Germany. Just to make sure that his readers knew that exactly two years had elapsed, Caries added that "12 o'clock here is half past six in the evening in Europe." Caries reinforced the significance of the timing of Sampson's death in a letter he sent to Spangenberg on January 23, 1757: "On the 4th of October the first of the baptized souls was kissed away, and it was on the exact same day, and in the exact same hour that I was sent to Jamaica.... I never thought that I, two years later, would send such a dear heart as our dear blessed Sampson's to the Savior."[96]

Sampson's funeral was an important event. "When leading members of the Black community die," Caries wrote, "thousands come together and make such a dreadful noise and carry on the entire night."[97] Caries wanted something different—and distinctly Christian—for Sampson. He was determined to lay Sampson to rest in *Gottes Acker*, or God's Acre, a burial plot the missionaries had set aside for the baptized. He planned the burial for the morning of October 5, when all the baptized brethren would be able to attend.

While Caries sought to maintain boundaries between Christian and heathen practices, the rituals he oversaw were infused with spaces of correlation. The details that emerge from the pages of Caries's diary are suggestive of the many ways in which Caries—often unconsciously—incorporated African practices into Moravian rituals. In preparation for Sampson's funeral, for example, he and the Black Moravian leaders "dressed the body in white and put red ribbons on the hat and sleeves."[98] The reference to the white clothing—which was also used in Cuffy's baptismal ceremony—is one such space of correlation. When Oldendorp interviewed Africans in the Danish West Indies during the mid-eighteenth century, several reported the significance of white clothing, particularly for funerals and purification rituals. In the Kingdom of Kongo, Oldendorp's informant explained, "Their dead are sewed into a white cloth, just like the Christian custom, laid in a coffin and carried out by a funeral procession and placed in a crypt. Those who have lived badly will not be buried in this way and they get neither a burial sermon nor such an entourage."[99] Oldendorp recognized how the white cloth acted as a space of correlation between African and Christian customs. In another reference, this time to members of the Kassenti nation in West Africa, Oldendorp wrote, "They dress the corpse in white and put it in a Kavanne or mat."[100] Similarly, among the Papaa, "the dead are always wrapped in a white cloth and buried inside it."[101]

On the next day, Black Moravians were chosen to carry Sampson's body to the burial ground where the enslaved, all dressed in white, "formed a double circle around *Gottes Acker*."[102] The circle recalls Oldendorp's descriptions of Watje rituals, in which congregants form a "circle under the open sky."[103] Following the ceremony, the burial party returned to the chapel where Caries preached from Revelations: "Blessed are the dead, which die in the Lord, from henceforth. Yea, says the Spirit, that they may rest from their labours; and their works do follow them."[104] Caries chose the verse well: The promise of rest from work and the blessings of the Savior were surely appealing to those who listened to Caries's words.

After Sampson was laid to rest, Caries was delighted when, he said, "various Black people came to me and requested that I bury Manatie as well."[105] Manatie, a baptismal candidate, had died suddenly the day before. The invitation to preside over a second funeral was confirmation of Caries's influence within the Afro-Moravian community. Caries's description of the funeral emphasized both the powerful imagery of Christ's crucifixion and Caries's desire to control the symbolism of the ceremony:

> Everything was in good order, and they had left the coffin open to show me the body, which looked delicate and was dressed in white. They hadn't put either salt or rum in the coffin like they normally do. We formed a circle around the grave and because there were a lot of unknown Black people there, I held a Discourse about the immortality of our souls, and where the souls of the believers go; also about the incarnation and the

reasons for his death, and about his and our own tranquility in the grave and about his and our resurrection with transfigured bodies, and the reunification of the body and soul.[106]

Caries's relief that the enslaved "hadn't put either salt or rum in the coffin" betrayed the fact that he lacked full control of the symbolic world of death. His tone implied that if he had found Manatie's coffin containing salt or rum that he would not have intervened.[107] The fact that the corpse was "dressed in white," meanwhile, struck Caries as "in good order."

Caries's "Discourse" at Manatie's funeral about the "immortality of our souls"—and his claim that he knew "where the souls of the believers go"— suggests another important correlation: prophecy. As mentioned previously, Caries defined Obeah in prophetic terms: "it means a Seer, or one who knows things that will happen in the future." In his diaries, Caries never talked about prophesying events on earth, but he frequently talked about death with conviction, describing how the hierarchies of slavery would be inverted after death. Just three days before writing his letter about "Obea," for example, he wrote about a conversation with a Black woman who asked him whether "souls go to Heaven" while the bodies in the grave "become alive again." Caries's response used blood and wounds imagery to paint a picture of an afterlife— and future—without slavery and racism.

> If we have been happy & washd in our Saviours Blood, then, when we die our Souls go to the d[ea]r Savr in Heaven & our Bodies rot in the Earth & we will get new Bodies made better than they are now, such as our dear Savr body, you will be no more Blacks, no more slaves, & your souls & Bodies will meet together. The soul which has been with our Saviour in his Wounds & pierc'd side, will come and fetch the Bodies to our Savr & then will be happy for ever & ever with him.

In Caries's telling, blood and wounds are at the center of a rich eschatological vision, in a future freed from racism, slavery, and suffering.[108]

Obeah and Africana Irruptions

When Caries referred to Obeah as a prophetic practice in March 1755, his definition was based on his interactions with Afro-Moravians. For scholars, Caries's reference to Obeah offers an Africana irruption that can be interpreted by pairing a close reading of the archives with an immersion in Africana scholarship. This chapter has examined Caries's behavior and theology in Jamaica through the lens of Obeah, asking what Caries did to give the impression that he was an Obeah man. As we have seen, in the first two years of his mission, Caries emphasized the healing powers of blood and wounds theology; he performed baptismal rites; he supported Black leadership and kinship networks; and he dealt in the symbolic worlds of death and dying. These activities offered spaces of correlation between Christian and African traditions that should be understood as part of the semantic field of Obeah.

Spaces of correlation were especially significant for enslaved Africans and their descendants, who had been torn from their homelands and found themselves surrounded by other Africans of diverse linguistic, religious, and national origins. To re/form sacred communities, they drew upon frameworks of correlation and grew skilled at recognizing similarities across cultural, political, and religious practices. They employed this orientation toward correlation in their interaction with Caries and the Moravian congregation. In the ritual practices and institutional structures of the church, they recognized an opportunity to support and develop a sacred community—a religio-nation in formation, as described in chapter 2.

Black Moravians' identification of Caries as an Obeah man in Jamaica suggests that the term *Obeah* applied not just to Afro-Caribbean practitioners but to anyone—European or African—who displayed an ability to perform these important roles of healing, prophecy, and community building. Once a practitioner failed to perform these tasks, however, he or she was at risk of losing his or her title and the community's respect, as we shall see in part II. Significantly, while most Europeans identified Obeah as a distinctly Afro-Caribbean practice, which they contrasted to "civilized" European religion and medicine, the evidence from Caries's letters and diaries suggests that Afro-Caribbeans could view European religion as a form of Obeah. In other words, while most whites attempted to create categories for Obeah that placed it outside of acceptable European practices, Afro-Jamaicans integrated Caries and his religion into their category of Obeah.

2

Religio-Nations in the Archives
RE/FORMATIONS OF SACRED COMMUNITIES

On February 15, 1756, six men from the Quambo nation were baptized by the Moravian missionary Zacharias George Caries. Fortune, Cubanna, Hampton, Monday, Thunder, and Jamie were given the baptismal names Isaak, Nahum, Nehemia, Mark, Caleb, and James. All six were described as "married" and "old." We do not know if they had lived most of their lives in Jamaica or whether they were adults when they were enslaved and forcibly transported across the Atlantic Ocean. Nor do we know whether the six men had known each other in Africa, whether they survived the Middle Passage on the same ship, or whether they met in the Caribbean. What their communal baptism on February 15 tells us is that these men identified as Quambo and they wanted to be baptized together. Their decision to engage in this sacred ritual together shows how Africana categories were central to the re/formation of sacred communities in the Atlantic world.

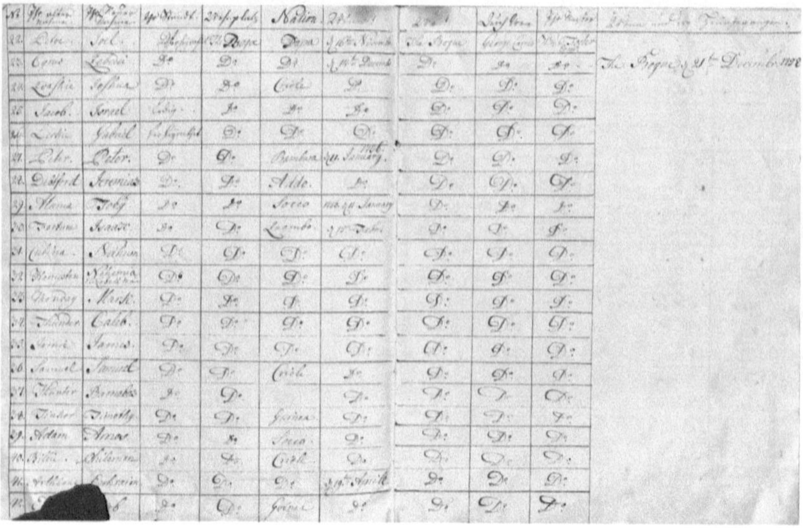

FIGURE 2.1. Moravian church register from Jamaica, 1759. Unitätsarchiv der Evangelischen Brüder-Unität, Herrnhut, Germany, R.15.C.a.02.05.02.

The reference to the Quambo nation is one of many Africana irruptions in the Moravian baptismal records. Figure 2.1 is a detail of the first page of the Moravian church register from Jamaica, which was created in 1759. It lists information about the seventy-seven Black men and women who were baptized in the Moravian church in the 1750s, as well as several dozen candidates for baptism. For each individual, missionaries recorded ten different data points: their old name (*Ihr alten Nahmen*), their new name (*Ihr neuen Nahmen*), their marital status (*Ihr Standt*), where they lived (*Wohn Platz*), their nation (*Nation*), the date of their baptism (*Wenn?*), their place of baptism (*Wo?*), the person who baptized them (*Durch wen*), their enslaver (*Ihr Meister*), and their time and place of death, if applicable (*Wenn und wo heimgegangen*).[1]

While most of these categories do not reflect Africana epistemologies, the inclusion of each congregant's nation provides an opportunity to center African categories and histories within a missionary archive. Through an analysis of the Moravian baptismal registers, we can learn, for example, that most individuals who received baptism in the Moravian church were African born: forty-seven of the seventy-seven individuals listed. Of the forty-seven Africans, seventeen were listed simply as being from Guinea, while the rest were given more specific nation designations, such as Coromantee, Papa, and Ibo (see appendix 1). The Jamaican church register can also be fruitfully compared to the church registers from the Danish West Indies, where the Moravians established a mission in 1732. In the Danish West Indies, Moravian missionaries recorded even more information: not only the nations of baptized members of the congregation, but also their parents' nation. Paired with interviews of Afro-Moravians conducted by Moravian ethnographer C. G. A. Oldendorp, it is possible to gain insight into how Africans and their descendants were creating families and networks of kin with diverse people from different nations.[2]

Reading these sources for Africana irruptions entails asking what it meant for Africans like Fortune, Cubanna, Hampton, Monday, Thunder, and so many others to identify their nation. We must also consider how this aspect of their identity connected with their decision to become part of the Moravian congregation. For each of the forty-seven Africans who were listed in the Moravian church register between 1755 and 1759, we can trace a general life story. Comparing the baptismal registers to Moravian diaries and other archival sources, we can glimpse how the men and women living at the Bogue plantation were re/forming kinship networks and sacred communities. Their nations were part of this process, but not simply through a process of transfer or retention.

I argue that the term *nation* that appears in the Moravian baptismal register was an Africana irruption and should be understood within a framework that I call religio-nation formation, a phrase that draws together Judith Weisenfeld's concept of the religio-racial with Dianne Stewart and Tracey Hucks's theorization of Africana nations.[3] In Africa and the African diaspora, the category of "nation" was dynamic and often had profound religious and political connotations, signifying a connection to sacred places, communities, polities, and identities. As Alexander X. Byrd and J. Lorand Matory have demonstrated, Africana nations were constantly in flux, as African captives adapted to enslavement and sought to create new communities of belonging in the Atlantic world.[4] In this chapter, I tie the rich scholarship on Africana nations together with recent scholarship on the history of race and religion.

The first section offers a review of scholarship on Africana nations alongside recent scholarship on religion and race to theorize the concept of the religio-nation in formation. Each subsequent section focuses on a group of Afro-Moravians who identified with a specific nation. I trace the evolution of each nation category over time to more fully imagine what it meant for Africans and their descendants to be part of the Moravian community. I end by arguing that the Moravian congregation can itself be understood as a religio-nation formed by Africans and their descendants in Jamaica.

Religio-Nations in Formation: Theorizing Religion, Nation, and Race

Scholars of the African diaspora have long debated how to interpret references to African nations, which many scholars have glossed as "ethnicities."[5] *Nations* could refer to geographic spaces or polities in Africa, but in the Americas, these signifiers evolved as Africans and their descendants utilized them to form new communities, kin relationships, and identities.[6] Recognizing that the term *nation*, like *religion*, is a category in flux is essential for examining diasporic lives.

I take inspiration from recent scholarship on Africana nations to rethink the meaning of *nation* as it is connected to religion and racial formation. In *Black Atlantic Religion*, J. Lorand Matory examines the connection between religion and nation in the late nineteenth and early twentieth centuries, when modern nation-states were coming into being. As Matory writes, while "white creoles were 'imagining' and reifying a nation called Brazil, Africans in Brazil and along the Lower Guinea coast were 'imagining' and sustaining a nation of a sort *un*imagined by Benedict Anderson."[7] For these Africans, both the diasporic Yoruba nation and the Afro-Brazilian Candomblé religion were defined and identified by practitioners through the language of nation.

More recently, Tracey Hucks and Dianne Stewart have offered a new appraisal of Africana nations in their two-volume study, *Obeah, Orisa, and Religious Identity in Trinidad*. Stewart and Hucks italicize the word *nation* to differentiate Africana constructions from Euro-Western conceptions of the nation. For them, Africana *nations* refer to "(1) related heritages in Africa and/or shared identities during the Middle Passage, (2) sovereign Powers, (3) spiritual families in the invisible realm, and (4) inter-*nation*-al exchanges with ambient nations."[8] Like Matory, Hucks and Stewart emphasize that the categories of religion and nation were deeply interconnected for Africans and their descendants.

In the context of the Moravian missionary records, we should interpret the "nation" designators in the baptismal records as complex and dynamic religio-nations in formation. Here, I connect the work of Stewart, Hucks, and Matory with recent research on the history of race and religion. Just as scholars of Africana nations have demonstrated the interconnections between nation and religion, religious studies scholars have emphasized that the categories of religion and race were co-constitutive.[9] In my previous scholarship, I have argued that the construction of whiteness emerged from a foundation in Christian identity, a history that continues to influence the performance and power of white Christianity.[10] Other scholars have examined how Africans and their descendants pushed back against white categorization to forge their own sense of identity. In *New World A-Coming*, Judith Weisenfeld examined how Black men and women constructed their identities during the Great Migration by resisting the racial categories defined in the US Census. Weisenfeld showed how religio-racial movements like the Nation of Islam and the Moorish Science Temple endowed black skin "with meaning derived from histories other than those of enslavement and oppression."[11]

Weisenfeld uses the phrase "religio-racial identity" to "capture the commitment of members of these groups to understanding individual and collective identity as constituted in the conjunction of religion and race."[12] Her approach is an important critique of previous scholarship that has focused on questions of authenticity, asking whether Black people "might be considered 'really' Muslim, Jewish, or Christian." Weisenfeld shows, instead, how people of African descent "have often contested racial categories, worked to reshape racial meaning by challenging racial hierarchy, or sought to dismantle race altogether, seeking other bases for collective identity still rooted in shared African descent."[13]

Weisenfeld's religio-racial framework is helpful because it centers the experiences and epistemologies of African-descended people and moves away from questions of authenticity based on Euro-Christian frameworks. In the literature on Afro-Christian communities in the Atlantic world, many scholars have utilized the concept of syncretism. As I have argued previously, I find this approach to be problematic because it maintains the hegemony of European categories and tends to make both European and African traditions appear static by asking how Africans and their descendants fit into Christianity as defined by missionaries or other European Christians.[14] It is important for scholars to utilize terminology that more effectively maps onto the epistemological orientations of Africans and their descendants whose perspectives are marginalized or, in Michel-Rolph Trouillot's words, "silenced" in the colonial and missionary archives.

I argue that the African and African-descended members of the Moravian congregation were articulating an important component of their African heritage and identity when they claimed their nation. Moreover, following the scholarship on Africana *nations*, we know that the concept of the nation was, itself, imbued with both political and religious connotations. As a result, I suggest that Weisenfeld's religio-racial framework should be adapted to the eighteenth-century African diaspora. The concept of a religio-nation in formation integrates Africana religious studies research on the interconnection between religion and nation with scholarship on the formation of religion and race. Significantly, the term *religio-nation* retains the term *nation* (rather than *ethnicity*) because it was an important term for Africans and their descendants, while also differentiating

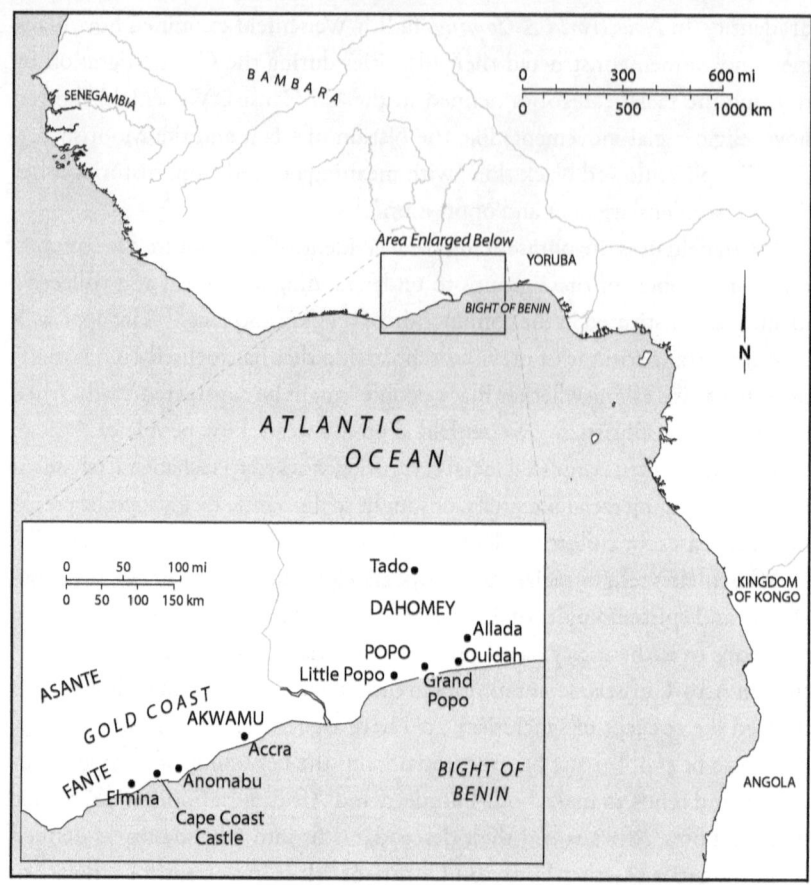

MAP 2.1. Map of West and West Central Africa. Drawn by Bill Nelson for *Archival Irruptions*.

it from modern conceptions of the nation-state. Finally, the reference to formations and re/formation reminds us of the dynamism of religio-nations, in both the past and the present.

Thinking about the category of nation through the concept of religio-nation helps to reframe the Moravian congregation through an Africana lens: Rather than viewing the congregants solely as Afro-Moravians or Afro-Christians, I argue that the Moravian congregation was itself a site of religio-nation re/formation: Africans and their descendants were re/forming their religio-national identities and communities, drawing on African precedents, including Kongo Catholicism and Islam, as well as Moravian rituals and theology.

Dynamic Religio-Nations on the Gold Coast: Fante and Coromantee

In Jamaica, Africans from what Europeans called the Gold Coast—the coastal region of modern-day Ghana—made up the largest percentage of enslaved people who arrived on the island between 1661 and 1760. During that century, an estimated 428,300 individuals were forcibly transported from Gold Coast ports like Anomabu, Elmina, and Cape Coast.[15] In the 1750s, when Caries established the first Moravian mission, nearly half of the Africans who disembarked in Jamaica were from the Gold Coast.[16] The stories of two of the men baptized in the summer of 1755, Dumbarton and Sherry, offer a window into the experiences of the almost quarter million people forcibly relocated to and enslaved in Jamaica.

While it will never be possible to understand the full complexity of their lives, it is important to begin imagining their worlds. Dumbarton and Sherry identified themselves as Fante and Coromantee, respectively. Although both designations can be traced back to the Gold Coast, they are linguistically and historically distinct. Tracing the evolution of each term shows that Fante and Coromantee were dynamic categories that were undergoing transformations both on the African continent and in the diaspora.

Dumbarton's identification as Fante suggests that he came from a religio-nation with a sacred history and community that was well established on the African continent. The term *Fante*, like other ethnic, linguistic, and political designations, has evolved over time, but in the mid-eighteenth century, the Fante people were part of what Rebecca Shumway has called the "Coastal Coalition," which controlled portions of the Gold Coast, including the port town of Anomabu.[17] Unlike other coastal inhabitants who spoke Guan or Etsi, the Fante people spoke a dialect of the Akan language, which was dominant in the hinterland.[18] The Fante were united by a sacred history: They regarded the town of Mankessim as the original settlement of their ancestors in the region, and they paid homage to their forebears at the sacred grove known as Nananom Mpow, where the Fante ancestors Oburumankuma, Odapagyan, and Osun were laid to rest. Over the course of the eighteenth century, the Fante exerted a significant influence over the culture, politics, and religious practice of southern Ghana. As they did, the Fante language became the lingua franca of the Coastal Coalition, and Fante speakers integrated elements of Guan and Etsi into their lexicon as well as words from European languages like Portuguese, Dutch, and English. Similarly, the sacred grove of Nananom Mpow was transformed from a local shrine into a "regionally revered oracle."[19]

Reading the baptismal register with an Africana lens suggests that Dumbarton may have brought memories of coastal politics, sacred oral histories about Nananom Mpow, and experience conversing with the diverse linguistic and ethnic groups in the Coastal Coalition, including Etsi and Guan speakers. He may also have had martial experience. Dumbarton was an adult when he sought baptism, suggesting that he was born in Fanteland in the early to mid-eighteenth century.[20] During that period, the Fante were in the process of expanding their influence along the coast and creating a coalition of coastal states.[21] This decentralized system of governance, which was based on robust diplomacy and treaties, helped to protect the Fante from the rapidly expanding Asante kingdom, but it also led to conflicts with some neighboring states.[22] Throughout this period, the term *Fante* was imbued with both religious and political significance, and Dumbarton would have brought this understanding with him into the Moravian congregation.

While Dumbarton's identification as Fante connects him to a religio-nation and a language with a strong presence in West Africa, Sherry's connection to the "Calamantie" nation connects him to an Atlantic nation in formation. Unlike *Fante*, the term *Calamantie* (an alternative spelling of *Coromantee* or *Kormantyn*) did not correspond to a specific nation in Africa. Instead, it was derived from the town of Kormantse, spelled Cormantyn in many English documents, a village located about halfway between Accra and Elmina on the coast of modern-day Ghana.[23] There, the English established Fort Kormantse in 1638. The Dutch displaced the English in 1665, renaming the site Fort Amsterdam, but the English continued to use the moniker Cormantyn and its derivatives to refer to the enslaved people who were sold through Cape Coast, Anomabu, and other ports on the Gold Coast.[24]

As English slave trading increased over the course of the seventeenth century, the term *Coromantee* began appearing frequently in English texts. It gained notoriety in 1688, when Aphra Behn's *Oroonoko: or, The Royal Slave*, was published to widespread success. *Oroonoko* told a fictional story of an African prince, the last of the Coramantien line, who was enslaved and transported to the island of Surinam.[25] The novel was adapted for the stage in 1695 and published as *Oroonoko: A Tragedy* in 1696. The story remained in print for over a century, helping to associate Coromantees with both nobility and war in the Anglophone Atlantic world.[26] Partly as a result of *Oroonoko*, Coromantees gained a reputation among English slave owners for strength, discipline, and intelligence, though they were also believed to be prone to rebellion. Jamaican slave owners, like their counterparts elsewhere in the Anglophone Atlantic, asserted a preference for Coromantees when they purchased enslaved laborers.²⁷

Despite its popularity with English authors and slave owners, Coromantee was not merely an enslavers' term. Scholars have shown how Africans took ownership of the Coromantee moniker to create new forms of belonging in the Atlantic world.²⁸ The process of ethnogenesis, or the creation of ethnic identity, was ongoing, and recent scholarship has shown that people known as Coromantee in mid-eighteenth-century Jamaica spoke multiple languages and came from different West African kingdoms. As Vincent Brown has written, Coromantees "comprised people who shared what are today known as Akan and other regional languages, recognizably familiar religious practices, some similar political ideals and symbols, and many principles of communal incorporation."²⁹ Similarly, Walter Rucker has emphasized that the creation of a Coromantee nation in the Americas must be understood within the complex history of West Africa. While most Coromantees in the eighteenth century could speak Akan, some Coromantee leaders in the Americas were Ga or Ewe speakers, suggesting a more dynamic story of ethnogenesis that was already well underway in West Africa, even before the process of enslavement.³⁰

African religious heritage often created a space of correlation for Afro-Moravians in their interpretation of Moravian theology. In Jamaica, the Coromantee members of the Moravian congregation told Caries that they knew God, and that his name was "Jamconpon."³¹ Indeed, on the eighteenth-century Gold Coast, Jancómpon (i.e., Jan Commaie, Jan Commé, Yancümpong, or Nyame in modern Akan orthography) was known as the sky god. Yet Jancómpon had not always been so prominent. Just as Nananom Mpow shifted from a local shrine to a regional deity as Fante influence grew on the coast, Jancómpon became more powerful within the cosmology of both Ga and Akan speakers after the Akwamu conquest of Accra. According to Rucker, this shift represented "either the *Akanization* of a Ga-speaking spiritual worldview or a set of independent cultural inventions that resonated within and beyond Akan, Ga, and Adanme cultural circles."³²

In both cases, religion and nation were not fixed entities, but rather dynamic processes that were already in motion when Dunbarton and Sherry were enslaved. Their baptism in the Moravian church did not mean that they rejected gods like Jancómpon or the shrine of Nananom Mpow; instead, their baptism should be understood as a re/formation of their religio-national identity. Their decision to become part of the Moravian congregation was part of a much longer story with deep and complex roots in the forests and coastal lands of West Africa.

Competing Religio-Nations in the Bight of Benin: Popo, Nago (Yoruba)

While the Fante and Coromantee may have been the majority in Jamaica, the Popo were the largest religio-nation in the Moravian congregation aside from the Quambo. Following the stories of Cyrus, Portland, and Peter, all of whom identified as Popo, alongside Sharper, who identified as "Naga" (Nago/Yoruba), offers insight into two competing religio-nations from West Africa to the east of the Gold Coast. Based on their identification as Nago or Popo, Cyrus, Portland, Peter, and Sharper were probably born and raised in the region that now comprises Togo, Benin (formerly Dahomey), and western Nigeria before they were forcibly transported through one of the ports on the Bight of Benin.[33] Indeed, Sharper, Portland, Peter, and Cyrus likely started their transatlantic voyage from the same site: Ouidah, a port city that was conquered by the expansionist kingdom of Dahomey in 1727 and became the "most prolific slave-trading port on the African coast."[34] Members of distinct nations from the same region—the Bight of Benin—may have viewed each other as foreigners in West Africa but likely recognized common features in their culture, intellectual traditions, and religious practices in the context of transatlantic slavery.

Understanding the complex history of Popo—both the place and the term—is crucial for recognizing how identity, like the categories of nation and religion, was shifting throughout the eighteenth century. In the mid-eighteenth century, *Popo* was primarily a reference to the kingdoms of Little Popo and Great (or Grand) Popo, located on the western edge of the Bight of Benin.[35] Robin Law has argued that the term *Popo* was originally used by the Yoruba to refer to their Gbe-speaking neighbors to the west, and that it was the Yoruba who introduced this term to the Portuguese.[36] The people of Popo, however, called themselves Pla, Fla, or Afra, and they traced their origins to the ancestral city of Tado.[37]

Grand Popo and Little Popo, while sharing the same name, had distinct histories. Grand Popo, which was located farther east than Little Popo, was settled by Aja (Ewe) migrants from Tado.[38] Little Popo was also settled by Aja (Ewe) people, but beginning in the 1680s, refugees from the Gold Coast immigrated into Little Popo, fleeing the expanding Akwamu empire, which had conquered Accra and Ladoku.[39] As these Ga and Adangme refugees fled east of the Volta River, some settled in Anlo while others moved farther into Little Popo. Among the refugees were members of the Ga ruling family, including Ofori (Foli Bebe), who established Glidje, the capital of the Little Popo kingdom.[40] As a result, Little Popo became what Silke Strickrodt has called a "plural community," where Hula, Aja/Ewe, Fante, Ga, and Adangme people lived together, though in separate settlements, and Ga migrants retained strong connections with Accra.

It is important to keep this complexity in mind when we only have single national identifiers for most Afro-Moravians in the Jamaican church registers. By understanding the interconnected but distinct histories of Little Popo and Grand Popo, as well as their relationship to other regions, languages, and ethnicities such as Ga and Accra, we can begin to imagine some of the ways that Popo men like Cyrus, Portland, and Peter may have narrated their own histories. Perhaps they were from Little Popo and traced their lineage back to the Ga migrants who fled Accra in the late eighteenth century; or they may have been Aja speakers who viewed Tado as their ancestral home. The influence of Ga migrants from Accra in Little Popo shows how the regions of the Gold Coast and the Slave Coast were deeply intertwined. Moreover, Africans used multiple and evolving terms of belonging to identify themselves, their kin, and their people.

The lives and stories of two Afro-Moravians from Popo, Christian Jacob Protten and Damma (aka Madlena or Marotta), show the complicated, evolving, and dynamic nature of religio-national identity in West Africa and the African diaspora. Protten, who was born in Accra-Osu, was related to the ruling families of Accra and Little Popo through his mother, the daughter of the Ga king Ofori.[41] Protten, whose father was Danish, traveled to Europe in 1727, where he met members of the Moravian church and converted to Christianity in the 1730s. He later married the free Afro-Moravian woman Rebecca Freundlich, who was one of the leaders in the St. Thomas Moravian church.[42] Eventually, Protten returned to West Africa and wrote about the relationship between Accra, Christiansborg, and Little Popo; then, in 1764, he drew on his multiethnic and multilingual background to create a manuscript titled *En nyttig grammaticalsk Indledelse til tvende hidintil gandske ubekiendte Sprog, Fanteisk og Acraisk* or A Useful Grammatical Introduction to Two Completely Unknown Languages, Fante and Ga, which introduced Danish speakers to Fante and Ga.[43] Protten himself maintained ties to the king of Little Popo, Assiambo, as well as his kin in Accra-Osu. Protten's connection to Accra and Little Popo, his conversion to Moravian Christianity, and his knowledge of multiple languages, including Ga and Fante, show how one person could embody multiple ethnic, linguistic, and religious identities.

We can gain further insight into the meaning of Popo by examining the writings of Damma (also known as Madlena or Marotta), an Afro-Moravian woman who lived on the island of Saint Thomas. In 1739, Damma, who was born and raised in Popo, referred to her African upbringing in a letter she wrote to the queen of Denmark. In her original Gbe text, Damma referred to

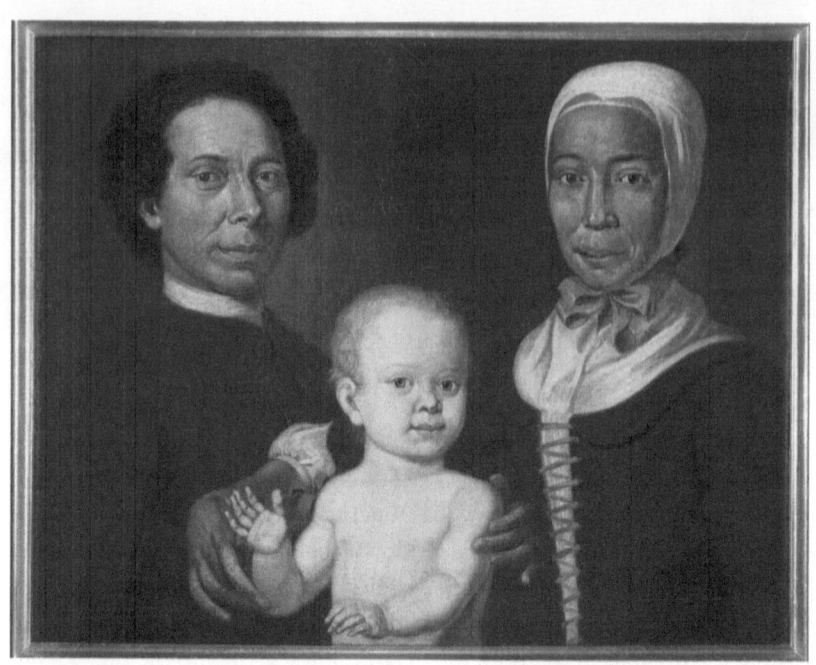

FIGURE 2.2. Christian Protten (left) with Rebecca Protten (right) and their child, ca. 1750. Unitätsarchiv der Evangelischen Brüder-Unität, Herrnhut, Germany, GS.393.

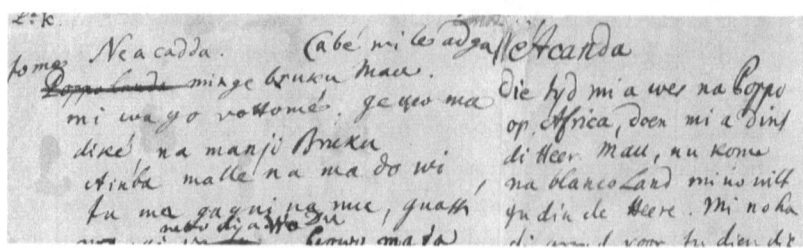

FIGURE 2.3. Detail of Damma's petition to the queen of Denmark in Gbe (left) and Dutch creole (right), 1739. Unitätsarchiv der Evangelischen Brüder-Unität, Herrnhut, Germany, R.15.B.a.03.61_a-b.

her homeland as "adga Tome," which can be translated as "Aja country."[44] In the Dutch creole version, "adga Tome" was translated as "Poppo op Africa," or "Popo in Africa."[45]

Damma's dual identification as being from "Poppo op Africa" and from "adga Tome," or "Aja country," is emblematic of diasporic Africans' overlapping and multiple methods of religio-national identification. It also shows how they used these terms in strategic and meaningful ways. Within the context of the petition to the queen of Denmark, Damma probably used the term *Popo* (or *Poppo*) because it was well known to Europeans. But she also chose to use the less well-known terminology "adga Tome" in her native language. By referring to "adga Tome," Damma connected herself with a language (Aja) and a region ("Aja country") that overlapped with the term *Popo* but also had distinct meaning. Damma may have recalled, for example, her connection to the ancestral site of Tado, while the term *Popo* was primarily helpful in gaining recognition from people outside her ethnic group, whether Yoruba speakers or Europeans.[46]

Like *Popo*, the term *Nago* also demonstrates the complicated and dynamic nature of ethnic identity and transregional African politics. The term *Nago* itself was likely derived from Aja speakers like Damma. In the eighteenth century, *Anago* was a general term used by the Aja to refer to the Yoruba speakers to their east. Initially, *Anago* referred to a specific Yoruba subgroup in the Ifonyin area, but its usage broadened after it was adopted by the French in Dahomey.[47] The term *Yoruba*, which is common today, was not widely used until the nineteenth century, and it derives from the Hausa term *Yarriba*, which was adopted by the missionaries who created the first Yoruba dictionary in the 1840s.[48]

The first European reference to *Nago* appeared in a French source listing the ethnicities of the enslaved people who were sold through Whydah (Ouidah) in 1725. At the time, *Nago* referred to people from western Yorubaland, where many Yoruba speakers were enslaved in Dahomean raids.[49] Over the next several decades, people who identified as Nago became a growing community in the Americas, especially in Brazil, where nearly half a million Yoruba speakers arrived between the seventeenth and nineteenth centuries.[50] In Brazil, the Nago subdivided themselves even further, distinguishing between Nagô-Ba (Egba), Nagô-Jebu (Ijebu), and Nagô-Gexá (Ijesha), as well as others.[51] Yet *Nago* was just one of two terms used to refer to Yoruba speakers in the African diaspora. The other term, *Lucumí*, was predominant in Spanish colonies and was likely derived from the Yoruba greeting *oluku mi*, meaning "my friend." *Nago* was the term that was most common in Brazil, Saint-Domingue, and the British Caribbean.[52]

Only one person in the Moravian congregation identified as Nago: an enslaved man named Sharper who was baptized on September 21, 1755, and given the name Abraham.[53] In the early to mid-eighteenth century, when Sharper was born and raised, Yoruba speakers in West Africa were part of a connected group of city-states, dominated by the city-state of Ife, which was settled in the ninth century. In the fourteenth century, the city-state of Oyo began to expand, asserting dominance over other city-states and growing into a small empire that stretched beyond Yorubaland into Dahomey and Benin.[54] By the late eighteenth century, the Oyo empire had begun to disintegrate, while the kingdom of Dahomey expanded to the west and the Muslim Fulani gained power to the north. During this period of unrest and warfare, an estimated 1.67 million Yoruba men, women, and children were enslaved and transported to the Americas, one of whom was Sharper.[55]

Based on Sharper's identification as Nago, it is likely that he was enslaved as part of the Dahomean wars of expansion. The term *Nago* appeared most commonly to refer to the victims of Dahomean raids who were sold from the port of Ouidah.[56] Sharper may have had facial scarification—a common practice among many West Africans, and especially the Nago and other Yoruba groups.[57] The Nago used metal instruments to inscribe markings, known as *abaja*, on the faces of Yoruba children. This ritual was generally performed by a priest, known as the *alakila*, or master of scarification, when a child was six or seven years old.[58] Although in West Africa Sharper would have viewed Aja speakers from Popo as foreigners, within the context of transatlantic slavery, he likely recognized common features in their culture, intellectual traditions, and religious practices.

Islam and Religio-Nations in Senegambia: Mandingo, Bambara

While the majority of Afro-Moravians were from the Gold Coast or the Bight of Benin, at least two—Cambridge and Peter—were from Senegambia, the northwestern region of the African continent between the Senegal and Gambia rivers. Cambridge identified himself as Mandingo, while Peter was Bambara. Senegambia, which is the sub-Saharan region closest to the Mediterranean, had centuries-old trade routes to Morocco, Egypt, and elsewhere that predated the European appearance on the maritime coast in the fifteenth century. Islam, which was introduced in the eighth century CE, was the dominant religion in the region.[59] The lives and stories of Cambridge, baptized Shem on May 30, 1756, and Peter, who retained the name Peter after his baptism on January 11, 1756, offer a window into the relationship between Islam, African religious traditions, and nations in Africa and the diaspora.

Cambridge's nation, Mandingo, has, along with its correlates (Mandinka, Malinke), become one of the most recognizable African ethnicities.[60] Yet the visibility of the word *Mandingo* can make it difficult to discern the term's historical contours.[61] In fifteenth-century Portuguese sources, the term *Mandega* was used to refer to the area of Senegambia that stretched from the Gambia River to the Rio São Domingos, or Rio Cacheu.[62] Yet this regional usage was derived from an ethnic origin. As Stephan Bühnen has written, the toponym Mandinga was "derived from the ethnonym Mandenga/Mandinka ('person of Mande'), which in turn was derived from the name of the Mand(ing) region on the left bank of the Niger, southwest of Bamako, possibly the nucleus of the Mali empire."[63] Philip Curtin has concluded that "'Mandingue' (or Mandingo in English) was originally a term attached to the Malinke-speaking people of the Gambia valley, but it later spread to all speakers of Mande languages."[64] What seems clear is that Mandingos were Mande speakers who traced their ancestry to the people of the Mali Empire.[65] Islam was the dominant religion among the Mandingos and had been since the eleventh century, when several African rulers in the Senegambian region converted.[66]

The term *Mandingo* was also connected to sacred practices. As Cécile Fromont has described, "Mande groups notoriously used amulets containing Islamic-inspired inscriptions enclosed in leather pouches along with other empowered material."[67] In the Luso-Atlantic world, enslaved people of the Mandingo nation were arrested for carrying small pouches known as *bolsas de mandinga*, which were viewed by inquisitors as evidence of "witchcraft."[68]

The Moravian missionary and historian C. G. A. Oldendorp interviewed several Mandingo men and one Mandingo woman on Saint Thomas in the mid-eighteenth century.[69] According to Oldendorp's interviews, the Mandingos were skilled in spinning, knitting, and weaving. Some had ritual scarification. Of the Mandingos on Saint Thomas, two had "straight downward-going lines on either side of the face between the ear and the eye," while a third "didn't have these signs, but rather a hole on the bottom of each ear."[70] The Mandingos on Saint Thomas confirmed the importance of Islam, and several of them called God "by the Muslim name Allah." Some were literate. "Many of them learn to read and write," wrote Oldendorp, and "some have a little board where they write and then they pray using it."[71] The emphasis on literacy was another indicator of Islam. Sylviane Diouf has written about how European visitors were consistently "surprised by the number of schools in West Africa compared to the norm in their own countries" and that the director of a French trading company was especially impressed with the Mandingos because they had public schools where they learned Arabic.[72] Still, not all Mandingos were Muslim. One Mandingo in the Danish West Indies called God "Margetangala," which also meant "sky." Two others called God "Kanniba," and they "prayed to him early until the sun came up."[73] Given the diversity within the term *Mandingo*, we cannot say with certainty if Cambridge (Shem) was Muslim, although it is likely that he was at least familiar with Islam, Arabic, and the Qu'ran. If he had learned to read and write in Senegambia, he may have been drawn to the Moravians' library at Carmel, which included over a hundred books, including language primers, Bibles, plays, novels, and histories.[74]

While Cambridge (Shem) may have been Muslim, Peter was most likely non-Muslim. In coastal Senegambia, the term *Bambara* carried religious connotations: Muslim traders used it to identify an enslaved person as non-Muslim—an important distinction because Islamic law forbade the enslavement of fellow Muslims.[75] As a result, scholars have debated whether Bambara was a self-conscious ethnic group or just a generic term for *slave*. It seems likely that it was both.[76] On the island of Gorée and elsewhere on the Senegambian coast, European merchants adopted the term *Bambara* from African merchants as a catchall term for *slave*. But Bambara was also an ethnic identity and a kingdom located in the interior of Senegambia. The changing meaning of the term *Bambara* can be compared to the etymology of the word *Slav* in Europe and the Mediterranean world. *Slav*, like *Bambara*, referred to a people, but as Slavs became increasingly associated with slavery in the Mediterranean and western Europe, the term became increasingly generic over time.[77] Similarly, the Bambara were a self-conscious ethnic group in the eighteenth century. Over time, they became a major source of slaves for the Mandingos and others, who had a prohibition against enslaving other Muslims. This usage, however, coexisted with the self-identification of Bambara.[78]

In the early eighteenth century, the Ségu Bambara kingdom was an expansionist military state that integrated captives into its ranks in order to replace and increase its own members. Captives would become part of the warrior class, and they either spoke or learned to speak Bamanakan. The Africans who identified as Bambara in the Americas may have been ethnic Bambaras who were connected to the Ségu Bambara kingdom, or they may have chosen to associate with the designation of Bambara at some point after their enslavement. Peter Caron has suggested that in Louisiana, where a large proportion of enslaved people were identified as Bambara, the term "may not have referred to an ethnicity *per se* but instead to a group identification of another sort."[79] Yet in Jamaica, unlike Louisiana, there was not a large population of Bambaras. In the Moravian congregation, Peter was the sole person identified as Bambara. Within this context, it is more likely that Peter was, in fact, ethnically Bambara and/or connected to the expansionist Ségu Bambara kingdom. At the Bogue, he was the head sugar boiler, a skilled position that suggests that he was not a newcomer to the plantation. He had likely arrived several years earlier—possibly even a decade or two—which would mean that he was enslaved during the 1730s or 1740s, when the Ségu Bambara king Mamari Kulubari (r. 1712–55) was consolidating his power over rival factions. Between 1739 and 1744, thousands of men and women were enslaved in the Ségu Bambara kingdom and transported to the coast, and Peter may have been one of them.[80]

The fact that there was one Mandingo and one Bambara in the Moravian congregation challenges some assumptions about the meanings of these terms. Douglas Chambers has suggested that when there are two terms available for a particular region (e.g., Lucumí or Nago for Yoruba), only one of those terms will predominate in a particular region or colony. As he explains, ethnic nomenclature "varied systematically over time and space, so that if Eboe/Moko was used to denote people from 'Calabar' (Bight of Biafra), then Carabalí generally was not used, and vice versa, and so with Mandingo/Bambara, Coromantee/Mina, Nagô/Lucumí, and others such as Mungola/Mondongue, and including even lesser groups like Cangá/Misérables."[81] As this quotation suggests, the terms *Mandingo* and *Bambara* were unlikely to be used in the same time and place. Yet here, within the small Moravian congregation, we have two men, one Mandingo and one Bambara. This indicates that the two terms were more meaningful than some scholars have assumed. Cambridge, for example, may have wanted to emphasize his Mandingo identity due to its association with Islam, his native language, or any number of complicated and unknown reasons.

The coexistence of the Bambara and Mandingo nations within the Moravian congregation suggests that these terms should be understood as religio-nations in formation rather than simple geographic referents or static ethnicities. It also demonstrates how community microhistories can provide important data for broader studies of Africana nations. Within the context of one community, we can see how African nations that had overlapping geographical referents were evolving within an Atlantic setting. Aside from Mandingo and Bambara, this type of intracommunal analysis can be extended to other religio-national pairings: The fact that Dumbarton identified as Fante while three other Afro-Moravians described themselves as Coromantee, for example, provides insight into the terms as well as the individuals. As a Fante from the Gold Coast, Dumbarton could have identified as a Coromantee. In fact, perhaps he did. Like all members of the congregation, Dumbarton almost certainly utilized multiple and overlapping terms that connected him with different groups, communities, and polities. Yet, at least within the context of the Moravian mission, he chose to highlight his Fante identity despite the fact that there were no other baptized Fantes in the congregation. Perhaps he wanted to distinguish himself from the other Akan speakers in the congregation; or perhaps his decision to emphasize his Fante religio-national identity connected him to religious sites like Nananom

Mpow. It is impossible to say, but noting these possibilities is important for broadening our imaginations and better appreciating the complex intellectual, political, and social worlds of Afro-Moravians like Cambridge, Peter, Dumbarton, and Sherry.

African Christianity and Religio-Nations in West Central Africa: Kingdom of Kongo

Coal, who was baptized on the same day as Cambridge (Shem), identified himself as a member of the Congo nation, suggesting that he was from the Kingdom of Kongo in West Central Africa. His baptism, on May 30, 1756, was one of the most diverse rites Caries performed: In addition to Cambridge and Coal (who was baptized Sadook), Caries baptized Romalus/Seth (Coromantee), Penny/Elizer (Ibo), Eden Charles/Ruben (Ibo), Cromwell/Onesimus (Creole), George/Ignatius (Creole), and Quaco/Sylus (Creole). Together, they represented vast swaths of the African continent, from Senegambia in the north to present-day Angola and Congo in West Central Africa.

While Cambridge may have been Muslim, Coal, the sole Congo man in the congregation, almost certainly encountered Christianity in Africa before he was enslaved. The Kingdom of Kongo, which was founded in the fourteenth century and stretched from the Congo River in the north to the Luanda Island in the south, had a long history with the Catholic Church.[82] Starting in the 1480s, the Kingdom of Kongo established diplomatic and trading relations with the Portuguese, and in 1491, King Nzinga a Nkuwu requested and received Catholic baptism. Nzinga a Nkuwu, who was given the baptismal name João I, instituted widespread reforms throughout the kingdom that were expanded by his son, Afonso I Mvemba a Nzinga, who ruled the Kingdom of Kongo from 1509 until his death in 1542.[83] Over the next two centuries, even as the relationship between Kongo and Portugal unraveled, Catholicism continued to play an important role in Kongo. After the Portuguese invaded the southern region of the kingdom to create the colony of Angola in the 1620s, the king of Kongo moved to strengthen the kingdom's relationship with the papacy and with specific Catholic orders, including the Capuchins, who worked under the control of the Kongo crown.[84]

By the time Coal was born in the early to mid-eighteenth century, the Kingdom of Kongo had experienced a long period of civil war, which destabilized the kingdom.[85] By that point, Christianity was woven into the fabric of life in complicated and unexpected ways. The political leader and antislavery advocate Dona Beatriz Kimpa Vita, for example, drew power and inspiration from

Saint Anthony, who appeared before her in a vision and advised her to restore the Kingdom of Kongo. Her vision built on her experience as an initiate to the rite of spirit possession as well as her Catholic faith—a faith her family had proclaimed for generations. Dona Beatriz united Kongolese cosmology with her vision of a Black Jesus and Mary, a revised catechism, and a promise of wealth. Her bold articulation of Catholic practice disturbed European Christian missionaries but brought her a mass following, which resulted in the suppression of her movement and her execution in 1706.[86]

If Coal was born in the early eighteenth century, he may have heard stories about Dona Beatriz. Even if he had not, he would almost certainly have been familiar with Catholicism. By the eighteenth century, Kongo society had integrated Catholic practice and visual culture into everyday life. As a result, it is misleading to bifurcate the categories of Catholic and African religious traditions. Instead, the art historian Cécile Fromont has argued that scholars should move away from Eurocentric ideas about Christian conversion in Kongo and instead examine spaces of correlation within the sacred landscape.[87] Similarly, scholars of Afro-Catholicism have emphasized that scholars should not separate African religions from the practice of Christianity, either in Kongo or in the Americas.[88]

Even if Coal was familiar with Kongo Christianity before his enslavement, the practice of Moravian Christianity would have been distinct. The Moravian theological focus on the suffering Jesus was likely familiar, but the specific worship of Jesus's side wound was probably new. Either way, the Moravian congregation likely offered a space of correlation where Coal could re/form aspects of his ritual, intellectual, and political practice from Kongo into the Moravian church. His story is a reminder that not all congregants in the Moravian church were new to Christian practice. It also suggests that the most important story about the Moravian congregation is not about conversion but rather about the reformation of sacred meaning and sacred community within an African diasporic context.

Nation, Country, Religion: The Case of the Ibo

An African diasporic lens is essential for understanding the creation of a Moravian community in Jamaica. It was a religio-national community that formed through affinities of theology, practice, and worship, but it was also the product of the violence, fear, and cruelty of the Middle Passage and plantation slavery. The cultivation, adoption, and redefinition of new forms of identity and community began in Africa, was forged in terror and hope during the Middle Passage, and continued in the cities, forests, waterways, and fields of the Americas. To examine this process further, we can turn to the baptism of two men, both of whom identified themselves as Ibo. Penny, who labored as a shepherd at the Bogue, was baptized Elizer, while Eden Charles was given the name Ruben. The two men were baptized together on May 30, 1756, along with Coal and Cambridge.

The meaning of Igbo (also Ibo, Eboe, etc.), like the terms for other African nations, evolved within an Afro-Atlantic context. While the word *Igbo* (Ibo) existed in Africa, few enslaved people who boarded slaving ships would have identified themselves as such. In the eighteenth-century Biafran interior, *Igbo* was generally an insult and expression of contempt. As Alexander Byrd has argued, communities living on the Niger used the term *Igbo* to denote "those who did not wash," while people living west of the Niger might use it to "denigrate the peoples dwelling just on the other side of the waterway."[89] Even in the nineteenth century, when Reverend Sigismund Koelle interviewed enslaved people who were shipped from Biafran ports and then emancipated at sea, he noted that while these Africans were "called Ibos," they identified themselves as "Isoama, Mbofia, Isiele, and Aro."[90]

The creation of an Igbo nation was a process facilitated, in part, by affinities of language, politics, and cosmology, but it was also created in the violence, dislocation, and loss of the slave trade and the Middle Passage.[91] We can see this process in the writings of Gustavus Vassa, better known as Olaudah Equiano, the most famous Igbo of the eighteenth century. As Alexander Byrd has shown, Vassa used the terms *Eboe*, *nation*, and *country* in multiple ways.[92] When he spoke of nations, Vassa sometimes meant *town*, as when he was writing about his own travel from the Nigerian hinterland to the coast and passing through different nations. Yet Vassa also used *nation* and *country* in a geopolitical sense, when he traveled "through different countries, and various nations."[93] *Nation* could also be a proto-racial term, as it was when Vassa found his "own nation" belowdecks on the slave ship.

As this analysis indicates, *nation* and *country* were malleable and expansive within eighteenth-century discourse. A nation did not represent a linguistic community, although it could sometimes be deployed in that manner; nor was it decisively a racialized term, although it could be used in this manner as well.[94] Recognizing the changing ways that Africans identified themselves and narrated their enslavement sheds light on the ways that African captives "responded cognitively to the challenges of their migrations."[95] Through the processes of alienation and religio-nation re/formation, terms like *Igbo* were adopted and redefined by Africans and their descendants in the diaspora, who used them to create new communities of belonging.

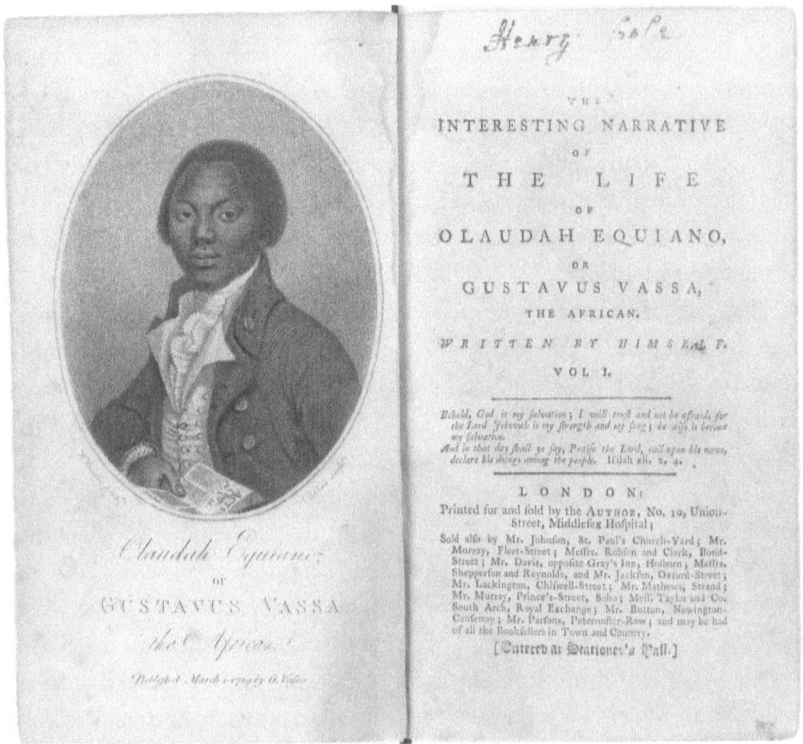

FIGURE 2.4. Frontispiece for Olaudah Equiano, *The Interesting Narrative of the Life of Olaudah Equiano, or Gustavus Vassa, the African* (London, 1789). Courtesy of the John Carter Brown Library.

A Methodology of Possibility: The Case of the Quambo

While we can have a degree of certainty about the meaning of some terms like *Ibo, Coromantee*, and *Nago*, others are more elusive. One of the most elusive is *Quambo*, which was not a common designation in Africa or the Atlantic world. It was, however, the largest nation represented in the Moravian congregation. The Quambo baptism on February 15, 1756, which began this chapter, was the only one to feature one nation exclusively. The fact that all Quambos were listed as "men" and "old" suggests a gendered and age-based bond that is unlike the other baptisms in the Moravian church register.

It is impossible to say with certainty what *Quambo* means, but there are a few possibilities. The historian John Catron identified Quambo as an alternate spelling of "Chamba," an ethnic designation originating in the Bight of Benin.[96]

If this is the case, then the six older African men who requested baptism together likely spoke a Gur language.[97] The historian Robin Law offers another possibility. "Quambo," he suggests, is an alternative spelling of "Akwamu," the expansionist kingdom in the Gold Coast, or present-day Ghana.[98] Beginning in 1679, the kingdom of Akwamu emerged as a major power in the region. Soon thereafter, Akwamu armies began moving from the hinterland of Ghana to the coast, conquering Accra in 1681.[99] By the early eighteenth century, the Akwamu kingdom stretched over a hundred miles on either side of the Volta River, making it one of the most powerful states in the region. Over time, however, the Kingdom of Akwamu was challenged by Asante and Akyem, and in 1730, they were forced out of Accra. Many Akwamu migrated east of the Volta, setting up a capital in Nyanowase, at the foot of the Akwapim-Togo hills.[100] Others were enslaved and transported to the Americas.

If the six older men who were baptized together were Akwamu, they may have been soldiers in the Akwamu army during the 1720s and 1730s. If so, they were part of an Akwamu diaspora with significant military expertise. The historian Ray Kea has suggested that the 1733 slave rebellion on the Danish island of St. John should be understood as an extension of the Akwamu kingdom's state-building efforts on the Gold Coast. According to Kea, many of the leaders of the uprising in St. John were Akwamu elites who sought to re-create the Akwamu kingdom in the Caribbean.[101] On Jamaica, scholars have traced the connections between the Gold Coast diaspora, which included the Akwamu, and the massive uprising of 1760.[102]

We cannot know which—if any—of these narratives best describes the experiences of the Quambo members of the congregation, but it is important to reconstruct the possibilities. Doing so allows us to recognize the complicated political, religious, and social histories of West Africa and to identify the dynamics that may have influenced the lives of Afro-Moravians. So while the meaning of *Quambo* remains obscure, historical research about West Africa still gives us crucial insight into the lives that Fortune, Cubanna, Hampton, Monday, Thunder, and Jamie may have led both before and after they were enslaved.

Religio-Nations and the Re/formation of Sacred Communities

This chapter has argued that scholars must center dynamic African histories when examining religious communities in the Americas. This is especially true for Afro-Christian congregations, where it is easier to maintain a Euro-

Christian framework based on the perception that conversion represented a turn from one belief system to another. And yet, as this chapter has demonstrated, Africana religio-nations remained of fundamental significance for the Africans who chose to join the Moravian congregation in Jamaica during the 1750s. Afro-Moravians—like Africans throughout the Americas—had a diversity of experiences with religion and religious traditions in Africa, including Christianity and Islam as well as other African religions. Coal (Sadook) was born into a Catholic kingdom (Kongo), while Cambridge (Shem) was probably a Muslim (Mandingo). These histories remained significant when Africans and their descendants re/formed sacred communities throughout the Atlantic world.

An Africana lens also offers crucial insight into the categories of religion and nation as these two terms developed within an early modern Atlantic context. Here we can ask: How is a nation different from a religion or a country, particularly for a people who have been uprooted from their homeland, forced into bondage, and transported across the seas? As this chapter has argued, for many Africans, a national origin like Fante was not only a geographic or political referent: It also represented a connection to a sacred history, a shrine (like Nananom Mpow), and a sacred chronology that centered around ancestors. As a result, it is crucial to push back against the impulse to separate the categories of religion and nation, and instead recognize the ways in which these categories were intimately bound up with each other as religio-nations.

The framework of religio-nation formation allows us to ask different questions about the congregants in the Moravian congregation: What did it really mean, for example, for Cambridge (Shem) to identify himself as Mandingo and to seek baptism within the Moravian church? How did the meanings of Mandingo and Moravian interact for him? If he was raised as a Muslim in Senegambia, how did he narrate the relationship between the traditions and rituals of his past and present? While we may not be able to answer these questions, asking them is, itself, a significant step toward telling histories that do not center European and Christian categories.

Building on chapter 1, which argued that Afro-Moravians viewed Christianity through the lens of Obeah, this chapter has suggested that the Moravian congregation was itself a site of re/formation for Africana religio-nations. African members of the Moravian congregation were re/forming both nations and religions as they connected their homelands and their new lives in Jamaica through sacred practices and communities. This process was not just about identity. Instead, the connection to African nations like Ibo, Fante, and Kongo were integral to the ways enslaved men and women experienced religion and interpreted Moravian theology and practice. By rejecting an epistemology of separation (that is, the rupture of the Middle Passage), we can move away from static conceptions of religion and nation and toward an embodied and dynamic model of religio-nation formation that highlights practice, being, and becoming.

3

Maroons, Blood Oaths, and Gendered Irruptions
ACCOMPONG AND MARGERY

On March 27, 1755, Accompong, a Maroon leader in Jamaica, met the Moravian missionary Zacharias George Caries for the first time. By the mid-eighteenth century, when Caries arrived on the island, central Jamaica had been home to Maroon communities for more than a century. The Jamaican Maroons were descendants of African and indigenous people who escaped slavery and created their own religio-nations in the island's mountainous interior, where they developed sovereign governments that harnessed the religious and political authority of Obeah.[1] Maroons consulted and followed Obeah men and women in making political and military decisions, used oaths to affirm community bonds, and drew on African precedent to create rituals of incorporation to unify members from different religio-national backgrounds.[2]

This chapter examines two archival irruptions about the Jamaican Maroons. The first focuses on the Maroon leader Accompong and highlights the significance of treaty-making and blood oaths in African diasporic history. The second features a Maroon woman named Margery. Based on an analysis of "gendered" irruptions, it shows how Margery used multiple strategies to maintain Maroon sovereignty and cultivate enslaved–Maroon kinship networks. Together, these irruptions demonstrate the central role of Obeah oaths in Jamaican politics and offer a nuanced portrait of Maroon life in eighteenth-century Jamaica.

In his diary, Caries described Accompong's appearance in detail. Accompong wore "an embroidered Waistcoat, gold Lace around his Hat, [and] a silver chain ab[ou]t his Neck." He had "Ear Rings & on each of his Fingers 5, 6, or 7 Rings of silver." On his feet, he wore "some Iron Rings," but otherwise went "barefooted." Perhaps the most striking aspect of his appearance, however, was the "silver Medal" that hung from the chain around Accompong's neck. On one side "was King George ye 2nd's Picture"; on the other was "his Commission with this subscription *Captain Acampong*."[3] Following their first meeting, Accompong invited Caries to his town, where he honored the missionary by "fir[ing] his Guns 41 times."[4] Accompong's interest in Caries presents a puzzle: what motivated the free and sovereign Maroons to engage with a newly arrived missionary from a small and controversial Protestant denomination?

Caries's description of Accompong is an archival irruption, and I read this moment through an Africana lens by pairing it with Maroon oral histories to examine the religious and political dimensions of Accompong's decision to pursue a relationship with Caries. While Caries viewed Accompong's medal from King George II as a fascinating accessory, listed along with rings and embroidered lace, its significance was much farther reaching. The medal can be interpreted as a representation of the 1739 Maroon-British treaty and should be understood within the long history of African oath making, diplomacy, and coalition building. As Maroon oral histories make clear, the treaty remains sacred in the twenty-first century.

While the reference to Accompong and his silver medal is an important Africana irruption, reading the archives with a *gendered* lens reveals an essential and overlooked story: the role that a Maroon woman named Margery played in negotiating Maroon sovereignty and cultivating Maroon–enslaved bonds. Margery is never named in Caries's diary. Caries refers to her only as the "wife" of Titus, an enslaved man at the Bogue plantation who was one of the first individuals baptized in the Moravian Church of Jamaica. Focusing on Margery reveals hidden dynamics in Maroon political and religious history. Piecing together fleeting references, I show how Margery strategized to maintain spatial freedom, cultivated intimacy and boundaries in her relationships, and ensured increased mobility for enslaved and Maroon men, women, and children. Reading for gendered irruptions is important because—with the exception of the Maroon leader and Obeah woman Nanny—British colonial archives consistently occlude the presence and significance of women and female leadership in their histories of the Maroons.

Together, these two archival irruptions—one about Accompong, the second about Margery—offer new insight into the complicated role of the Maroons in eighteenth-century Jamaica.[5] The history of the Maroons is generally told as one of rebellion and complicity: The Maroons are celebrated as freedom fighters for their rejection of slavery but also labeled traitors for their decision to sign a treaty with the British in 1739. As part of the treaty, the Maroons agreed to return enslaved runaways to plantations and to fight with the British in the case of a slave rebellion. In 1760, during Tacky's Revolt, the Maroons were instrumental in the eventual defeat of the rebels.

This chapter tells a different story about the Maroons and their role in Jamaican society between the 1739 treaty and Tacky's Revolt of 1760. Following a review of Maroon historiography, the chapter focuses first on the famous Accompong and argues that we should interpret his silver medal as a "legal technology" that was part of a long history of Africana oath-taking, Obeah, and political formation. It then turns to the less-famous Margery, who—while never named in Caries's diary—played a pivotal role in the Maroon–Moravian alliance. Margery's role in linking the Maroons and the Moravians was significant but it only becomes visible when we center Margery to unearth what Katherine McKittrick has called "black women's geographies" in the African diaspora.[6]

Jamaica's Maroons: From Rebellion to Treaty

In 1755, when Margery and Accompong met Caries, the Maroons were known for their practice of Obeah, their fierce resistance to colonial slavery before and during the First Maroon War, and their 1739 treaty with the British colonial government. Their origins in Jamaica predate the British colony: When the English conquered Jamaica in 1655, some ex-slaves of the Spanish retreated into the interior of the island to form Maroon communities, possibly joining communities that already existed.[7] Between 1660 and 1739, as the English system of plantation slavery grew, so did the Maroon settlements. Fleeing terrorizing treatment and the brutal labor regime of sugar cultivation, scores of enslaved people risked torture, dismemberment, and death by fleeing into the mountains. Most new Maroons were runaways who escaped on their own or in groups, sometimes following a rebellion. Others were captured during Maroon raids.[8]

The Maroons created governments that harnessed the religious and political authority of Obeah, which they used to incorporate new members. Political leaders sought out Obeah men and women for guidance on military and diplomatic strategy. Maroon governance structures were heavily influenced by Coromantee religio-nation formations on the Gold Coast of West Africa, which I described in chapter 2. While Coromantee traditions formed a core of Maroon political and religious life, Maroons incorporated political and military strategies, as well as ritual practices, from other African nations. They also developed a unifying language, referred to as "Kromanti," which was "derived from several Gold Coast tongues."[9]

By the 1730s, a man named Kojo, known by the English as Colonel Cudjoe, had consolidated control over the Leeward Maroons in Cockpit Country on the western side of the island. Together with Accompong and Johnny, Kojo governed through political and familial ties of kinship.[10] In contrast to the Leeward Maroons, the Windward Maroons in eastern Jamaica maintained a looser political structure. Inhabitants of their two main towns, Nanny Town and Guy's (or Gay's) Town, provided aid and supplies to each other when needed, but neither exerted formal authority over the other.[11] An Obeah woman named Nanny provided political and spiritual guidance to the Windward Maroons. Nanny's prominence—both then and now—is profound. Contemporary Maroons refer to themselves as *Yoyo*, which means a descendent of "Grandy Nanny," as she is called.[12]

Over time, the Maroon communities grew powerful enough that the British colonial government sought to eradicate them. Hoping to expand their own settlements and minimize opportunities for enslaved people to run away, colonial officials became increasingly aggressive in their military tactics during the late 1720s and 1730s. During what became known as the First Maroon War, the British sent militias into the Jamaican mountains to track down the Maroons and destroy Maroon settlements.[13] During the war, colonial records describe Maroon Obeah men and women, especially the Obeah woman Nanny, who fought the British state with tremendous success. Maroons followed Obeah men and women in making military decisions, and used Obeah to protect themselves from English bullets without injury.[14] The Maroons, with their guerrilla tactics and superior knowledge of the landscape, eluded capture and conquest.[15] While the British militias successfully destroyed Nanny Town, one of the Windward Maroon settlements, they failed to subdue either Maroon community through warfare.

Nanny, the Obeah woman and leader of the Windward Maroons, is widely celebrated throughout Jamaica as one of the fiercest fighters of the First Maroon War.[16] Even in the colonial archive, Nanny is recognized as a powerful and dangerous Obeah woman, though her identity remains fragmentary and incomplete—a "puzzle," as Jenny Sharpe has written.[17] In fact, the first written reference to Nanny—from 1733—celebrates her death, noting that she was "the rebels old obeah woman."[18] The following year, however, another source reported that "Nanny" was alive, along with "her husband."[19] Philip Thicknesse, a British army officer, described the "Obea woman" of the Windward Maroons—possibly Nanny, though he did not use a name—as an "old Hagg." According to Thicknesse, she wore "a girdle round her waste, with ... nine or ten different knives hanging in sheaths," adding that the "horrid wretch, their Obea woman would demand their deaths."[20] Obeah emerges in these records as a powerful force and Nanny—or perhaps multiple "Nannys"—as a fearless leader who terrified colonial authorities.

By 1739, when it became clear that neither the Maroons nor the English would claim complete victory, representatives from each Maroon government agreed to sign a peace treaty with the British colonial government. On March 1, 1739, Leeward Maroon leaders Kojo, Accompong, Johnny, Cuffee, and Quaco met with the English colonial administrator John Guthrie and committed to a treaty that (1) recognized the Maroons as free, (2) acknowledged their land tenure, and (3) allowed them to sell produce in the island's markets. In return, the Leeward Maroons were expected to defend the island against invasion and rebellion, return runaway slaves to the British, hunt down Maroons who did not agree to these terms, and allow a white man to live in their settlements. Kojo, Accompong, and the other Leeward Maroon leaders were granted life tenure and the authority to administer any punishment except death.[21]

The treaty with the Windward Maroons was similar, although it added clauses requiring Maroon militias to be headed by whites when tracking runaway slaves.[22] Notably, Nanny was not involved in the treaty signing for the Windward Maroons. It is unclear whether she had died by 1739; whether she refused to participate; or whether the British refused to negotiate with her in favor of a male representative.[23] Regardless, British colonial records frequently ignored or suppressed the role of women in positions of authority, so Nanny's story acts as an important reminder of female leadership within Maroon communities.

Blood Oaths, Silver Medals, and Treaties: Remembering and Representing Sacred Bonds

The 1739 treaty was a pivotal moment in Jamaican Maroon and British colonial history. For the Maroons, the treaty remains sacred and significant today. Maroon oral and written histories demonstrate that the treaty should be understood within the long tradition of African diasporic oath making and political coalition building. This section draws on Maroon oral histories recorded by anthropologists in the twentieth and early twenty-first centuries alongside contemporary Maroon depictions of their history in Jamaica, placing them in conversation with archival evidence about treaties and the oaths that solidified their power. Pairing oral histories with archival research is essential for interpreting the Africana irruption in Caries's diary that featured Accompong and his "silver medal."

Maroons drew upon Africana political, intellectual, and religious traditions to ratify the 1739 treaty. Every aspect of the treaty-signing process contributed to its sacred authority. Sydney McDonald, a Jamaican Maroon who spoke to anthropologist Kenneth Bilby in 1978, described the importance of the feather used to sign the treaty. According to McDonald, the treaty was written and signed with the feather of a particular bird, known as *okrema*, the Kromanti word for "chicken hawk."[24] The location of the signing also contributed to the significance of the event. Known both as Peace Cave and Ambush Cave, the location remains sacred for contemporary Maroons and is part of their annual celebrations on January 6.[25] The use of the Kromanti language is another indication of how Maroons, both in the eighteenth century and today, draw upon Africana practices.

According to Maroon oral histories, the 1739 treaty was ratified through a blood oath. Thomas Rowe, an Accompong Town Maroon, recounted the following narrative to the anthropologist Kenneth Bilby in 1991: "[The Englishmen] came out and shook hands with Kojo [Cudjoe], and offered the peace terms. And as a token of peace, they used white rum. [The Maroons] had a thing they called 'calabash'—or otherwise, 'gourdie.' ... So they both cut their arms now, and drained the blood into the calabash, and threw white rum onto it and mixed it up. And both of them drank it. So they said that from that time on there would be a link between the Maroons and the white men."[26] Dozens of other oral histories confirm the same story—that the treaty was consecrated with a blood oath that remains in effect today. Other narratives discuss the significance of the "blood and the feather," the physical objects used to ratify the treaty by blood oath and by signed document (signed with ink and a feather quill).[27]

Historically, blood oaths were central to Gold Coast politics in West Africa. Walter Rucker has argued that they were "inviolable military and political pacts" in seventeenth- and eighteenth-century Akan political culture. Oaths helped to secure community bonds, incorporate new members into polities, and formalize treaties between governments. In the Caribbean, blood oaths were incorporated into Obeah practice as an important "ritual technology."[28] Within the context of Maroon negotiation with the British, a blood oath served to ratify the treaty, working together with the feather and the written legal document to secure the alliance between the British colonial government and the Maroons.

For Maroons, the blood oath meant that the treaty was a sacred charter that could not be broken, and the 1739 treaty continues to play a foundational role within Jamaican Maroon society.[29] The anthropologist Archibald Cooper, who did fieldwork in Accompong Town in the 1930s, wrote that "the signing of the treaty at [the] Peace Cave is an event that is well remembered to the present day."[30] Anthropologist Kenneth Bilby, whose fieldwork spans the 1970s until today, confirms the prominence of the 1739 treaty in Maroon oral history.[31] In contemporary Accompong Town, an enlarged copy of the treaty is the first image that visitors see when they enter the Maroon-led Accompong museum.[32]

The chief of Accompong Town, Richard Currie, frequently refers to the treaty in his claims for Maroon land tenure and sovereignty. When Prince William and Princess Catherine, then the Duke and Duchess of Cambridge, visited Jamaica in 2022, Currie announced via Instagram that "the Leeward Trelawny Town Maroons of the Sovereign State of Accompong wishes to take this opportunity to highlight to the British Royal Family (Crown), their Agents and Assigns of their outstanding debts, engagements, and fiduciary obligations under the 1738 Maroon treaty. It is only right if the Crown visits the land of the Indigenous people who still domicile on the island, and who have a blood oath with the Crown's predecessors, that honor and respect be in accordance with the relationship our forefathers had with each other."[33] Currie's reference to the treaty and to the Maroons' "blood oath with the Crown's predecessors" demonstrates how the treaty remains a foundational political document for contemporary Maroons.[34]

Sovereignty and Sartorial Strategies

Understanding the long history of African diasporic oath-making practices as well as the sacrality of the 1739 treaty for Jamaican Maroons is crucial for interpreting the Africana irruptions in the Moravian missionary archives. By the time Caries arrived in 1755, Accompong had long been recognized as one of the principal leaders of the Leeward Maroons. After signing the 1739 treaty, he acted as the governor of the Accompong Town Maroons. In the ensuing decade, however, the British colonial government began a long process of undermining the terms of the treaty and encroaching on Maroon sovereignty. Archival records suggest that British officials began to undermine the treaty almost immediately. In a letter written to the Council of Jamaica soon after the treaty signing, the English colonial official John Guthrie wrote that he was "Obliged to tye myself up, by a Solemn Oath" to conduct treaty negotiations.[35] His disregard for the Maroon political process signaled a larger imperial strategy behind British negotiation and treaty-making: For British colonial authorities, the 1739 treaty was a means to contain and regulate the Maroons, not a sacred political charter.[36]

In 1744, the British colonial government passed two acts that sought to increase British influence in Maroon politics. The "Act for the better Order and Government of the Negroes belonging to the several Negroe Towns" gave whites living in the Maroon towns authority that had not been granted in the treaty. They introduced courts in the Maroon settlements that were to be presided over by a white superintendent. The second law, "An Act for raising companies in the several negro-towns," aimed to bring Maroon militias under increased regulation by the British government.[37] Both laws reduced the autonomy of Maroon leaders by assuming authority over legal proceedings and military decisions.

The acts of 1744 were emblematic of the conflicting approaches to treaty-making between the Maroons and the British colonial government.[38] While the Maroons insisted that the 1739 treaty was inviolable, British colonial lawmakers undermined it by passing new laws without Maroon approval. While some scholars have argued that Maroons and British colonials had different interpretations of the treaty, archival evidence suggests that the British colonial government deliberately sought to diminish Maroon sovereignty through a variety of strategies. In addition to passing new laws that contradicted the treaty terms, British colonial authorities denigrated Maroon and African diasporic coalition-building strategies. They tended to regard political rituals like blood oaths as "superstitious" while affirming European text-based lawmaking practices as "modern" and "reasonable."[39]

As scholars have shown, European ideas about modernity and universal reason were developed and refined through the exclusion of so-called premodern and superstitious practices of political "others."[40] This dynamic helped to justify European seizures of land, people, and political power throughout the early modern world. In Jamaica, as Bradley Craig has written, "British rituals of law were no less magical than Coromantee rituals of blood. The 'pen and ink witchcraft' of treaties made possible the negotiation and erosion of sovereignties, the appropriation and apportionment of land, as well as the manage-

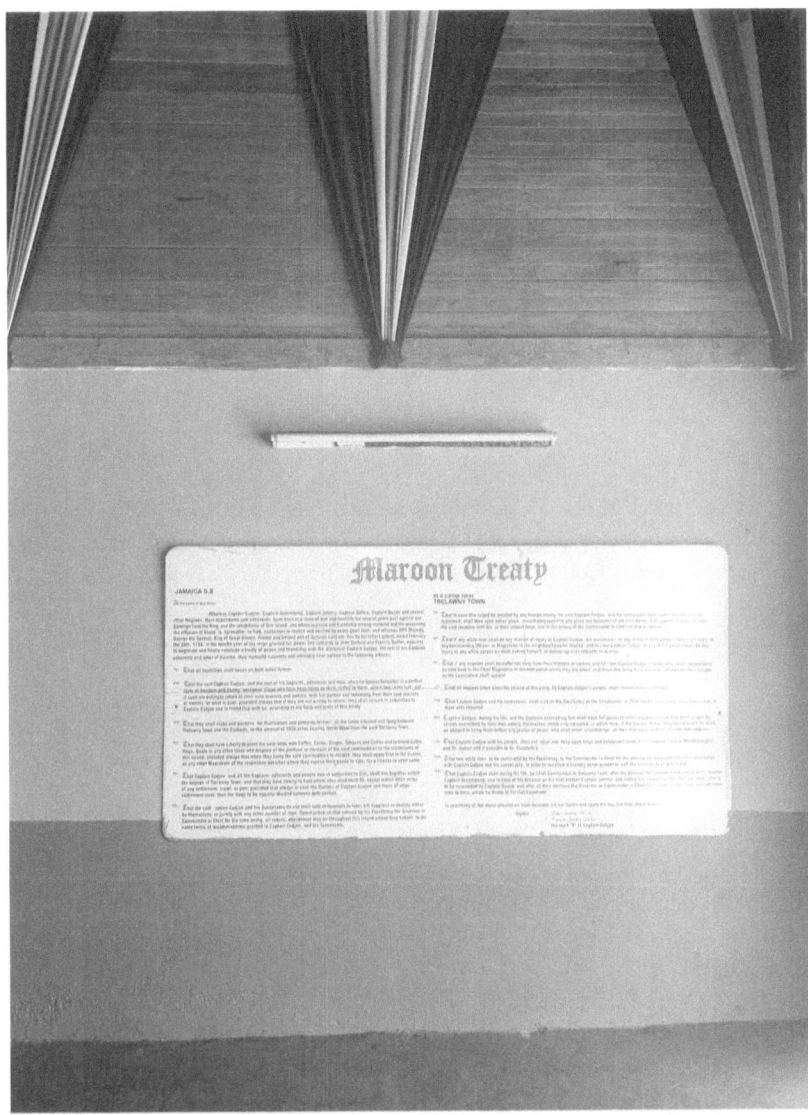

FIGURE 3.1. A transcription of the 1739 treaty displayed at the entrance to the museum in Accompong, Jamaica. Photograph by the author.

ment of commerce and conflict throughout the British Empire."[41] In order to counter the long European history of denigrating of Africana religio-political practices, the tradition of Maroon treaties—and the blood oaths that accompanied them—should be interpreted as "legal technologies" and understood within a diplomatic framework.

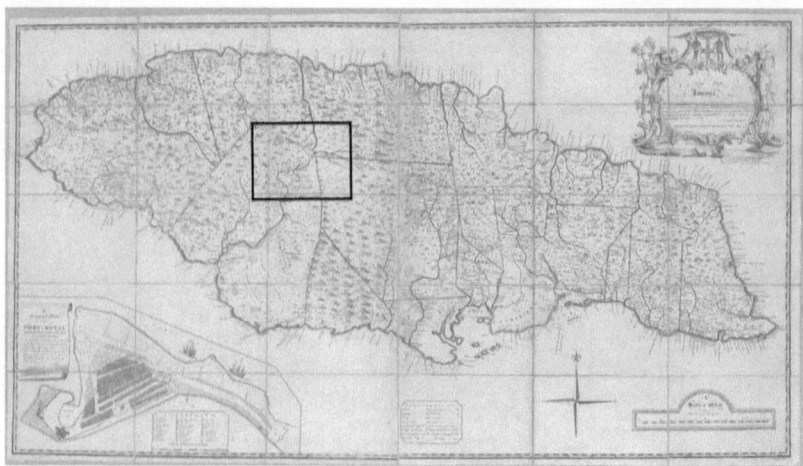

FIGURE 3.2. Patrick Browne, "A new map of Jamaica" (1755). Black outlined area contains the Moravian mission site at the Bogue and Accompong Town (a Maroon town), shown below in detail. Courtesy of the John Carter Brown Library, Brown University.

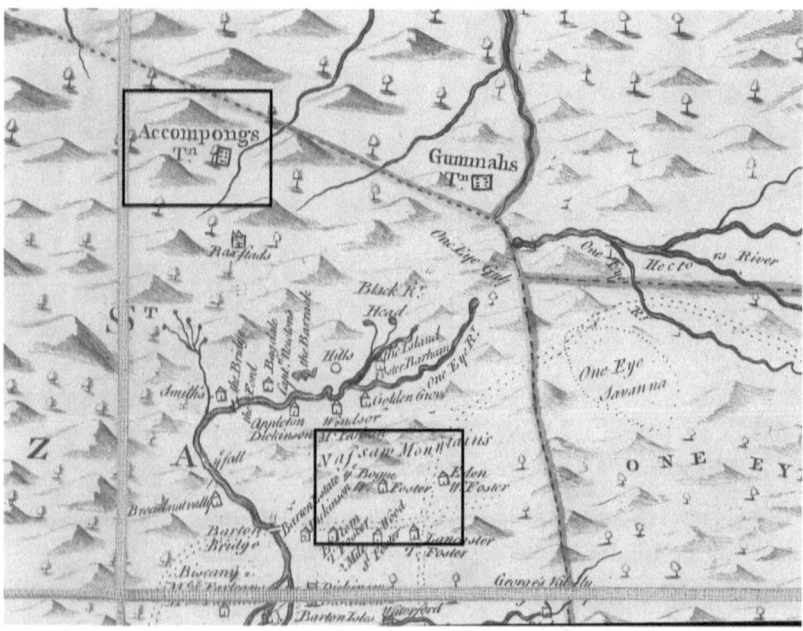

FIGURE 3.3. Detail of Browne, "A new map of Jamaica" (1755) showing the Bogue plantation and Accompong Town. Courtesy of the John Carter Brown Library, Brown University.

Recognizing that Accompong's medal was a legal technology helps us interpret Accompong's sartorial strategies through an Africana lens. The medal served as material evidence of the treaty-making process, and when Accompong met Caries, he displayed the sacred authority of the 1739 treaty on his body to reinforce the authority of the Maroon alliance with the British government. The medal, as Caries noted, was made of silver, and it was inscribed with Accompong's name on one side and King George II's picture on the other.[42] Caries clearly recognized that the peace medal was significant, although his commentary suggests that he did not recognize its full meaning. Instead, Caries listed it as one of a series of notable sartorial choices, alongside Accompong's "embroidered Waistcoat," the "gold Lace around his Hat," his "Ear Rings," and "Rings of silver" on each of his fingers."[43] Other white colonials gave similar descriptions of Maroon leaders.[44] Thomas Thistlewood, the white overseer at a nearby estate, recorded several meetings with Accompong and other Maroons in the 1750s.[45] In one entry, he noted that the Maroon Colonel Cudjoe was wearing "a Beavour ffether'd and a large med[al] hang[ing] Chains ab[ou]t his Neck."[46] The "large med[al]" around Kojo's neck was likely similar to Accompong's.

By examining the tradition of Africana oath-making, both past and present, we can interpret Caries's description of Accompong as an archival irruption. While Caries considered Accompong's peace medal a fascinating accessory, akin to lace or an embroidered waistcoat, it should be understood as a proclamation of Maroon sovereignty that was, in 1755, already under threat. Wearing the medal was a legal technology and should be understood as part of a broader Maroon strategy to display and reinforce the authority and autonomy of the Maroons.

Margery: Finding Women in a Patriarchal Missionary Archive

While Accompong's silver medal can be read as an affirmation of Maroon sovereignty, a gendered analysis of Caries's diary reveals that a Maroon woman named Margery played a central role in cultivating the alliance between the Moravian mission and the Accompong Town Maroons. Margery, like other women, is not a prominent figure in Caries's diary. Caries never actually named her in his text, referring to her only as "Titus' Wife." I found her name—Margery—in a list of "[Baptismal] Candidates from the female sex," which Caries compiled in 1756. In that document, Caries made sure to note each woman's husband to the left of her name. "Margery" is listed as belonging to "Titus."[47]

The existence of Margery's name is a "gendered irruption" because it reveals information that Caries felt was trivial—a Maroon woman's name. By pairing

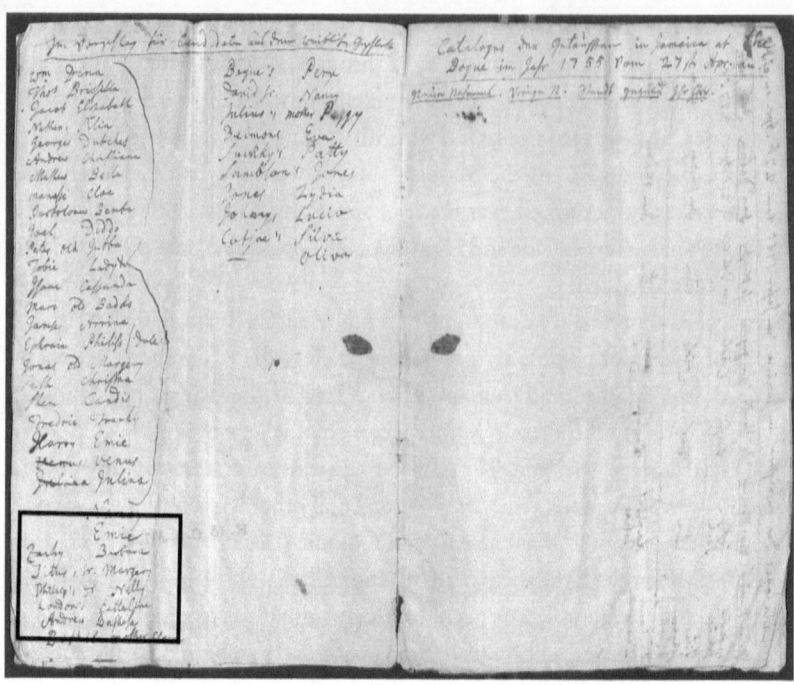

FIGURE 3.4. Margery's name in a document listing female candidates for baptism, ca. 1756. Unitätsarchiv der Evangelischen Brüder-Unität, Herrnhut, Germany, R.15.C.a.02.04_08.

Margery's name with Caries's references to "Titus' wife," we can create an alternative narrative about the Maroons focusing on Margery. In doing so, we push back against the patriarchal nature of the archive. Even though the Windward Maroons were led by an Obeah woman named Nanny, and several Maroon towns throughout the Americas were named after women, most colonial sources report only on male Maroons.[48] As a result, as historian Shavagne Scott has written, scholarship on marronage "tend[s] to relegate maroon women to the background, positioning them as objects of male agency."[49] In recent years, Black feminist scholars have offered new ways of theorizing female marronage by focusing on Black geographies of resistance, reproductive labor, and the gendered nature of racial capitalism.[50] By reading Caries's diaries for gendered irruptions, we can see how Margery created what Stephanie Camp has called a "rival geography" as she moved between the Bogue plantation, where Titus was enslaved, and Accompong Town.

The first reference to Margery appears on May 13, 1755, when Caries notes that "Titus's wife is a free Negro & is come here on a visit."[51] Titus, a Creole man, was enslaved to William Foster, the owner of the Bogue estate. While Caries did not explicitly mention Titus's role on the plantation, he was probably an enslaved overseer. Titus sometimes traveled to perform "inspections" at other estates, demonstrating a freedom of mobility that was not available to other enslaved men.[52] It is unclear how Margery and Titus first met, or how long they had been together, but on May 13, Caries noted that Titus's wife was visiting the Bogue, suggesting that Margery lived occasionally on the plantation with Titus.[53]

Margery and Titus played an important role in Caries's mission and his relationship with Accompong. On March 11, three weeks before his meeting with Accompong, Caries noted that "Titus a Negro Candidate for Baptism came to see me."[54] Two weeks later, Caries wrote that Titus "does already labour among his People," suggesting that Titus's role as a spiritual leader predated Caries's arrival.[55] Then, in early May, Titus became the third Black person baptized in the Moravian church on Jamaica, rising soon thereafter to leadership status within the congregation as a Helper, an official position in the Moravian church hierarchy.[56]

While Caries did not baptize women in the first two years after his arrival, Margery's significance emerges through a careful reading of his diary entries. On July 8, 1755, he noted that Margery had been attending Moravian worship meetings "for a long time."[57] Since this entry came just seven months after Caries's arrival in Jamaica, this suggests that Margery had been a member of the Moravian congregation from its inception, or shortly thereafter. She was probably among the first Maroons to attend Moravian meetings, since she regularly spent time at the Bogue plantation with Titus. Given this context, it is possible that Margery introduced other Maroons to Caries and the Moravian congregation.

Margery and Titus's interest in Moravian Christianity was multifaceted, encompassing theological inquiry, prayer, social engagement, and political pragmatism. In March, Titus told Caries that he spoke "continual[l]y with [the Savior] ... on the Road, when I go to Bed, and when I get up in the Morning." Titus's words suggest a close personal relationship with God and an emphasis on prayer—particularly in the mornings, in the evenings, and while traveling. Caries added that Titus had joined the missionaries "in our singing hour and evening blessing," noting, "tho[ugh] I did not give out the Verses, he however sung with us."[58] Two weeks later, Caries again wrote about a conversation in which Titus told him that he "pray[s] often" and that he "speaks with [the Savior] till the Tears come."[59]

Margery, like Titus, emphasized prayer and the power of blood in her approach to Moravian Christianity. On May 13, for example, Caries noted that Margery "is really mov'd" and that she goes "very often in a Corner to pray to give her his good Blood into her heart to forgive her all her sins."[60] As I detailed previously, blood and blood oaths were central to Obeah practice, and to Africana religious traditions more generally. Margery's connection between prayer and blood thus signals the space of correlation that existed between Moravian ritual worship and Africana religious traditions.

On May 20, 1755, Margery had a near-death experience. As Caries related the incident in his diary, "Titus's Wife was washing in the River," and accidentally "dropp[ed] a Shirt into the water." When she "endeavor'd to take it up," she "slipped into the water," and was swept away by the strong current. As she was carried downstream, Margery cried out to the "saviour" to save her life, which he "did accordingly."[61] This story has several significant components. It offers a glimpse into the type of labor Margery performed, washing clothes in the river. While this may have been a quotidian task, it is also important to remember that rivers were often sacred sites within both African and European religious traditions. In Jamaica, Christian baptisms were sometimes performed in rivers, possibly in the same river where Margery was swept away. This sacred significance is important for interpreting Margery's accident, in which she "slipped into the water." In this precarious moment, Margery chose to call upon the Moravian God to intervene. The fact that she then relayed this incident suggests that she hoped to inform Caries that her prayers to the Moravian "saviour" had been efficacious.

Margery and Titus likely contributed to the consensus in the Moravian congregation that Caries was an Obeah man who could offer spiritual, social, medical, and political benefits. In fact, it was on March 17, 1755, soon after mentioning Titus for the first time, that Caries penned the letter referenced in chapter 1, in which he wrote, "They call me Obea, which means a Seer, or one who knows things that will happen in the future."[62] The timing of his letter—combined with the references to Titus and Margery in his diary—suggest that Titus and Margery could have been the ones who initially called Caries "Obea[h]."

Maroon Landscapes and Sovereignty

For Maroons like Margery, knowledge of the Jamaican landscape operated as a "rival geography" that was foundational to their sovereignty.[63] In 1751, the colonial government passed a law that aimed to curtail Maroon movement, seeking to undercut a key aspect of Maroon autonomy.[64] The act noted that Maroons "frequently left their several Towns," and "rambled about in the several Parishes of this island" where they visited "neighboring Plantations," sometimes "persuading and enticing others to run away." The act required Maroons to have written permission to leave their towns and specified that any Maroon who "shall entice or endeavour to entice and persuade any Slave or Slaves to run away" would "forfeit his or her Freedom, and be transported off this island."[65]

The 1751 act was an attack on the Maroon landscape. Within the context of the act, passed just four years before Caries's arrival, Margery likely recognized that the Moravian congregation offered an important layer of protection for her and other Maroons to move between Accompong Town and the Bogue plantation. Additionally, Caries's presence—and the existence of the Moravian congregation—provided a justification for Margery to relocate from Accompong Town to the Bogue. In November 1755, Caries wrote that Margery "has been convinced thro[ugh] the Testimony of our Sav[io]r & for this Reason had left Compong's [Accompong's] town & came here to live w[i]th her husband."[66]

Margery's and Titus's freedom of movement was a boon to the Moravian church, and the couple urged others to join the congregation. In this way, they helped to create a new religio-national community that brought together Maroons and enslaved people within the Moravian fold. By July 1755, Caries noted that several Maroons now attended his worship services. Among those, he singled out Margery, noting that she had been with them "for a long time" and "has really been taken hold of by our Sav[io]r."[67] A month later, Caries visited Accompong Town. In his diary, Caries wrote that the Maroons were "very civil," and several knew him and had "been at our Meetings."[68]

Caries's description of the trek to Accompong Town offers a brief glimpse into the "rival geography" that Margery regularly traversed, as she traveled between Cockpit Country, the mountainous region that was home to the Windward Maroon towns, and the Bogue plantation. Caries wrote that he "travell[e]d over the high Mountains," noting that the roads were very "Bad." He also commented on the distance between Maroon towns as he walked from Accompong Town over "still higher Mountains" to reach Cranky Town. He added that "there are several more Places" where the Maroons lived, "but they lay so scatter'd," he could not visit them all.[69]

The remote location of Accompong Town was an intentional feature of the Maroon landscape. Maroons had agreed, in the terms of the 1739 treaty, to allow for a white superintendent to reside in their towns. However, Caries's account suggests that the superintendent was unable to surveil all of the Maroons towns, since there were so many "scatter'd" settlements. Moreover, the minister who was supposed to preach in the Maroon towns on a regular basis had not visited for "many years." Caries speculated this was "on Account of the Badness of the Roads."[70]

While Caries had difficulty navigating the Maroon landscape, Margery would have known the terrain intimately, utilizing routes and paths unknown to Caries and other whites. This "rival geography" offered her and other Maroons protection from colonial intrusion. However, legislation like the 1751 act sought to undermine this crucial component of Maroon life by policing Maroon movements and limiting their ability to travel to plantation and urban spaces. By cultivating a relationship with Caries and bolstering Maroon–enslaved bonds within the Moravian congregation, Margery strategized against colonial efforts to contain and control the Maroons. In this way, her actions—while less visible than Accompong's silver medal—should be understood as part of a larger effort to protect and proclaim Maroon sovereignty.

Intimate Bonds and Enslaved–Maroon Relationships

The distance between the Bogue plantation and the Maroon towns proved helpful when Margery's relationship with Titus—and the Moravian church—began to change at the end of 1755. On November 6, 1755, Caries reported that he was "very much griev[e]d by a circumstance . . . w[i]th our Titus." He had encountered Margery while she was "pack[ing] up all her things" and preparing to move back "home." Margery told Caries that she "would no more live with her husband" because "he was jealous of her." Caries urged her to "return w[i]th her child" and promised to speak to Titus.[71] Caries later learned that Titus "mistrusted" another Afro-Moravian who had been in a relationship with Margery years before. According to Caries, Titus had "consent[ed]" to Margery's relationship with this other man, adding that this was "the custom here among the best friend."[72]

Caries's diary suggests that Margery practiced polyandry and that Titus had given his "own consent & approbation" for her relationship with his "friend."[73] For Caries, this was a sin, and according to his diary, Titus and the other man—who was also a baptized member of the church—now agreed with him. Caries reported that the accused friend asked Titus for forgiveness for having had "intimacy w[i]th your wife" and added, "since I am baptized with the blood of our Sav[io]r I could no more do such things." Caries was relieved that the practice of polyandry "begins to leave off at the Bogue entirely."[74]

While Caries viewed Titus and Margery's relationship within a Christian framework that prized monogamous marriage, Margery's actions suggest that she did not. As Alexis Wells-Oghoghomeh has written, both polygyny and polyandry were grounded in African social conventions, and in the context of Atlantic slavery, "sexual choice became a sacred value."[75] As a free Maroon woman, Margery was not forced to remain at the Bogue, and she used mobility to her advantage. Sometime in late 1755 or 1756, Margery moved back to Accompong Town, contradicting Caries's portrayal that she and Titus "live now again in Peace & Harmony together."[76]

After her return to Accompong Town, Margery maintained a relationship with Titus outside of the purview of the Moravian missionaries. Her decision suggests that she did not conform to Caries's ideal of monogamous, cohabitating marriage. She may also have wanted to raise her child—who is mentioned only in passing by Caries—within the context of a free Maroon town, rather than plantation slavery. After Margery relocated, Caries supported Titus in his efforts to split his time between the Maroon town and the Bogue plantation. In 1757, Titus took several trips to Accompong Town, sometimes spending a month at a time with Margery. He was able to gain the support of Mr. Robertson, the white attorney at the Bogue, by gaining Caries's approval and insisting that his health was dependent upon a "change of air" in Accompong Town, "where his wife and relatives were."[77] Caries continued to refer to Margery as "Titus's wife," but her actions suggest that this was not her primary identity.

Through brief glimpses in Caries's diaries, we can imagine slivers of Margery's world as she sought to protect her autonomy and create a relationship with Titus on her own terms. As a free Maroon woman, she had more flexibility than an enslaved woman, and she used that to her advantage, relocating between Accompong Town and the Bogue. We can also discern a general trajectory in Margery's relationship with the Moravian church. In the first half of 1755, Margery's and Titus's leadership in the Moravian mission, as well as their effort to strengthen ties between the Maroon and enslaved populations, suggest that they saw both theological and practical reasons for pursuing a relationship with Caries. Margery's near-death experience in the river seems to have deepened her commitment to the Moravian God. She and Titus also recognized that Caries—as a white man—could provide support for their long-distance relationship by advocating on their behalf to other whites. Moreover, Caries provided access to important spiritual rites, such as baptism, which, as I argued in chapter 1, was understood through the framework of Obeah.

By 1756, Margery had recognized some limits in the spiritual offerings of the Moravian church. Caries's emphasis on monogamous marriage and his prioritization of Titus's spiritual journey may have been factors in her decision to return to Accompong Town on her own. By distancing herself from Caries and the mission, Margery presaged some of the problems that would come to plague the mission in coming years, which I describe in part II. It is especially significant that Margery and Caries seem to have disagreed about the role of women within a household. While Caries preferred a patriarchal structure in which one man was married to one woman, Margery's actions suggest that she held different ethical ideals about how to construct kinship networks and sacred community.

Gendering Africana Irruptions

Margery's story changes the meaning of the Africana irruption that began this chapter: Caries's description of the Maroon leader Accompong and his "silver medal." If Accompong already knew about Caries from Margery—and if he had heard that Caries was an Obeah man—his "attentive" reaction to Caries's evangelical message takes on a different resonance. So too does his decision to invite Caries to Accompong Town, where Accompong promised to "make [Caries] very welcome." For both Accompong and Margery, creating an alliance with Caries offered significant political, social, and spiritual advantages. Caries could potentially negotiate with British colonial authorities, and as a white man with the support of the attorney and overseer at the Bogue, he could advocate for his congregants and protect their ability to travel between the Bogue plantation and Accompong Town.

While Accompong's silver medal is an important irruption, reading with a gendered Africana lens reveals that Accompong was not the only person advocating for Maroon sovereignty. Margery's effort to build a religio-nation that included both enslaved and Maroon people, and her effort to facilitate mobility for Maroon and enslaved men, women, and children shows that she was bolstering Maroon spatial and bodily freedom. Centering Margery suggests that the Moravian church provided an opportunity for enslaved people and Maroons to come together within the religio-nation of the Moravian congregation. It also demonstrates that women played an important role in Maroon politics that is easily obscured by the male-centered archival sources that have dominated historical accounts of the Accompong Town Maroons. As Margery developed ties with Caries and deepened her connection to the Moravian congregation, she helped to create a literal space of correlation that gave Maroons and enslaved Moravians expanded sovereignty over their bodies in both Maroon and plantation spaces. Margery's decision to move back to Accompong Town in 1756, meanwhile, presaged some of the conflicts that would develop in the mission in the coming years. Part II, *Heuchelei*, expands on these tensions within the Moravian congregation, especially after the arrival of new missionaries.

This chapter has argued that reading for irruptions allows us to tell an alternative narrative about the Maroons, their use of Obeah, and their relationship with enslaved people. Just a few years after Margery and Accompong developed an alliance with Caries, Tacky's Revolt (chapter 6) would severely undermine the relationship between Maroons and enslaved people. Maroon leaders led militias against the enslaved rebels, helping the British colonial government to defeat the largest slave rebellion in the eighteenth-century British Empire. Reading the archives for irruptions makes it is possible to tell a different story about Maroons, their relationship with the enslaved population, and their dynamic Africana political practices in the years before Tacky's Revolt.

PART II

Heuchelei

At the end of 1756, Caries reflected on the success of his mission and hoped that "several more Brothers and Sisters [i.e., missionaries]" would be sent to assist him.¹ When Caries wrote those words, his long-awaited reinforcements had already arrived in Jamaica. Christian Heinrich Rauch and his wife, Anna Rauch, were accompanied by Charles and Maria Schulz.² After their arrival, the Moravians were able to establish a new mission station at Mesopotamia plantation, Joseph Foster Barham's estate in Westermoreland parish.

Far from being the godsend that Caries had anticipated, however, Christian Heinrich Rauch's presence led to severe disagreements about the meaning of conversion, the proper preparations for baptism, and the boundaries of Christian behavior. As Part I demonstrated, one key to Caries's "success" was that he performed dozens of baptisms, preached about blood and wounds, and offered medical support and prophetic knowledge to his congregants. These actions led Afro-Moravians to call him Obeah.

Rauch felt that Caries had baptized too many Afro-Jamaicans, and he argued that the missionaries should not be involved with the Maroons. In the years after his arrival, Rauch halted nearly all baptisms and severed Caries's alliance with Accompong Town. During this time, most Afro-Moravians at the Bogue plantation abandoned the mission. While the missionaries created a narrative of "backsliding," part II argues that from an Africana perspective, the missionaries had lost their status as Obeah men. On one hand, they failed to protect the congregation from sexual violence, as I show in chapter 4. On the other hand, as I describe in chapter 5, Rauch abandoned "spaces of correlation" and turned, instead, to policing the boundaries of Christianity. In 1759, after a series of conferences, Caries was expelled from the mission and sent back to Europe.

Even as their mission faltered, the missionaries continued to create archival records. Christian Heinrich was the most prolific archival producer, but Charles Schulz also wrote letters and diary entries. In 1759, seven more missionaries landed on the island, creating a multivocal archive that is preserved in Herrnhut, Germany, and Bethlehem, Pennsylvania. Significantly, the arrival of female missionaries, and especially Anna Rauch, offered new insight into the lives, struggles, and hopes of the female congregants at the Bogue. While Anna Rauch did not write diaries, her presence fundamentally changed the information that her husband, Christian Heinrich Rauch, recorded. As a result, Rauch's diaries contain more information about enslaved women's lives than Caries's diaries—especially about the brutal realities that faced enslaved women: what Alexis Wells-Oghoghomeh calls the "culture of sexual dismemberment."[3]

During these years, as the missionaries produced simultaneous diaries and letters, it is possible to read different interpretations of the same event. Often, the missionary accounts align. At times, however, the narratives compete, offering divergent and sometimes incongruous information. Accordingly, part II is titled *Heuchelei*, German for "dissimulation" or "hypocrisy." I analyze inconsistencies and censorship in the mission narratives to (1) demonstrate how conflicting archival documents can offer a lens into Africana perspectives of the mission, and (2) identify larger themes in the production of knowledge about religion, gender, crime, and rebellion. I argue that dissimulation in the archives offers an opportunity to identify archival irruptions that emerge in the fissures of competing missionary narratives.

4

Archival Silence, Sexual Violence

READING FOR RE/MEMBRANCE

On a hot afternoon in July 1758, a young Black woman named Camilla visited Anna Rauch, a white woman and the first female missionary on the island. Camilla arrived with her mother, Elizabeth. The three women spoke at length about sexual violence, rape, and trauma. After their meeting, Anna's husband, Christian Heinrich Rauch, recorded the following passage: "July 14, 1758: In the evening we had a visit from Elizabeth, and her daughter Camilla, who spoke with Sister Anna and told her everything about how she was forced [*gezwungen*] into prostitution [*Hurerey*] when she was still a child, including who and how."[1]

From Rauch's diary, we learn that Camilla, who was either fourteen or fifteen years old, had been the victim of rape. Rauch used the verb *zwingen*, which can be translated as "to force" or "to coerce," to describe Camilla's predicament. Camilla was now seeking to evade the sexual predations of white men. She and her mother, Elizabeth, hoped that Anna Rauch could provide advice and protection. We do not know exactly what they said, but the passages reveal that they discussed sexual abuse at length, and especially, Camilla's experience of being "forced" when she was "still a child." Camilla and Elizabeth may have thought that as a white woman and a missionary, Anna Rauch could help to prevent further abuses.

The meeting was unsuccessful. The next day, Christian Heinrich wrote a devastating entry: "July 15, 1758: We thought about our dear Brother Joseph during our morning service.... Sister Anna learned today that Camilla was bound and beaten until she agreed to be the whore [*Hure*] of the whites again. The poor child of just 14 or 15 years wanted to be honest. She ran out of the brothel (*kammern der unzucht*) and hid in the sugar fields; then they searched for her. Neither her tears nor her pleadings helped in the slightest. She was forced."[2]

It is a horrifying scene. So horrifying, in fact, that when Rauch's diary was recopied, as all mission diaries were, it was excised from the record. We do not know who copied the diary, nor do we have documentation about their editorial choices, but in this case, the scribe's priorities seem clear. Compare the previous passages to the following line in the recopied diary from the same day: "July 15, 1758: We thought about our dear Brother Joseph during our morning service." Camilla and Elizabeth's visit to Anna Rauch is completely erased, as is their difficult conversation about child rape and the terrifying experience of Camilla, who tried to run from her attackers, only to be hunted down in the cane fields.[3]

The Moravians' decision to excise this sexual assault from their records raises questions about the production of silences in the archive and the erasure of enslaved women's and girls' experiences.[4] We can begin by asking: How was this traumatic episode recorded in the first place? And why was it later censored? Most importantly, how can a comparative archival methodology and a focus on Africana irruptions offer insight into Camilla's life *beyond* her experience of sexual violence? It is also important to ask: What is the meaning of crime in a society where the premeditated rape of a Black child was not a punishable offense? And what role does religion have under these circumstances?

This chapter examines the terror of sexual violence while also interrogating how and when archival silences are created.[5] I do so by examining conflicting narratives within a multivocal archive to trace the production of silence. I then use fissures in competing archives to identify and imagine alternative narratives. This methodology allows us to tell a story about Camilla and Elizabeth that is not solely grounded in the outrages of Atlantic slavery. In my analysis,

FIGURE 4.1. Rauch's original diary entry for July 14–15, 1758. Unitätsarchiv der Evangelischen Brüder-Unität, Herrnhut, Germany, R.15.C.b.02.1_1758_07_02.

I build most explicitly on Michel-Rolph Trouillot, Saidiya Hartman, Marisa Fuentes, Sasha Turner, and Alexis Wells-Oghoghomeh, whose scholarship on the archives of slavery has influenced and inspired my approach.[6]

The first sections interrogate the production of two different kinds of silences regarding sexual violence. I then compare the Moravian archives to the diaries of enslaver-overseer Thomas Thistlewood, whose recording of sexual violence

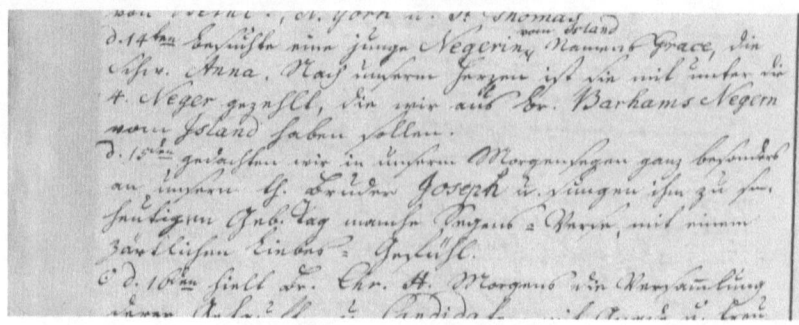

FIGURE 4.2. The recopied and edited version of the Bogue diary for July 14–15, 1758. Diary of Jamaica [Bogue estate], Moravian Archives, Bethlehem, PA, MissJmc 7.2.

suggests the enormity of the erasures in the missionary records. I argue that the missionaries' inability to protect their congregants from sexual violence—even in the sacred space of the meeting house—was one reason that they lost their status as Obeah practitioners.

The final section places the ubiquity of sexual violence in the context of religion and religious experience. Like the missionary sources, many contemporary histories of religion under slavery either marginalize or ignore discussions of sexual life. Yet sex is integral to the ways that humans understand their existence and their place in the world.[7] As Alexis Wells-Oghoghomeh has written, the "culture of sexual dismemberment" that characterized Atlantic slavery presented existential challenges for enslaved women in eighteenth-century Jamaica.[8] My analysis of Camilla and Elizabeth—which begins with an examination of the production of silences—ends by "reading for re/membrance," a method that interrogates competing archival narratives to identify Africana irruptions and imagine Camilla's life beyond her experience of sexual violence.

The Production of Archival Silences:
Sexual Violence and Censorship

The erasure of Camilla's assault was an intentional act. To understand it, we must examine the production of the missionary records at each stage in their development. In his now-classic text *Silencing the Past*, Michel-Rolph Trouillot posited that silences enter the process of historical production at four distinct moments: "the moment of fact creation (the making of *sources*); the moment of fact assembly (the making of *archives*); the moment of fact retrieval (the making of *narratives*); and the moment of retrospective significance (the making of *history* in the final instance)."[9] The Moravian records produced between 1758, when Anna Rauch arrived, and 1762, when she died, offer an opportunity to study the first moment—the creation of sources—in a unique way. With Caries, Rauch, and Schulz all producing diaries simultaneously, it is possible to compare and reflect upon the divergent narratives that each white man produced. Moreover, all their diaries were recopied, so the originals can be compared to later versions and examined for moments of censorship—such as Camilla's rape. This section looks at how the archival silencing of Camilla's sexual assault was produced in the Moravian archive. It shows, first, why the event was censored (the silencing), and then examines how it was recorded in the first place (the "moment of fact creation").

To understand why Camilla's assault was silenced, we must first consider how and why Rauch's journal was recopied. It is possible that the diary was copied by Rauch himself. More likely, it was copied by another Moravian missionary in Jamaica, possibly Caries, or a scribe in Bethlehem or Herrnhut. In fact, on the very same day that Camilla was assaulted, Caries was sitting quietly in the Moravian mission house in Carmel, recopying mission diaries. "After our morning prayer," he wrote, "I wrote in our diary and finished a copy of the June [diary] for Europe." Later that day, Caries "copied the diary until the evening, and Brother Carl [Schulz] copied letters for our archive."[10]

The juxtaposition between Caries's and Camilla's experiences on July 15, 1758, speaks volumes about the problematic nature of the archival record, particularly concerning enslaved women's experiences. The missionaries, with their ink and paper, wrote and recopied their documents, creating an archive while Camilla was attacked in the cane fields. Their self-conscious creation of archival records was never intended to be neutral; instead, mission diaries and letters had three objectives. First, they allowed church leaders to oversee the mission from afar. Second, they circulated information about global missions that would be shared with other Moravians, thereby promoting the image of the Moravian Church as a successful evangelical body that spread the gospel not only to Europeans but to Africans, Native Americans, and others. Third, the diaries and letters were intended to produce unique communal opportunities to cultivate Moravian piety. Many of the documents were recopied and excerpted in the *Gemein Nachrichten*, a Moravian manuscript newsletter that would be read aloud during worship meetings in Bethlehem, Herrnhut, and other mission stations. Congregants could imagine the lives of their brethren in faraway places and seek to commune with them through written descriptions.[11]

After Camilla's rape was deleted, Rauch's edited diary was circulated globally within the Moravian Church.[12] Parts of his diary were later included in the *Gemein Nachrichten* that were compiled from all mission stations every year. As the differences between the two passages makes clear, the editor did not want to include news about shocking, violent, or offensive events. The inclusion of Camilla's horrifying—but hardly uncommon—experience of rape would have been difficult to integrate into a prayer meeting. Nor would it have promoted the Moravian Church as successful. The fact that it was recorded at all is an archival anomaly.

The written record of Camilla's assault is a result of two changes: first, the arrival of a female missionary, Anna Rauch; and second, the decision of Anna's husband, Christian Heinrich, to record his wife's conversation with Camilla and Elizabeth.[13] Even though Anna did not write the diaries herself, her presence had a profound impact on the knowledge about enslaved life that the male missionaries (the archival producers) were able to access. In this case, Anna Rauch's intimacy with Christian Heinrich, her husband, meant that Christian Heinrich's mission diary is more attuned to the experiences of enslaved women than the diaries that Caries produced. Even then, however, secrets remain. When enslaved women like Camilla spoke in confidence to women like Anna Rauch, they chose to reveal some aspects of their interior lives while keeping others hidden.[14]

Comparative Archival Methodology and Critical Fabulation

The production—and erasure—of Camilla's assault is an archival irruption that should be approached with care and caution. In *Dispossessed Lives: Enslaved Women, Violence, and the Archive*, Marisa Fuentes reminds scholars that "epistemic violence originates from the knowledge produced about enslaved women by white men and women ... and that knowledge is what survives in archival form." In a warning, she adds that "sole reliance on the empirical matter of the eighteenth-century Caribbean ... can only create historical narratives that reproduce these violent colonial discourses."[15] For Fuentes, the very call to "find more sources" can be problematic.[16] Fuentes advocates, instead, for "reading along the bias grain" and emphasizes the importance of "explicitly demonstrating how power works in making certain historical subjects invisible, brutally hypervisible, and silent."[17] I take seriously Fuentes's warning—as well as her methodological approach—and suggest that reading for archival irruptions can offer an opportunity to write alternative narrations that draw on colonial and missionary sources. I also take inspiration from Saidiya Hartman's call for "critical fabulation" to expand the possible interpretations of traditional sources.[18] This section draws on the scholarship of Fuentes and Hartman to interpret the archival erasure of Camilla's rape through the lens of Black feminist scholarship.

The Moravian archives are outsider sources—written in German by religious minorities and newcomers to the island of Jamaica. As such, they provide a unique window into enslaved life in the English colonies. Still, their production was governed by power relations. This means that when we imagine the conversation between Anna, Camilla, and Elizabeth, we must remember that Anna wielded more power than Camilla and Elizabeth, who likely approached their encounter with a white woman with both hope and caution. Similarly, when Anna told her husband, Christian Heinrich, about her conversation with the mother-daughter pair, she did so as a woman who had less power than her husband, regardless of the intimacy of their relationship.

Elizabeth's decision to speak to Anna Rauch was part of a multipronged maternal strategy to protect her daughter, Camilla.[19] From the missionary diaries, we glimpse only parts of her strategy, though we can surmise others. But one thing is clear: Elizabeth's decision to cultivate Anna Rauch's support did not begin on July 14, 1758, the date of the diary entry that began this chapter. The missionaries recorded that Elizabeth (then known as Coco) visited them over six months prior, in December 1757. They wrote that "Anna was visited by Coco [Elizabeth] and she announced that she wanted to belong to the Savior."[20] On May 12, 1758, the missionaries decided that Coco was ready for baptism.[21] Three days later, she was baptized and given the name Elizabeth.[22] Elizabeth was the third woman baptized at the Bogue, and it is likely that she had been a member of the congregation from the early days of the mission. Her husband, Nehemia (formerly Hampton), was baptized in early 1756.[23]

It was soon after her baptism—once she was a recognized member of the Moravian congregation—that Elizabeth sought Anna's advice about Camilla. First, she went alone. On July 2, two weeks before Camilla spoke to the missionaries, Elizabeth visited Anna by herself. Christian Rauch recorded that "Sister Anna gave Elizabeth good advice: that when the whites wanted to force her to give her daughter to them... how she should respond."[24] From this passage, we learn that Elizabeth was aware of—and was likely in conversation with—the white men who were trying to rape her daughter.

What, exactly, was Anna's advice? While we cannot know for sure, it may have been similar to the advice that a later Moravian missionary, Joseph Powell, gave to Benjamin, a baptized member of the local Moravian church. In October 1761, Benjamin was "much... distressed" and reported that the overseer was threatening both him and his wife, Venus, because "they resisted him in yielding th[ei]r Daughter to his will." Powell assured Benjamin that "no slave was Obligi'd to prostitute th[ei]r Child" and that he should "immediately let us know" if he continued to have problems. He added that Benjamin should fear "God rather than Man."[25]

Powell's advice was not useful. While it may have been mildly heartening to have a white missionary agree that a parent should not feel "oblig'd" to "prostitute th[ei]r Child," he did not offer a practical strategy for Benjamin's daughter to resist the white man's advances.[26] On October 27, 1761, ten days after Benjamin's visit, Venus appeared at the mission station "with a Driver behind her." The driver "had orders to employ her in the field." It is possible that Venus's efforts to protect her child meant that she was being sent to the fields for punishment. Venus hoped that the missionaries would defend her. But Powell refused: he "chose not to hear" Venus's "complaints." Instead, he and the other missionaries at the Bogue in 1761 "advis[ed] her to be Obedient as becoming a Slave."[27]

Unlike Venus, Elizabeth was not punished for helping her daughter resist rape—or at least, the missionaries did not mention any punishment. In fact, the missionaries did not write about Elizabeth or her daughter for nearly three months. Then, on October 3, 1758, Elizabeth visited Anna, and the two women had a "blessed conversation." It was at this time that Elizabeth informed the missionaries that her daughter had married Daniel, an enslaved Christian whose siblings and parents were all members of the Moravian church.[28] This entry—and the lack of information that preceded it—suggests that Elizabeth recognized that the missionaries had failed to protect her daughter and sought other strategies.

Why did Camilla marry Daniel? Perhaps she hoped that a union with Daniel could provide her a degree of protection from white men. The politics of plantations were complex, and Camilla's marriage to Daniel would have changed the social dynamics on the estate.[29] Daniel, who was also baptized, had been born and raised at the Bogue and had the support of a large and relatively powerful family. He had three adult brothers, Ignatius, Joseph, and Whan, as well as four younger siblings. His parents, Casandra and Isaac, were also members of the Moravian congregation, and his brother Joseph, the fifth person baptized on the estate, was a leader in the congregation.[30]

While it is impossible to know for sure why Camilla married Daniel, later narratives written by formerly enslaved women like Harriet Jacobs suggest that enslaved women sought out sexual partners of their own choice to affirm their free will and to make it more difficult for their rapists to pursue them.[31] Harriet Jacobs, though living in a very different time and place, wrote about how she pursued a relationship with Mr. Sands (Samuel Tredwell Sawyer) in order to evade her enslaver, Mr. Flint (James Norcom). Several aspects of Jacobs's narrative can be helpful for understanding Camilla's situation at the Bogue. First, Jacobs explains why she did not tell her grandmother, her most trusted relative, about Mr. Flint's abuses. "Both pride and fear kept me silent," she wrote.

Jacobs's silence, especially concerning her experiences of sexual assault, is a reminder of how experiences of sexual violence remained hidden, even when they were ubiquitous.[32] Like Jacobs, Camilla may have chosen not to tell her mother, Elizabeth, about certain aspects of her experiences.

Second, Jacobs notes that she refused to marry a free Black man, despite the urging of her white mistress, Mrs. Flint. Not only did Jacobs conclude that a free Black man could not provide the same protection against abuse as a white man, but she also objected to Mrs. Flint's matchmaking, noting that her mistress "seemed to think that slaves had no right to any family ties of their own."[33] As Jacobs intimated, the *choice* of a sexual partner was meaningful. Jacobs's decision to have a relationship with Mr. Sands was an act of defiance as well as an assertion of morality.[34] For Jacobs, the decision to enter into a relationship with Mr. Sands was intertwined with her experience of sexual assault and her strained relationship with Mrs. Flint. It was also a rebuke of white morality and a critique of white Christianity. "She was a member of the church," Jacobs wrote about Mrs. Flint, "but partaking of the Lord's supper did not seem to put her in a Christian frame of mind."[35]

Camilla's relationship with Anna Rauch was not equivalent to Harriet Jacobs's relationship with Mrs. Flint. Still, placing the two stories side by side helps to draw out some potential parallels. First, while Anna Rauch was clearly sympathetic to Camilla's predicament—certainly more sympathetic than Mrs. Flint—she was not able to protect the young girl. Moreover, Anna Rauch's advice may have inadvertently worsened Camilla's situation. In other words, despite positive intentions, Anna Rauch's efforts on behalf of Camilla and Elizabeth were unsuccessful.

Given this context, the archival silence about Camilla that lasted from July, when she was raped, until October, when Elizabeth informed the missionaries that Camilla had married Daniel, is itself important. The silence *is* an archival irruption, and we can surmise that Camilla and Elizabeth disengaged with the missionaries to some degree, seeking a solution from within the enslaved community. The fact that they did not ask the missionaries for their opinion about Camilla's marriage to Daniel, nor did they ask them to preside over the ceremony, is yet another important archival absence. Finally, it is significant that Elizabeth, rather than Camilla, informed Anna Rauch of Camilla's marriage. This suggests that while Elizabeth decided that it was worthwhile to maintain a relationship with the missionaries, Camilla was less interested. Indeed, the church registers show that Camilla was not baptized until 1769, more than ten years later and seven years after the death of Anna Rauch.

Reading for Dissimulation: Competing Archival Narratives

On July 30, 1758, the Moravians experienced a different kind of disturbance—possibly from the same men who had attacked Camilla. It was a hot summer evening, and the Moravian meeting house was packed. The building was so full that several men and women were leaning on the wall at the back of the hall, close to the door. They were listening to Caries's sermon. At some point while Caries was speaking, a crowd of white men began congregating outside the house.[36] They were likely noisy as they idled and laughed. They would have known that their very presence was an ominous sign. As they stood there, visible through the windows, the tension within the small meeting house was surely rising. Some congregants probably looked through the windows nervously, hoping the crowd would disperse. A group of rowdy white people was never a good sign in eighteenth-century Jamaica.

Later, Caries wrote that when he "held the normal Sunday meeting ... we were disturbed by white people who stood by the door and by the windows." One of them "stuck his hand through bars of the window," gesturing to an enslaved woman to "come out of the Meeting." She refused. Perhaps she tried to ignore the man; perhaps she answered him and said no. She may have thought that since she was in a worship meeting, listening to a white man preach about God, she would be able to have a temporary sanctuary from this man who, everyone knew, was her rapist. She was wrong. "When she refused [to come outside]," wrote Caries, "he stuck his hand through the door and pulled at her skirt." Caries insisted that he was unperturbed by the events. "This didn't disturb me," he wrote, "because I was holding the meeting and was fully captivated by my material." It was his "dear Brethren," he noted, "who saw the spectacle and they saw how our dear blacks listened as well."[37]

There is another layer to this story. Caries was not the only person who wrote down the events of July 30. Christian Heinrich Rauch was also sitting in the meeting house, and he watched as Caries continued his sermon. Like Caries, Rauch recorded that "the evening meeting was again disturbed by the white people in a crude and outrageous way." But he added some new details. "Amos [a baptized congregant] tried to stop it. But they already had the young black woman by the skirt and wanted to pull her out."[38] Here we learn that Rauch, like Caries, watched these men disturb their meeting and grab a young woman. We also learn that he, like Caries, did nothing. In fact, Amos, an enslaved Christian, was the only person who tried to stand up to the white men. It was a dangerous move for Amos, who surely knew that he could be the subject of retaliation.

Amos's effort to protect the young enslaved woman demonstrates how sexual violence rippled out into the broader enslaved community. Amos was appalled that these men were able to shamelessly interrupt a sacred moment in the missionary's home. As a baptized member of the church, perhaps he felt protective of the worship meeting. The Moravian records indicate that Amos frequently defended the Moravian congregation against the mockery of whites.[39] His decision to speak out against the white rapists—despite the silence of missionaries—was a sign of how much he was willing to risk his own body to vocalize his protest.

While enslaved men and women struggled to protect themselves and their loved ones from rape, the culture of "sexual dismemberment" also weakened the authority of white male missionaries. Men like Caries and Rauch had more privilege within Jamaican society than enslaved men and women, but their convictions put them at odds with white culture on the island. While the patronage of the Fosters and Barhams, the absentee slave owners, protected Caries and Rauch in some respects, episodes like the one in the summer of 1758 were a clear sign to both Blacks and whites that the missionaries lacked the authority to challenge white rapists. The missionaries' inability to protect their congregants from sexual assault—even during a worship service—was one reason why they lost their status as Obeah men, a theme traced in more detail in chapter 5.

Thistlewood, Violence, and Multivocal Archives

Thomas Thistlewood, a white overseer and slave owner, lived just a few miles away from the new Moravian mission station in Westmoreland Parish. Thistlewood was not a particularly remarkable individual, aside from the fact that he kept a journal that he wrote in obsessively, recording facts about each day, including the weather, his dinner guests, and a list of the women he raped. Placing the Thistlewood diaries in conversation with the Moravian records helps to illuminate important aspects of archival production in 1750s Jamaica, particularly relating to sexual violence. While Anna and Christian Heinrich Rauch recorded their struggles to provide guidance and support to enslaved people who were seeking to evade white rapists, Thistlewood recorded his own sexual behavior, including his serial rapes of enslaved women.

Thistlewood's diaries have become one of the most important sources for understanding everyday life in eighteenth-century Jamaica. Many scholars consider Thistlewood's diaries to be, in the words of Heather Vermeulen, "the largest extant archive for studying slavery in eighteenth-century Jamaica."[40] While the Moravian records constitute a larger archive, their early records have not

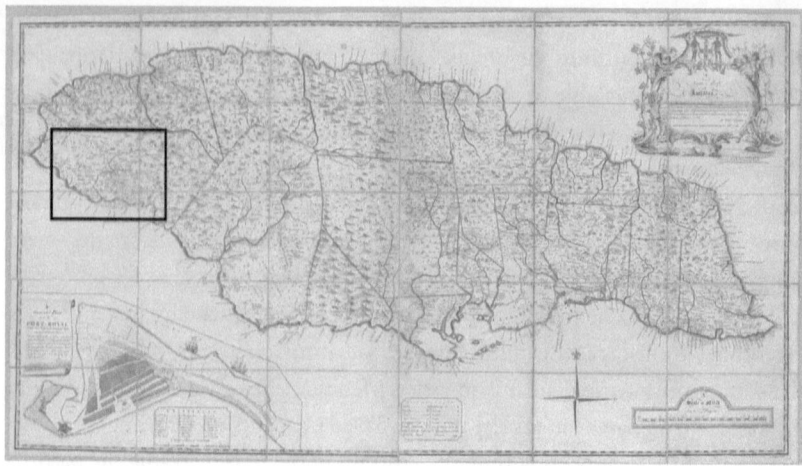

FIGURE 4.3. Patrick Browne, "A new map of Jamaica" (1755). Black-outlined area contains the Moravian mission site at Mesopotamia and Egypt plantation (Thomas Thistlewood's location), shown in figure 4.4 in detail. Courtesy of the John Carter Brown Library, Brown University.

been examined by scholars because they are written in German Script. Thistlewood's diaries, by contrast, are written in English, though he recorded sexual encounters in Latin.[41] As a result, several scholarly journal articles and monographs have been devoted to examining Thistlewood's troubling words. One scholar has analyzed Thistlewood's weather references in order to understand Jamaica's climate; another has used the journals to analyze the economic opportunities for poorer white men; several have scoured the diaries in order to examine medical practice under slavery. Many have debated whether Thistlewood was a typical overseer or an unusual one.[42] The most comprehensive book on Thistlewood, Trevor Burnard's *Mastery, Tyranny, and Desire*, places him within the context of the Atlantic Enlightenment as well as slavery.[43]

While Thistlewood's diaries have been used in a variety of ways, the documents are most famous—or infamous—for their depiction of rape and sexual violence. From Thistlewood's diaries, historians gain access to names and numbers. Thus, historian Trevor Burnard was able to calculate that Thistlewood engaged in sexual activity 3,852 times during his thirty-eight years in Jamaica. At Egypt plantation, where he worked as the overseer from 1751 to 1767, forty-two of the enslaved women on the plantation were forced to have sex with him (ten were not). Burnard even calculated Thistlewood's sexual activity by decade, noting that his sexual activity "peak[ed] in 1754," then "gradually declin[ed]." The number of "partners" also declined, "from a high of 26 in 1755 to under 10 in the 1780s."[44]

FIGURE 4.4. Detail of Browne, "A new map of Jamaica" (1755) showing the Mesopotamia plantation and Egypt plantation, where Thomas Thistlewood worked as overseer from 1751 to 1767. Courtesy of the John Carter Brown Library, Brown University.

The data that Thistlewood's archives make visible is revealing and deeply problematic. In a pointed critique, Heather Vermeulen notes that many historical accounts of Thistlewood's sexual practices do not use the term *rape*. Instead, she writes, "one encounters references to his 'sexual athleticism,' 'spur-of-the-moment lust,' 'voracious libido,' 'couplings,' and 'sexual conquests' recorded in 'school boy Latin.'"[45] In her essay "Venus in Two Acts," Saidiya Hartman articulates the problem clearly:

> While the daily record of... abuses, no doubt, constitutes a history of slavery, the more difficult task is to exhume the lives buried under this prose, or rather to accept that Phibba and Dido [two enslaved women] exist only within the confines of these words, and that this is the manner in which they enter history. The dream is to liberate them from the obscene descriptions that first introduced them to us.[46]

Hartman's challenge—to "exhume the lives buried under this prose"—represents an ethical project as much as a historical one.

Placing the Moravian missionary records next to Thistlewood's diary does not solve the historical and ethical problems that Hartman articulates, but it can illuminate important patterns of production in two very different archives, created just a few miles away from each other in mid-eighteenth-century Jamaica. While Moravian missionaries often obscured, edited, or deleted their knowledge of sexual violence, Thistlewood's journal reminds scholars of its ubiquity. In other words, Thistlewood's accounts and the statistics about his sexual behavior make it possible to recognize the silences in the Moravian archives. Thus, while the Moravian missionary diaries reference a handful of cases of sexual assault and rape between 1755 and 1762, we can be sure that this represents only a small fraction of the actual cases.[47] Factoring in that some rape references were later edited out, the degree to which missionary records erase sexual violence is staggering. It is not possible to know how much the missionaries knew and chose not to record, and how much they did not know, but either way, the production of silences around sexual violence was a deliberate not-knowing.

While the Moravian archives obscured sexual violence, they do offer a different perspective from Thistlewood's diary. Thistlewood, writing as a rapist, did not consider the consequences of his assaults for enslaved women; nor did he seem to consider his actions to be problematic. On this point, it is instructive to place Thistlewood's entries for July 15, 1758, next to the entries from the Moravian records of the same day. At the Bogue, July 15 is the day that Anna Rauch heard that Camilla had been attacked, "bound and beaten," tracked down in a cane field, and raped. Meanwhile, on the same day at Egypt plantation, just a few miles south, Thistlewood recorded:

Saturday 15th

gave the Negroes to day (Mrs: Cope had a Jarr off Butter by Bacchus) * A.M. Was at hill, ffetched my Alligator Teeth, &c. gave Phib: Some.

xxx About 11 a.m. Cum Jenny Sup: Terr: by Morass Side, hill Negroe ground. gave do: 2 Bitts

x This Morning had Port Royal and Cambridge fflogg'd ffor stealing molassus last night at the Curing house door:they being Watchmen. gave Pluto a Bottle of Rum ffor detecting them . . . [48]

Tucked in between Thistlewood's reference to fetching "Alligator Teeth" and his order to "flog" Port Royal and Cambridge for "stealing molassus" are the words: "Cum Jenny Sup: Terr: by Morass Side, hill Negroe ground."

Thistlewood's decision to record his sexual activity in Latin means that historians have to translate his code. The word *cum* is Latin for "with," and *sup* is generally translated as "over" or "on," while *Terr*, an abbreviation of *terra*, means "ground" or "country," so the notation could be translated as "with Jenny on the ground." Trevor Burnard translates *sup terr* as "on the ground," while Saidiya Hartman translates the full phrase as "I fucked her on the ground," emphasizing Thistlewood's intentionality as well as his vulgarity.

Thistlewood's archive thus forces historians into an uncomfortable place, one in which the archival knowledge most readily available takes the perspective of an enslaver and rapist. With its Latin phrases and its interspersal of spectacular violence with banal facts, notations like the one he made on July 15, 1758, "Cum Jenny Sup: Terr" make Thistlewood's behavior seem sober, transactional, even rational. The Latin phrases divert our attention, presenting a code to crack and statistics to gather, and privileging Thistlewood's frame of mind and perspective. Within this context, Christian Heinrich's haunting description of Camilla provides historians with words that reintroduce terror. By following the references to Camilla and her mother, we can also see more than a sensationalized tale of violence against a young woman. Knowing about Camilla's family, her decision to marry Daniel, and the fact that she kept her distance from the missionaries gives her life more texture, even if our understanding will remain forever inadequate.

Sexual Ethics and Re/membrance

If Thistlewood and his diaries represent one type of archival inheritance from slavery—one that is brutal, callous, and casually violent—the missionaries represent a different kind of inheritance. They contested the actions of people like Thistlewood but also failed to prevent them. Still, neither archive reveals the full scope of experiences that enslaved women had related to sex, rape, and religion. Rape, as Thistlewood's ample documentation shows, was ubiquitous, part of what Wells-Oghoghomeh calls a "culture of dismemberment" that defined Atlantic slavery. Sexual dismemberment refers to the collective "experiences of familial separation, rape, and other forms of violence" that altered how enslaved women and men "understood the cosmos and their places within it."[49]

The culture of dismemberment was not merely an assault on enslaved people's bodies; it presented existential and ethical dilemmas, such as how to find meaning and preserve kinship bonds in a system built on brutal exploitation and social alienation. In response, enslaved women developed strategies of "re/membrance" such as "sense" and "sexual ethics" that drew on African precedents and were aimed at "mitigating the effects of sexual dismemberment."[50] The framework of re/membrance reorients morality away from Christian definitions and centers, instead, the embodied experiences of enslaved women. This final section rereads the Moravian archives through the lens of re/membrance, showing how Camilla and Elizabeth drew upon enslaved women's sexual ethics in their decision to join—and leave—the Moravian church.

One fundamental component of re/membrance is sexual choice. As Wells-Oghoghomeh argues, "sexual choice became a sacred value among the enslaved."[51] In the midst of the brutal system of slavery in which exploitation and rape were commonplace, enslaved women sought to choose their own partners, to engage in nonprocreative sex, and to define their own sense of right or good sex. Here, we can interpret Camilla's choice to form a union with Daniel—and to forego missionary intervention in her marriage ceremony—as part of her sexual ethics. The full scope of her psychic world is unavailable to us, but through fissures in the archives, we can see slivers of Camilla's decisions. Still, we should also not assume that her union with Daniel was intended to match missionary ideas about monogamy, and Camilla's sexual ethics may have included multiple partners or any set of complex arrangements that "included and transcended the monogamous marital relationship."[52]

Elizabeth's decision to become a member of the Moravian congregation and partake in Christian rites should also be interpreted within the context of re/membrance. She, like the other enslaved women who joined the church, initially hoped that she could protect her family, and especially her daughter Camilla, by joining the church and cultivating relationships with the missionary Anna Rauch. The culture of dismemberment can be understood, in part, as an ongoing attack on enslaved kin networks. White men undermined unions between enslaved men and women, and they split up families, selling children and spouses. More fundamentally, it forced parents to wrestle with existential problems, such as the one that Elizabeth, Benjamin, and Venus faced: Should they prepare their children, and especially their daughters, for a world in which rape and assault were ubiquitous? How much should they place their own physical bodies on the line to protect their children from rapists? Moreover, what did it mean to put oneself, and one's family, back together within this culture of predation?

As Elizabeth's story suggests, the protection and cultivation of family—of kin—was a key aspect of enslaved religious life that emerges again and again in the Moravian records. Elizabeth's choice to join the Moravian congregation was an effort to bolster bonds of kinship and develop a sacred community to mitigate the culture of dismemberment. As I showed in chapter 1, membership in the church often extended along family lines. Parents followed their young adult children into the church, while mothers and fathers often brought their sons and daughters to worship meetings. Baptism offered a strategy for re/membrance as well as a space of correlation with clear analogues in African religions. Some women may also have viewed baptism as a way to heal from violence. As Wells-Oghoghomeh has written, enslaved women might seek to disremember sexual trauma through the "ritual cleansing" of Christian baptism. Baptism could "resignify" a traumatized body and offer a "means of re-membrance" as women "ritually cleane[d] themselves of unwanted touches and penetration" and "purge[d] the guilt and rage that followed in the wake of their violations."[53]

While the Moravian congregation could be a place for re/membrance, this was true only up to a point. The Moravians, like other Christian missionaries, held ideals about sexual morality that formed the core of their religious convictions.[54] In the Moravians' first Caribbean mission on Saint Thomas, missionaries initially insisted that marriage was between one man and one woman. Almost immediately, however, they realized that this conception of marriage could not be realized within the context of Caribbean slavery.[55] By the time the Moravians arrived in Jamaica in the 1750s, they had adjusted their rules about marriage to some degree, but mostly to accommodate enslaved men who had multiple wives.[56] The Moravians were less willing to accommodate the challenges facing enslaved women. They often used words like *prostitute* or *whore* to describe enslaved women's sexual relationships with white men, which did not acknowledge the power relations inherent in their actions. Only occasionally did the missionaries use words like "force," as Christian Heinrich did in describing Camilla's experience on July 15, 1758.

Crime and Archival Silence

The culture of dismemberment and the tension between enslaved sexual ethics and missionary ideas of morality and sin are critical to keep in mind when we examine conflicts between missionaries and enslaved congregants. Throughout the late 1750s, Camilla's mother, Elizabeth, continued to cultivate a good relationship with the Moravian missionaries.[57] But when Anna and her husband, Christian Heinrich, moved from the Bogue to Mesopotamia in Westmoreland parish, Elizabeth's relationship with the new missionary, Joseph Powell, began to deteriorate. On July 25, 1761, Powell wrote that he "sharply reprov'd Old Elizabeth, not only for taking her sons part, but also her commending his black, wicked crime." When Elizabeth tried to attend a worship meeting for the baptized, "she was Desier'd to withdraw."[58] In other words, Powell barred Elizabeth from participating in the Moravian service. The passage provokes far more questions than answers. What was the so-called crime? Which son were the missionaries referring to? Could it have been Elizabeth's son-in-law Daniel, Camilla's husband, who was at that time embroiled in conflict with the missionaries? Considering that Elizabeth was not accused of anything aside from protecting her family, why was she barred from entry to a worship meeting?

Powell's reference to "crime" recalls one of the questions I asked at the beginning of this chapter: What is the meaning of a crime in a society in which the premeditated rape of a Black child was not a punishable offense? It should not be controversial to state that Camilla was the victim of a crime, but the archival reality—and the reality of legal structures in Jamaica—meant that the word *crime* was never mentioned in the sources relating to Camilla's rape. Instead, we see the term *crime* referenced in relationship to Elizabeth's son, but never regarding her daughter Camilla. The following two chapters take up the construction of crime more fully by examining the practice of policing within the Moravian congregation (chapter 5) and the criminalization of Obeah following Tacky's Revolt in 1760 (chapter 6). Throughout these chapters, it is important to keep in mind that the rape of a Black child never warranted the designation of crime in eighteenth-century Jamaica.

While the following chapters focus on policing and crime, this chapter has emphasized how dissimulation in conflicting archives can offer an opportunity to (1) identify fissures in the archives, (2) interrogate the production of silences, and (3) reread the archives for re/membrance. As we have seen, the Moravian missionary documents systematically silence—and in some cases, intentionally erase—the existence of sexual violence. While some references, like those in Rauch's diary, remind readers that rape was a problem, theoretical approaches that center enslaved women's methods for creating meaning, kin networks, and religious communities in the face of sexual dismemberment are necessary for putting archival knowledge in its proper place. Using a comparative archival methodology, examining the production of silences, and drawing on concepts such as critical fabulation and re/membrance can help modern historians avoid repeating the devastating narratives—and the silences—that make up colonial and missionary records.

5

Policing Bodies, Saving Souls

DISSIMULATION IN THE ARCHIVES

In June 1758, Christian Heinrich Rauch wrote a scathing letter to Joseph Spangenberg, the Moravian bishop in Pennsylvania. In it, he criticized Zacharias George Caries and his approach to mission work, complaining that Caries had baptized men and women who were not true Christians.[1] After Rauch's arrival, the number of baptismal ceremonies at the Bogue plantation plummeted. While Caries performed twenty-six baptisms in 1755 and forty-three in 1756, only five men and women were baptized at the Bogue plantation in 1757. In 1758, there was only one baptism: Elizabeth, Camilla's mother (the focus of chapter 4). In 1759, there were no baptisms. In 1760, two congregants were granted the sacrament, both women: Marina (November 1760) and Sarah (November 1760).[2]

The decision to halt nearly all baptisms was another reason that the Moravians lost their status as Obeah men. As baptisms decreased, the missionaries bemoaned that many of their congregants stopped attending worship meetings. The missionaries viewed these changes as evidence of "backsliding" and "sinful" behavior among their congregants. Rauch blamed Caries for the devolving situation, arguing that he had been too quick to baptize, among other faults. He also criticized Caries for developing an alliance with the Maroons, saying that the missionaries should focus their efforts only on the enslaved population. Caries defended himself but also acknowledged that there were problems at the Bogue. As the years wore on, Caries came to believe that he had been a "poor child" and had been too "gullible."[3] By 1759, the mission was in such a bad state that the Moravian church leaders sent Nathanael Seidel, a Moravian bishop, to mediate. During a series of conferences, Seidel sided with Rauch, and Caries was sent back to Europe in shame.

Previous histories of the Jamaica mission have focused on theological disagreements between Caries and Rauch as the reason for the mission's temporary failure.[4] This chapter offers a different interpretation of the feud between Caries and Rauch by (1) reframing it from an Africana perspective, and (2) placing it in conversation with the Moravian missions to the Mohicans in Shekomeko (New York), where Rauch had worked before his arrival in Jamaica. It argues that Rauch's ideas about conversion were at odds with those of the Black men and women who had initially sought baptism from Caries, and the real shift was that Afro-Jamaicans had stopped viewing the missionaries as Obeah men. This change was connected, in part, to the dynamics that were the focus of chapter 4: The missionaries were unable to protect Black families from the culture of sexual dismemberment. But this was not the only issue. Rauch had fundamental disagreements with Afro-Moravians about what it meant to be a Christian, and he sought to police the line between heathen and Christian in ways that were at odds with the congregation.

I use the framework of policing in this chapter to define Rauch's orientation to baptism, colonial law, and the Maroons. I define policing as an approach that seeks to control and discipline behavior, rather than seeking spaces of correlation in practice and belief.[5] I ask several interconnected questions: How were different missionaries defining the line between African religious practices and Christianity? How were enslaved and free congregants negotiating and challenging missionary efforts to police the line between Christian and heathen? How did missionary policing mirror and/or depart from colonial governance and its policing of religion? And finally, how did Rauch's approach to Christianity interact with the epistemology of Obeah? Throughout, I maintain a critical eye toward the archive, using the growing distrust between Rauch and Caries as an opportunity to gain new insight into the experiences of Black Moravians.

The first part of this chapter examines Rauch's experiences as a missionary among the Mohicans at Shekomeko in the 1740s. It was there that Rauch began to crystallize a vision for conversion that would influence his ideas about baptism. Rauch, who initially struggled to gain interest among the Mohicans, embraced a vision of conversion which suggested that only a small number of "heathens" could ever be truly Christian. I draw on Rauch's diaries and letters, as well as Moravian histories of the North American mission to the Mohicans, to narrate this history.

Once Rauch arrived in Jamaica, his dispute with Caries left its mark on archival documents, which show signs of growing distrust and surveillance between the missionaries. The distrust also permeated Caries's perception of Black Moravians, whom he began to see through the lens of *Heuchelei*, a word that can be translated as hypocrisy or dissimulation. The second section examines the construction of archival sources through the lens of *Heuchelei* and argues that dissimulation offers an opportunity to identify Africana irruptions by reading the fissures in the missionary archive. Caries's and Rauch's disagreements are also a reminder that the meaning of baptism was deeply contested—not only between converts and missionaries, but among missionaries themselves. Caries and Rauch had different personalities, different experiences, and different convictions about what it meant to be Christian.

The third section of this chapter turns to the concept of sin and examines it from an Africana perspective, suggesting that neither Caries nor Rauch grasped why Afro-Caribbean men and women joined the congregation—or why they left. While Rauch and, eventually, Caries became convinced that their congregants were involved in sinful behavior, Moravian missionary records offer another perspective on the category of sin, showing that the concept did not exist in most West African languages. This is another example of an Africana irruption, emerging from the fractured effort to translate Christian theological concepts into multiple African languages.

The final part of this chapter shows how Rauch reoriented the Moravian mission toward policing and colonial law. Policing, in this respect, took several forms. Rauch's approach to baptism and conversion focused on discipline: He was dismayed by what he considered to be sinful behavior, and he turned to disciplinary measures in response, rather than seeking common ground. Significantly, Rauch severed the missionaries' alliance with the Maroons, seeking instead to cultivate more support from colonial authorities. His decision was based on his experience in the Mohican mission, where he had been exiled by the colonial government in 1744. Wanting to avoid a similar outcome in Jamaica, Rauch prioritized his relationship with the colonial government over Caries's alliance with Accompong and other Maroons.

While many scholars have debated the relationship between colonialism and missions, this final section demonstrates how a single mission had an evolving and dynamic relationship with enslaved people, free Black communities, and the colonial state. The Moravians, who were linguistic and religious outsiders, were in a precarious position, and Rauch sought to strengthen their relationship with British authorities, rather than with the Maroons or the Afro-Jamaican members of his congregation. I argue that Rauch's prioritization of the missionaries' relationship with those in power—British lawmakers, overseers, and enslavers—was the primary reason that the majority of Black Moravians at the Bogue turned away from the missionaries and abandoned the idea that they were Obeah men.

Indigenous Missions, Baptism, and Colonial Authority

When Christian Heinrich Rauch landed in Jamaica on Christmas Eve 1756, he was an experienced missionary. He had spent the previous fifteen years of his life in North America, where he was the first Moravian missionary to evangelize to the Mohicans in present-day New York state. Rauch, who was born in 1718 in Bernburg, Sachsen-Anhalt, Germany, experienced an evangelical awakening on October 31, 1738, when he was twenty years old, and was accepted into the Moravian community in Marienborn the following summer.[6] In November 1739, he felt called to begin mission work among Native communities in North America, and by 1740, when he was twenty-two years old, he arrived in New York, where he began nearly two decades of mission work among the Mohicans.[7]

In New York, Rauch met two Mohican men who were part of a diplomatic envoy that had traveled to New York City to meet with the governor. The men, Tschoop and Shabash, communicated with Rauch in Dutch, and told him that they would accept a missionary into their community at Shekomeko.[8] Rauch's mission had a difficult start. While Rauch wrote that his first sermon was well attended, the Mohicans soon mocked and threatened him, and at one point they chased him out of the village. Nor was Rauch welcomed by nearby whites. Most saw Rauch's mission as an impediment to settler colonialism, and some threatened to shoot the missionary.[9]

Despite the clear message from the Mohicans and the antagonism of nearby whites, Rauch persisted and traveled regularly to Shekomeko to speak to the

Mohicans. Historian Rachel Wheeler has suggested that Rauch's medical skills, his theological focus on "blood and wounds," and his unusual demeanor and determination eventually led some Mohicans to reconsider the missionary. Tschoop wrote later that he was won over by the fact that Rauch seemed to trust the Mohicans, and because he was disinterested in stealing their land.[10]

By the end of 1741, Rauch was convinced that four Mohicans—Shabash, Tschoop, Seim, and Kiop—were ready for baptism.[11] He traveled with three of them to the town of Oley where, in 1741, Rauch baptized the Mohicans "into the death of Jesus."[12] When the Mohicans described the ritual, they highlighted the power of blood and wounds—two of the hallmarks of Moravian theology that were also central to the Caribbean missions. In a letter Tschoop (baptized John, or Johannes) wrote, "Nothing is so important to me, as to hear of the blood of my Savior."[13]

In 1742, the Moravian leader Count Zinzendorf traveled to Shekomeko to see the Mohican Christian community for himself. Zinzendorf wrote favorably about the visit and conversed with the four baptized Mohicans. The experience contributed to Zinzendorf's evolving ideas about the global Moravian missions and the meaning of conversion. In fact, it was during his visit in Shekomeko that Zinzendorf developed an outline for regulating conversion—a framework that would influence Moravian missions throughout the early modern Atlantic World, including Jamaica.

Zinzendorf's new policies on "heathen baptism" emphasized that since "the conversion of whole nations does not at present appear to be at hand," missionaries should not seek the "speedy increase of numbers" but rather "do their utmost, that the firstlings be well established in faith and love."[14] Evidence of conversion, Zinzendorf wrote, should be based on the experience of the "heart," and missionaries "must be careful" not to "merely [fill] their heads ... with knowledge." Missionaries were expected to exhibit "still greater caution" before "admitting the converts to the Lord's Supper." Specifically, he wrote that "none but such who have proved their faith by their works, and walk worthy of the Gospel, can be admitted to this Sacrament."[15] The new policies also established the groundwork for indigenous leadership in the church and approved the creation of an indigenous congregation in Shekomeko. Tschoop, Shabash, Seim, and Kiop (baptized John, Abraham, Jacob, and Isaac), the "four firstlings," were given leadership roles to extend the "important work of God amongst their nation."[16]

As in Jamaica, the recognition of indigenous leadership in Shekomeko was essential to the Moravians' appeal. In both cases, leadership positions offered a "space of correlation" in which indigenous or Black leaders could integrate Native and African religious traditions and rituals into the framework of the

Moravian church. Tschoop's and Shabash's leadership was especially fundamental in 1744, when King George's War broke out. The New York government forbade white Moravians from preaching to Native Americans, and Rauch was expelled from the mission. Colonial authorities feared that Moravians were papists who were secretly aiding the French.[17] Beginning in 1744, this meant that Rauch could no longer visit Shekomeko, and the mission was under complete indigenous control.

Rauch's expulsion from Shekomeko had a lasting impact on his perception of colonial authority and its relationship to the Moravian missions. Unable to continue his mission in Shekomeko, Rauch sailed to Saint Thomas in 1745 with his wife, Anna, to visit the first Moravian mission to enslaved Africans, which was founded in 1732.[18] In Saint Thomas, he prioritized his relationship with the colonial governor, who was the first person he visited after landing on the island. As in New York, the Moravians held a precarious political position in the Danish West Indies.[19] The colonial governor warned Rauch "not [to] Dare on any acc[ou]nt to teach the Negroes or speak with them of our Sav[io]r" because only those who were "nominated by ye King" were permitted to do so. After a long exchange, Rauch was able to convince the governor that "the King has nothing against the Negroes being bro[ugh]t to ye knowledge of Jesus Christ who has so dearly bought ym with his Blood on ye Cross." The governor, however, warned Rauch that he could not be responsible if any of the white people "should beat" him, and noted that many inhabitants had "a great hatred against you."[20] Despite these difficulties, Rauch's efforts to align himself with the colonial governor were successful in Saint Thomas, and he was able to visit the island again, in 1755, just a few years before he moved to Jamaica.

On his second trip to Saint Thomas, Rauch spoke to Black Moravians about the people of Shekomeko, as well as his initial difficulties in the mission. After a love feast (*Liebesmahl*) one Sunday, Rauch recalled how the Mohican leaders of the congregation, Tschoop and Shabash, "acted as men of God" when the "white brothers had been driven out" in 1744.[21] While we do not have a recording of the exact words that Rauch used, the story likely emphasized the authority of the indigenous Moravians who led the mission after the white missionaries were forced to leave. The fact that Rauch was talking—and writing—about his expulsion from Shekomeko over ten years later indicates that it was a formative experience for him.

The lessons that Rauch learned from his previous missionary experiences were twofold. First, in Shekomeko, he embraced an approach to baptism that was selective. He, like Zinzendorf, aimed to identify just the "first fruits" rather than to seek the conversion of an entire group of so-called heathens. Second, he learned to be cautious in his relationship with colonial authorities. In both Shekomeko and Saint Thomas, Rauch saw how colonial authorities could impede or facilitate mission work. In Shekomeko, the colonial authorities' distrust of the Moravians led to Rauch's inability to continue his mission work. In the wake of this experience, Rauch became especially careful to seek colonial authority for his missionary endeavors.

Heuchelei: Dissimulation in the Archives

When Christian Heinrich and Anna Rauch arrived in Jamaica on January 1757, there was no indication of the turmoil that would follow in the coming years. In their first month at the Bogue plantation, several Black Moravians welcomed the new missionaries. Rauch reported that the women in the congregation were especially excited by the arrival of the first female missionaries. Anna spoke with female candidates for baptism regularly, while Christian Heinrich spoke with baptized men.[22] According to the diaries, the missionaries discussed their "plan" for the mission, Caries continued to visit the sick in their homes, and Nathanael and Simeon were introduced as new helpers in the congregation.[23]

On January 23, 1757, the sugar season began, and the brethren held "the last Meeting of the week for the baptized and candidates before they have to work day and night."[24] During the harvest, the missionaries met only occasionally with their congregants. On February 5, for example, they wrote in their diary that "since no sugar was made that night, we took advantage of the opportunity, and held a Meeting of the Baptized and Candidates."[25] The following day, they reported that they "had no opportunities" to see their congregants, "because of the large amount of [sugar] cane that had to be cut, they had to be at the mill at dusk."[26] While the enslaved toiled in the sugar fields and the boiling houses, the missionaries met with the sick and, occasionally, with free Blacks.[27]

Enslaved people at the Bogue continued to request baptism. On March 30, Christian Heinrich "spoke a lot with Zachy and Quashie, two Candidates who asked for baptism."[28] By April, the missionaries agreed that they should baptize Quashie and Aberdine—the first baptismal rite since the arrival of the Rauchs and Schulzes. Spring 1757 also marked the first baptism of an enslaved woman at the Bogue. In February, the missionaries noted that "Barbara . . . brought the sisters a gift of a basket full of West Indian fruit."[29] The gift indicated that Barbara was proactively seeking out the missionaries, and especially the women, Anna and Maria. Soon thereafter, the missionaries wrote that Barbara had several "heartfelt discussions" with Anna.

In early April, Barbara was counted among the baptismal candidates. Just three days later, the missionaries proposed her for baptism, and she was approved by the lot. "She is the first woman to be baptized here," they noted.[30] Barbara was baptized on April 24, 1757 by Christian Heinrich Rauch and given the name Salome, which means "peaceful" in Hebrew.[31] Like other members of the Moravian congregation, Barbara frequently attended sermons and discussions with members of her family. Her daughter accompanied her when she visited Anna Rauch, and her husband, Zacheus, was also a baptismal candidate who would be baptized the same year, on Christmas Eve. When Christian Heinrich and Carl Schulz visited her home in June, they noted that Zacheus and Salome lived with "3 daughters and grandchildren" and that they were a "beautiful and dignified family."[32]

In these first months, Caries and Rauch seemed to enjoy each other's company, and they wrote positively about each other in the archival documents they left behind. On January 23, 1757, Caries wrote to Joseph Spangenberg in Bethlehem that Christian Heinrich was "a dear and respectable heart with whom [he could] be whole."[33] Similarly, Rauch's first letters are full of praise for Caries.[34] Nor did Carl Schulz's letter from February 2, 1757, suggest that problems were brewing.[35]

The first indication of a disagreement between Caries and Rauch occurred in July 1757, about seven months after the arrival of the new missionaries. On July 9, 1757, Joseph Spangenberg, the Moravian bishop in Pennsylvania, wrote two letters: one addressed to Caries, and one to Rauch. From those letters, we learn that Rauch had begun to criticize Caries, and Spangenberg sought to reconcile the missionaries. He told Rauch that the "Savior wants to create a masterpiece through you in Jamaica," and that Caries—whose "method" was distinct—was part of that masterpiece.[36] Spangenberg suggested that Caries could focus his mission on the "Wilden," or Maroons, while Rauch met with the enslaved. In his letter to Caries, Spangenberg assured him that he and Rauch would "come to understand each other's methods," and that they belonged together. He also praised Caries for his work among the enslaved population, though he warned him not to spend too much time preaching to whites.[37]

Spangenberg did his best to paint a poetic portrait about how Rauch and Caries complemented each other: "One of you tests the ice before stepping on it, the other runs over it without worrying about whether it will hold up." The differences between Caries and Rauch were indicative of a strong church. "Martin Luther and Phil[ip] Melancht[h]on were very different in their ways and talents," wrote Spangenberg. "But one like the other had to contribute to the work of the Reformation." Similarly, Rauch and Caries would contribute to the "reformation" of Jamaica by "loving one another tenderly." They could not "reform each other" but rather should recognize that they were "both originals, about which nothing [could] be changed, although there are some things that could be improved."[38]

The mission diaries offer additional insight into the emerging rift between Rauch and Caries. A few weeks after Spangenberg's letters, the missionaries had a conversation about their "Plan," in which Rauch "told Caries about some difficulties that occurred at the beginning of the Indian [mission], and how [Christian Heinrich] had stopped them."[39] While the missionaries did not record exactly how Rauch was using his experience in Shekomeko to advise Caries, it may have had to do with the Mohicans' initial rejection of his mission or with the careful approach to baptism that Rauch had displayed. Rauch could have explained that he had labored months to find just four "true" converts, or he may have discussed the importance of indigenous leadership, given the precarious political position of the Moravians. Rauch's decision to emphasize his experience in Shekomeko at this juncture is an indication of how his experiences in North America framed his interpretation of the Jamaican mission.

Neither Spangenberg's appeal nor Caries's and Rauch's conversation about their "Plan" had the desired effect. As the months wore on, Rauch accused Caries of making grave errors in the mission, while Caries vacillated between defending himself and acknowledging that the situation had begun to devolve. Still, Caries created a chronology that protected him: "Things only got bad after my dear brethren arrived from Bethlehem," he wrote. He suggested that his "great love" for his Black congregants "often blinded" him, and emphasized that the timing of the Rauchs' and Schulzes' arrival could not have been worse. The new missionaries landed on the island "just before the beginning of the sugar harvest," Caries wrote, so they could only have "2 meetings for the baptized and candidates before sugar making got in the way," and the enslaved "had to work day and night." Moreover, as Caries explained in a letter, "the sugar crop took unusually long this year, six and a half months." During this "hard time," Caries continued, "some of the baptized have fallen openly into sin." The missionaries "could hardly get to speak to them apart from Sunday evening and then they were tired because they had to work during the night right after the Meeting, and they also had to work half of the previous night."[40]

Once the sugar season was over, the missionaries planned to meet more regularly with their congregants, but Rauch came down with a violent fever and was close to death.[41] In October of the same year, Rauch had recovered from his illness, but most of the enslaved had not returned to the congregation. "I often despair," Caries wrote to Joseph Spangenberg in Pennsylvania: "it has caused me many sleepless nights, that so many of the baptized have fallen into sin and shame, and many things have come to light for which I thank the Savior, but Satan still has, or has gotten, so much control over them makes me very sad...."[42] Rauch, who responded to Spangenberg around the same time, seemed pleased with Caries's letter. He wrote to Spangenberg that "Caries... wrote pretty honestly, which made me happy."[43]

Caries used the word *Heucheley* (in modern German, *Heuchelei*), or "dissimulation," to describe the root of the problem. He explained that the Black congregants could "learn our language and to speak it back to us without using their heart."[44] Yet the problem of trust and dissimulation was not limited to the relationship between the missionaries and their congregants. It also animated the relationship between Caries and Rauch. Caries's letters indicate that Rauch began reading Caries's correspondence, checking it to make sure that he had been "truthful." Caries defended himself and implied that Rauch had placed him under a degree of surveillance that did not allow him to write everything he wished. In December 1757, for example, Caries wrote again to Spangenberg, noting, "my dear Brother Christian Heinrich reads all my letters that I write about the Plan, so he has also read this." In the same letter, he also contested Christian Heinrich's depiction of him. "One could get the impression that Brother Christian Heinrich was trying to say that I did not act truthfully and honestly," Caries worried. On the contrary, "I have, as far as I am aware, always written honestly."[45] Caries also began reading Rauch's letters, showing how easy it is to erode trust within a community when one leader polices another. Once Rauch began to surveil Caries, reading his letters and checking their accuracy, Caries contested Once Rauch's depiction of him and sought to defend himself.

Reading for Dissimulation: Africana Perspectives on Sin

The themes of dissimulation and distrust make the Moravian archive of 1757–59, which is composed of letters and diaries, an especially precarious—and intriguing—source of knowledge. When our informants, Caries and Rauch, distrust each other, how should we interpret their words? Should we side with one missionary over the other? Whose interpretation of the mission was correct? Were they both wrong? Most importantly, how can we begin to apply an Africana lens to the archival evidence left by Caries and Rauch?

The fragility of our trust toward this archive, I suggest, offers an opportunity. The Moravian archives of 1757–59 *could* be read through the lens of the Christian missionary genre of backsliding: a mission-centered narrative that describes how new converts returned to heathen behavior. The stock narrative about backsliding emphasizes sinful behavior. Yet this term—sin (*Sünde*)—needs further analysis. What, exactly, did the missionaries mean by *sin*? More importantly, what did a word like *sin* signify for the members of their congregation? Similarly, what does it suggest about language when Caries and Rauch accuse their congregants of dissimulation—of saying something but not meaning it "with the heart"?

We can gain insight into this complex process of translating *sin* through the records of the Moravian missionary and ethnographer Christian Oldendorp, who was stationed on the island of Saint Thomas in the 1760s, just a few years after Caries and Rauch were debating the appearance of sinful behavior at the Bogue. Oldendorp conducted interviews with African members of the Moravian congregation, in which he asked a series of questions about upbringing, African religious customs, and stories of enslavement. Oldendorp also sought to get a better sense of African perceptions of Christian theological terms by asking congregants to translate words and concepts. Specifically, he asked people from different African nations to repeat the following biblical saying in their own language: "Christ has loved us and he has washed our sins with his blood" (*Christus hat uns geliebet und gewaschen von den Sünden mit seinem Blut*). The phrase that Oldendorp chose included the key Christian term *sin*, as well as the fundamental Moravian emphasis on blood.[46]

According to Oldendorp, "some of them could translate it quickly in their own languages," but "most of them found it much more difficult" than he had anticipated: "[I spent] an hour with some of them going over those few words," he wrote, "and in the end, when I inquired as to whether they had made a good translation, I found that they had understood something completely different." Oldendorp came to realize that most Africans had "no word in their language for 'sin' [*Sünde*], so for those [he] suggested uncleanness [*Unreinigkeit*], evil [*böse*], or bad things [*schlechte Sache*]."[47] In his linguistic analysis, Oldendorp provided a dual translation based on his conversations with Africans (see table 5.1). First, with the help of his interviewees, he translated the phrase "Christ has loved us and he has washed our sins with his blood" into eighteen different West and West Central African languages. He then translated the African phrases back into German to demonstrate which metaphors were used to signify the theological concept of sin.[48]

As Oldendorp's communal translations demonstrate (see table 5.2), the most frequent translation for *sin* in West African languages was "uncleanness." The languages that emphasized uncleanness were identified as Kanga, Papaa, Karabari, Camba, and Congo. Four languages had an analog for *sin*: Loango, Mokko, Sokko, and Tambi, while four others offered no word at all. In those languages, Oldendorp's translations focused instead on the act of washing, as

TABLE 5.1: Oldendorp's Translations of *Sin* into Eighteen African Languages

Language	Translation	Translation of *Sin*
Jalunkan	Christus ibenkola mokkellutjelee. Christus hat mich gewaschen mit seinem Blut. Christ has washed me with his blood.	None
Kanga	Christus oddibem onjummo degoy. Christus hat mich gewaschen mit seinem Blut von Unreinigkeit. Christ has washed me from uncleanness with his blood.	Uncleanness
Gien	Christus andoinge, akkanitjru ensera. Christus liebt mich, er hat mich mit seinem Blut gewaschen. Christ loves me, he has washed me with his blood.	None
Amina	Christus pemy, oguarrimi, otomikau niboja. Christus hat mich lieb, hat mich gewaschen, meine Schuld bezahlt mit seinem Blut. Christ loves me, he has washed me, and paid my debt with his blood.	Debt/Shame
Akkim	Christus pemi papa, semi guquerri wuasibonni bodjaa. Christus hat mich lieb, er hat mich gewaschen von schlechten Dingen mit Blut. Christ loves me, he has washed the bad things from me with blood.	Bad Things
Akripon	Christus midoo, meloblemmi lobobubbaing ublemminklee. Christus liebt mich, er hat mich gewaschen von schlechten Dingen mit seinem Blut. Christ loves me, he has washed the bad things from me with his blood.	Bad Things
Tambi	Christus ensumi eduham umboo openabuh. Christus liebt mich, er hat mich gewaschen mit Blut von Sünden. Christ loves me, he has washed me from sins with blood.	Sins
Tembu	Christus ullunama, owaschumaa negu naschuma. Christus liebt mich, er hat mich gewaschen von schlechten Dingen mit seinem Blut. Christ loves us, he has washed our uncleanness with his blood.	Bad Things

(*Continued*)

Language	Translation	Translation of *Sin*
Kassenti	Christus tjquwi geem, ka undum mitjam duppan. Christus hat uns geliebet und gewaschen mit Blut von Schuld. Christ loves us and has washed our debt with blood.	Shame/ Guilt/Debt
Sokko	Christus minwoadjee, karmo-ee djurrimi markente. Christus liebet mich, hat mich gewaschen mit seinem Blut von der Sünde. Christ loves me, he has washed me from sin with his blood.	Sin
Papaa	Christus ijuwannam, elewunam ekrewoba noi emmehun. Christus liebt mich, er hat mich gewaschen von Unreinigkeit mit Blut. Christ loves me, he has washed me from uncleanness with blood.	Uncleanness
Wawu	Christus edike, melaünam dolleahuinam. Christus hat uns geliebet, er hat mich gewaschen mit seinem Blut. Christ loves us, he has washed me with his blood. Others: Christus esoaree, amboaree anjembo. Christus liebt mich, hat mich gewaschen mit Blut. Christ loves me, he has washed me with blood.	None
Karabari	Christus obiamamma, emwamehu hudji emsimee. Christus hat mich geliebet, er hat mich gewaschen von Unreinigkeit mit seinem Blut. Christ loves me, he has washed me from uncleanness with his blood.	Uncleanness
Ibo	Oparra Tschukkoabiami ihanjeneme odiama, obsananje otjirri ubarra. Der Sohn Gottes hat uns geliebet, uns gewaschen mit Blut. The son of God loves us, he has washed us with blood.	None
Mokko	Christus mamafeti, semmejeridem sidjaugo adji. Christus liebt mich sehr, er hat mich gewaschen von der Sünde mit seinem Blut. Christ loves me a lot, he has washed me from sin with his blood.	Sin
Loango	Christus munto untiel, minoa sukkula umeenga massumu. Christus liebt mich, er hat mich gewaschen mit seinem Blut von der Sünde. Christ loves me, he has washed me with his blood from sin.	Sin

(*Continued*)

Language	Translation	Translation of *Sin*
Camba	Christus wantie, najobila makilla vi-indo. Christus hat mich lieb, er hat mich gewaschen mit Blut von Unreinigkeit. Christ loves me, he has washed me with blood from uncleanness.	Uncleanness
Congo	Christus ensolani, sukkula nituam winu mengaman. Christus hat mich geliebt, hat meinen Leib gewaschen von Unreinigkeit mit Blut. Menga heißt blut, und das angehängte man drückt mit aus. Christ loves me, and has washed my body of uncleanness with blood. *Menga* means "blood," and the suffix *man* means "with."	Uncleanness

TABLE 5.2: Translations for *Sin*

Translation	Quantity	Africana Nations
Uncleanness [*Unreinigkeit*]	5	Kanga, Papaa, Karabari, Camba, Congo
Sin [*Sünde*]	4	Loango, Mokko, Sokko, Tambi
None	4	Ibo, Wawu, Gien, Jalunkan
Bad Things [*Schlechte Sache/ Schlechte Dinge*]	3	Tembu, Akripon, Akkim
Debt/Shame/Guilt [*Schuld*]	2	Amina, Kassenti

in the Gien translation, "Christ loves me, he has washed me with his blood." In Tembu, Akripon, and Akkim, *sin* was translated as "bad things," a signifier that could refer to a number of different material objects or physical actions.

Of the eighteen African languages that Oldendorp recorded, several were likely spoken by members of the congregation at the Bogue. Coal, who was baptized Sadook on May 30, 1756, was Congo, meaning that he may have interpreted sin as a form of uncleanness. Similarly, the Popo (i.e., Papaa) members of the congregation—Jacob/Frederick (Popo), Portland/Bartholomew (Popo), Peter/Joel (Popo), Cyrus/Zebedei (Popo), and Harris/Simeon (Popo)—likely had a similar interpretation of the Christian theological concept of sin as uncleanness. The Ibo members of the congregation, by contrast, may have understood sin somewhat differently. According to Oldendorp's translations, Penny/

Elizer (Ibo) and Eden Charles/Ruben (Ibo), who were baptized on the same day in 1756, may have had a conceptual signifier that was closer to *sin* in Ibo.[49]

The inability to translate *sin* in Kanga, Papaa, Karabari, Camba, Congo, and most other West African languages is a reminder that this category was not salient for the majority of Afro-Moravians who joined the congregation. Instead, they emphasized the significance of water rituals like Moravian baptism, prized the institutional authority given to Black leaders, and valued the healing power of blood and wounds theology, as detailed in chapter 1. The framework of Obeah, which had yet to be criminalized and redefined by white colonial authorities, had initially been the dominant framework for understanding the missionaries. But this was in the process of changing, as the rift between Caries and Rauch—along with several other factors—led to a breakdown in the meaning, purpose, and community of the mission at the Bogue.

Failing as Obeah Men: Rejecting Maroons, Embracing Law, and Policing Religion

The dynamic between Caries and Rauch devolved further in 1758 and 1759. While there was a temporary reprieve from acrimonious letters when Caries visited Mesopotamia plantation in Westmoreland, where the Moravians set up another mission station, Rauch continued his attacks in a letter dated June 27, 1758. Rauch's critique revealed a fundamentally different vision for the mission: While Caries tended to embrace overlapping beliefs and accommodate the requests of enslaved and free Black Moravians, thereby creating spaces of correlation, Rauch was focused on policing the boundaries of Christianity and aligning the mission with colonial authority. As a result of his efforts, the missionaries halted nearly all baptisms; approved new disciplinary measures, including physical punishment; and demurred when congregants requested that they advocate on their behalf to white authorities. This reorientation, I argue, led most Black congregants to abandon the belief that the missionaries were Obeah men. One consequence of these events was the increasing incompatibility of the epistemological frameworks of Obeah and Christianity.

Rauch's stance against the Moravian-Maroon alliance, the subject of chapter 3, was part of his reorientation toward policing. In a letter from June 1758, Rauch offered several reasons for his position. First, he argued that there was a "storm brewing" among the Maroons, and that the time for the gospel had not yet arrived. Second, Rauch felt that the missionaries had "enough work" already with the enslaved population at the Bogue. Finally, he noted that the Maroons had been "promised a preacher" in their peace treaty of 1739, and he felt that the governor should be contacted about that. Rauch suggested that instead of preaching to the Maroons, the Moravians should make direct contact with the head of the colonial government. "Is it not time that one of us went to see the Governor?" he asked.[50]

Rauch's opposition to the Maroon alliance is indicative of several features of his missionary approach. First, Rauch demonstrated a desire to proceed with great caution, wanting to remove himself—and the Moravian church—from any political disputes. The facts that the Maroons had a treaty with the colonial government and that there was a "storm brewing" within the Maroon community made him hesitant. Rauch preferred to focus on a smaller number of enslaved converts living at the Bogue, where the Moravians had been invited to preach by the white enslavers of the plantation. Rauch's deference to colonial authority was also evident in his statements about the governor. Noting that the governor had committed to sending a preacher to the Maroons—and that the Moravians had not explicitly spoken to the governor—made him anxious.

Rauch's cautious approach was likely based on his experience dealing with antagonistic colonial governments. In Connecticut and New York, Rauch had been banned from preaching, while in Saint Thomas, the governor had warned him to be careful in spreading his evangelical message. Rauch wanted to prevent the type of disruption that he had experienced in Shekomeko, when he was exiled from his own mission. Rauch's deference to colonial authority undermined Caries's alliance with the Maroons, and by 1759, Rauch had succeeded in severing Caries's relationship with them. Significantly, Rauch's actions also threatened the mobility of enslaved and free Blacks like Titus and Margery, who were drawn to the Moravian church, in part, because Caries had facilitated their ability to travel between Accompong Town and the Bogue plantation.

In the face of ongoing conflict between Rauch and Caries, the Moravian leadership decided to send an intermediary to Jamaica to resolve the dispute. Nathanael Seidel, a Moravian bishop, landed on August 15, 1759. Beginning at the end of August, Seidel held a series of conferences with the missionaries that covered a wide range of topics but focused on Caries's mission strategy. The conference minutes offer further insight into the dispute between Caries and Rauch, as well as the fundamental differences in mission strategy that guided them—most notably related to baptism, the alliance with the Maroons, and the Moravians' relationship with white authorities as well as the colonial state.

Seidel agreed with Rauch on most issues and decided that Caries should return to Europe, leaving Rauch in charge of the Jamaica mission. During the fifth conference, Seidel reprimanded Caries for performing baptisms too quickly. "You have started too early with your baptisms," he stated. "However, now I wish that the Savior could soon satisfy his hunger and thirst for souls and that a few blacks would be presented to him, who could enjoy the Lord's body and his blood with us in the Holy Sacrament."[51] Seidel's preference to focus on a select few—the *Erstlinge*, or "first fruits"—was in line with Rauch's position regarding baptism, as well as Zinzendorf's official Moravian mission policy.

Seidel also commented on the theological message that the missionaries should spread: "A main point that I would like to recommend to the brethren and put to their hearts: the simpler and easier to understand you preach the gospel among the poor black people, now and in the future, the more effect it will have on their hearts."[52] The desire to simplify the gospel for the enslaved had many sources: On the one hand, it fit with the Moravian theological emphasis on the blood and wounds of Christ, which had been a hallmark of their worship for decades. Yet the emphasis on a simple gospel also had political components. As I argued in *Christian Slavery*, on Saint Thomas, Moravians taught their first enslaved congregants to read and write, a feature of their mission strategy that made them popular among the Black population in the Danish West Indies. Over time, however, the missionaries restricted their literacy training to accommodate the fears of white slave owners, who worried that literacy education would make the enslaved more likely to demand freedom. Preaching a simple gospel also meant that the missionaries could avoid specific biblical stories that might undermine slavery (like Exodus) or promote practices that the missionaries wanted to de-emphasize (like polygyny).[53]

Seidel, siding again with Rauch, reminded the missionaries to respect white authorities, and he forbade them from intervening in disputes between enslaved congregants and white overseers. In one of the conferences, Seidel asked the missionaries, "Do your authorities know who you are and for what purpose you are here?" Seidel also reminded the missionaries, "You should love and honor your authorities," and "if you hear anything bad about them from other people, forget it as soon as you have heard it." The goal, for Seidel and the other leaders of the Moravian church, was for the brethren "to be known in Jamaica as poor but honest and upright people by everyone."[54]

The brethren agreed "not to be judges and arbitrators between the Black people (on whose souls they are working) and their authorities [i.e., their enslavers]." Instead, they were to "leave this matter entirely to their attorneys who are appointed for this purpose." If an enslaved congregant complained about mistreatment, they were to "direct all complaints ... to the right man."[55] In this and other conference notations, Seidel sought to differentiate between the "souls" that they were "working" on and the enslaved bodies that were subject to punishment by the "authorities." The missionaries' duty was "solely with the [enslaved] ... but in no other way than seeking to win their souls." They concluded, "The brethren who are on post should not in the least take the [plantation] attorneys to task," and "if [the enslaved] complain to them, about their masters, they should reject them so wisely."[56] In other words, Moravian missionaries were forbidden to advocate on behalf of their congregants to white authorities.

The decision to divide enslaved bodies from enslaved souls had profound consequences. By giving white overseers full authority over enslaved bodies, the missionaries abdicated their role as advocates for enslaved Blacks. They decided not to intercede, for example, if a white authority threatened physical punishment. As previous chapters argued, Caries's advocacy on behalf of his congregants was fundamental to the initial success of the mission. Enslaved people at the Bogue saw the missionaries as intermediaries who could speak to other white authorities on their behalf. Indeed, Caries regularly interceded between the attorneys, overseers, and enslaved congregants. His efforts were undoubtedly part of his appeal, and part of the reason that he was initially called an Obeah man. Over the years, however, the perception that the missionaries were successful advocates was put into question—especially when, as we saw in chapter 4, the missionaries were unable to protect their congregants from the "culture of sexual dismemberment" that characterized the Bogue plantation and Jamaica more generally.[57]

Rather than fostering the missionaries' support for their enslaved congregants, the conference minutes were preoccupied with the need for discipline and order. During the fourth conference, for example, the missionaries condoned physical abuse. While they forbade "abusive words" toward the enslaved congregants the conference minutes concluded that Black Moravians "shall be punished if they deserve it." The notations went so far as to suggest that physical violence could be aligned with Christianity: "if ... such a thing is done with a sinner's heart then it has benefits and will have a blessed result for them."[58]

Rauch and Seidel also sought to improve their relationship with the colonial government. The brethren spent a significant amount of time discussing their relationship with the British colonial state, and they studied the legal framework of the colony. The missionaries' preoccupation with colonial law was woven throughout each day of the conference. During the first conference, Seidel noted, "The brethren ... should acquaint themselves diligently with the laws of the land." He was concerned that "the law [books] which have been issued since 1755 must still be acquired."[59] During fifth conference, Seidel asked, "Would it not be good to show our Acts of the Unitas Fratrum to the authorities, so they would also be informed about them and know how they should regard us?" The question was "approved by all the brethren."[60]

The orientation toward colonial law was part of a broader shift ushered in by Rauch's arrival. The policy shifts help to explain why most of the Black men and women at the Bogue decided to abandon the mission—at least temporarily. On the one hand, the missionaries stopped offering one of their most important rites: baptism. As I showed in chapter 1, baptismal ceremonies resonated strongly for many Africans and Afro-Jamaicans as a space of correlation. Obeah was the epistemological framework for Afro-Caribbeans who participated in the baptismal ceremony, and most viewed the rite as a way to strengthen community and kinship bonds and to offer spiritual protection to themselves and loved ones.

The missionaries' decision to defer to white authorities, rather than advocate for their congregants, was another reason that Black men and women revised their perception that the missionaries were Obeah men. As I showed in previous chapters, Caries helped to facilitate mobility, and he also offered to speak with white authorities on behalf of enslaved congregants. Seidel found this to be inappropriate, and he insisted that the missionaries should view enslaved souls as separate from bodies. Their charge was to save souls, but they were to allow white overseers to maintain control over enslaved bodies. The missionaries' epistemological division of bodies and souls was directly at odds with Obeah, which did not propose such a division of the human experience.

While the body/soul division had a long history in Christian theology, the way that the missionaries adapted it to the environment of Jamaica changed over time: by talking about Jesus as "the Great Physician" and highlighting blood and wounds, Caries had integrated body and soul in a way that offered a space of correlation with African religious traditions. By rejecting that approach, Rauch and Seidel reintegrated a firm boundary between bodies and souls that was intended to accommodate Moravian Christianity to Caribbean slavery.

Re/formations of Christianity, Obeah, and Law

The new mission policies narrowed the epistemological possibilities for both Obeah and Christianity by policing the boundaries between the two categories rather than leaving open possibilities for spaces of correlation. The missionaries' orientation toward colonial law is crucial to highlight in this respect. The boundaries of religion and Christianity have an evolving relationship with law. Religion is not necessarily a legal category, but some religions have been legalized while others have been deemed illegal. More fundamentally, some practices that are religious can be deemed illegible as religion in colonial law. Such was the case of Obeah, as we will see in chapter 6.

For precarious religious denominations like the Moravian church, the missionaries' fixation on law was born of fear and anxiety. It was a legitimate fear: Rauch had witnessed the power of colonial law in undermining his Shekomeko mission, and it was an experience he hoped to avoid at the Bogue plantation. Since the Moravians were on the margins of Christianity in eighteenth-century Jamaica, their assimilation and orientation toward colonial law was thus a strategic effort on the part of Rauch, Seidel, and other Moravian leaders to bolster their legitimacy and affirm their standing in the eyes of colonial lawmakers.

In orienting the mission toward policing and colonial law, however, Moravian missionaries chose to abandon the space of correlation that had existed between Obeah and Christianity. No longer could Black Moravians have conversations with the missionaries describing Jancómpon and the Christian God as different names for the same deity, as they had with Caries; nor was it possible for the Moravian missionaries to advocate for their congregants' spatial mobility, to support Maroon–enslaved alliances, or to protect the enslaved from the physical abuse of overseers, as Caries had sought to do in the first years of the mission. Instead, Christianity was confined to the soul, and the missionaries concluded that the bodies of their enslaved congregants belonged to their enslavers and their overseers.

6

Constructing Religion, Defining Crime

ASSEMBLING, CONGREGATING, BINDING

On May 26, 1760, the white overseer at Mesopotamia plantation rushed to give the missionaries a "distressing message." Enslaved people had broken out in rebellion "not far from here," wrote the missionary Christian Heinrich Rauch. "They had gruesomely murdered many," he continued, and "all the white people in this parish were to go to rifle practice."[1] The rebellion, later known as Tacky's Revolt, was the largest uprising of enslaved people in the eighteenth-century British Empire. It began in April 1760 in St. Mary's Parish, on the northern coast of the island. By the end of May, rebels had begun to attack plantations in Westmoreland and St. Elizabeth, where the Moravian mission stations were located. It took over a year before the rebels were defeated by the joint forces of the colonial militia and the Maroons.[2]

Tacky's Revolt changed the way that white colonials policed the enslaved population. Most notably, lawmakers passed "The Act to Remedy the Evils arising from irregular Assemblies of Slaves," which criminalized Obeah for the first time. The criminalization of Obeah had widespread consequences. The legislation officially excluded Obeah from the realm of religion, making it incompatible with the category of Christianity. It also created new methods for policing the enslaved population by connecting specific material objects and rituals with the illegal practice of Obeah. In the following decades, Jamaica's anti-Obeah legislation spread throughout the Anglophone Caribbean, from Barbados to Trinidad to Grenada, creating a legacy that continues to influence modern ideas about religion and crime.[3]

The criminalization of Obeah is one example of how colonial states utilized the category of religion—or its absence—to criminalize anti-colonial technologies of power. Throughout the early modern world and beyond, scholars have identified variations of this dynamic: some imperial states banned "Black Gods," while others claimed that African and indigenous people did not "have" religion and used the language of witchcraft and superstition to delegitimize their religio-political practices. Colonizers and enslavers drew on claims about religion and non-religion to justify dispossession, enslavement, and settler colonialism. As a consequence, the modern category of religion has been indelibly marked by the intertwined histories of colonialism and slavery.[4]

This history of oppression has made it difficult to write about religion in the early modern period without reinscribing the power relations inherent in the category. This chapter reads the 1760 Act for irruptions and argues that scholars must deconstruct colonial terminology to understand the shifting contours between religion, "rebellion," and "crime" before, during, and after Tacky's Revolt. Specifically, I focus on title of the act, which refers to "irregular Assemblies." While the act itself did not focus on religion, the phrase "irregular Assemblies" offers insight into the strategies that British lawmakers used to criminalize Africana religious traditions without calling them "religion."

I argue that scholars need to take a twofold approach to examining the formation of "religion" under colonial slavery. First, I draw on the field of political theology to emphasize that the categories of religion and politics both depend on formations of the sacred. As Pamela Klassen has written, "all political power is also sacramental power."[5] Second, I argue that scholars must read for irruptions to identify evidence of religion during the early modern period. In my analysis of Tacky's Revolt, I examine religion by focusing on the religio-political acts of *assembling, congregating,* and *binding*. There are both etymological and epistemological reasons for this approach. On one hand, the word *religion* may stem from the Latin *ligare*, meaning "to bind."[6] Indeed, religion has long been recognized as a force for social cohesion and group identification. On the other hand, the power of assembly—of bringing people together—is fundamental to both religious and political power. In *Ekklesia*, religious studies scholars Pamela Klassen, Paul Johnson, and Winnifred Sullivan argue that the European categories of church and state are both "techniques of convening people." They coin the term "churchestatedness" to describe the "patterns of materials, practices, and procedures" that join people together into collectivities that "make and dissolve corporeality."[7]

Defining religion through the processes of assembling, binding, and congregating is an important reorientation—not only for the study of African diasporic religions but also for missionary Christianity and colonial political authority. By emphasizing assemblies of people, this approach also draws on the concept of "lived religion" that expands the study of religion beyond traditional sites of worship and institutions.[8] Recently, Tracey Hucks and Dianne Stewart have argued that whites' preoccupation with Obeah, or the "colonial cult of obeah fixation," was itself a "lived religion" based on "imaginations and persecutions of Obeah/African religions."[9] Building on their insight, this chapter places the lawmaking practices at the Jamaican Assembly House, where Obeah was criminalized, in conversation with the rebels' Obeah tactics and the worship practices at the Bogue to highlight the power of binding and congregating as religio-political acts.

I focus on the places where people assembled during Tacky's Revolt: The first section begins with the Moravian missionary house, a recognizably "religious" place where enslaved and free Blacks gathered for worship with white missionaries. The Moravian sources show that while the mission remained an important place for some enslaved people, the bonds that held its congregants together weakened further during the rebellion. This section also considers the shifting relationship between religion and the law, as Moravian missionaries were forced to defend their religious practice by providing legal paperwork to colonial authorities during the rebellion.

The second section turns to the neoclassical building in St. Jago de la Vega, or Spanish Town, the seat of the British Empire in Jamaica, where white colonial authorities assembled to create new laws intended to control the enslaved population. They, too, were congregating. Although they gathered for lawmaking rather than religion, the lawmaking practices of the Assembly of Jamaica—like the missionary meetings or the Obeah rituals of the rebels—depended on sacred practices. Slave-owning lawmakers straddled the domains of religion and politics as they sought to eliminate African diasporic sources of power, not only by criminalizing Obeah but by targeting all assemblies of enslaved people.

Section three, "Criminalizing Africana Religions," places the 1760 act into historical context, showing how it replicated and diverged from previous legislation aimed to suppress Black rebellion—and religion. The 1760 act is one example of how, in the wake of slave rebellions, colonial legislators intentionally excluded or marginalized Africana technologies of power from the realm of legitimate religion. As a result, scholars must read for irruptions in legal archives to examine the history of religion under colonial slavery. Examining acts of *assembling* destabilizes the linguistic patterns found in colonial archival documents to challenge the anti-Black genealogy of the modern category of religion.

The Meeting House: Lived Religion, Lived Rebellion

The Moravian missionaries at Mesopotamia lived in a small structure that doubled as the church's meeting house. The meeting house was closer to the quarters of the enslaved people than the big house—a fact that had created some controversy in 1758, when the missionaries chose the spot. Inside the meeting house, missionaries hosted a variety of worship meetings with enslaved men and women. A typical meeting included recitation of scripture, discussion of theology, and singing of Moravian hymns. When missionaries and congregants met for worship, they highlighted the suffering body of Jesus. As chapter 1 described, the missionaries' Christo-centric practice focused on Jesus's bloody hands, feet, and side wounds during the crucifixion. While the missionaries were no longer regarded as Obeah men, at the new mission station in Mesopotamia plantation in Westmoreland Parish, they were still sought out as spiritual practitioners by some enslaved men and women.[10]

When Tacky's Revolt broke out in 1760, it changed the practice of religion in the Moravian mission. The rebellion presented both a problem and an opportunity for the enslaved members of the Moravian church. Some chose to absent themselves from the mission house to participate in the rebellion, while others supported the colonial militia and the missionaries. Many just tried to survive the ordeal. As they did so, enslaved people utilized uncertainty to their advantage, presenting themselves alternatively as rebels, runaways, or Christians. For the missionaries, by contrast, the rebellion highlighted their precarious social and legal position on the island. They were forced to define their religion through law.

As previous chapters have emphasized, the Moravians were ethnic and linguistic outsiders in Jamaica. The rebellion exacerbated tensions with other whites and forced the missionaries to defend their religion using legal documents. On May 27, for example, just a day after the first rebel attack in West-

FIGURE 6.1. "An Act for encouraging the People known by the Name of *Unitas Fratrum* or *United Brethren*, to settle in His Majesty's Colonies in *America*" (London: Printed by Thomas Baskett, 1749).

moreland, the missionaries wrote, "a great Company of armed white people on horses passed by our house." They informed the missionaries that they "had to take rifles and appear at Cross-Path in the morning." When the Moravians explained that they "had no rifles" and that their religious principles included a peace testimony, the whites assumed that the Moravians were Quakers. The captain of the white militia informed them that "Quaker-Principles were not accepted in Jamaica" and that if they "were Bishops, [they] had to go with him."[11]

The Moravians defended themselves by explaining that they were not Quakers but rather an ancient Protestant episcopal church that had been authorized to settle in Jamaica by an act of Parliament. Upon hearing this, the white captain "desired to see the Act," but the missionaries didn't have a copy on hand. They resolved the tense moment when Nicholas Gandrup, a recently arrived missionary, "promised to show [the captain] the Act the next day."[12] In desperation, the missionaries turned to Mr. Macfarlane, the white attorney of the estate, for help.

When the missionaries met Mr. Macfarlane "on his way to Cross-Path," they asked if he knew about the act of Parliament. Fortunately for the missionaries, Mr. Macfarlane not only knew about the act but also had a copy "in his house." He promised to speak to Richard, the militia captain, on their behalf. The following week, Mr. Macfarlane reported that he had persuaded the captain "never again [to] trouble [the missionaries] about military service."[13]

The Moravians' interactions with the white militia captain show how rebellion could shift the relationship between religion and the law. By May 1760, the Moravians had been in Jamaica for five years. In that time, they had mediated tensions with the white colonial population, but they had never been challenged about their peace testimony nor required to present proof of the British Parliament's support of their presence. Previously, the missionaries had relied on their patronage from the absentee slave owners Joseph Foster Barham and William Foster to defend themselves against hostile white colonials. The rebellion, however, created new challenges for their mission. As the needs of the military conflict altered the social order, the missionaries were forced to articulate a religious objection to joining the white militia and to defend themselves with the material paper outlining specific laws. As rebels defied the colonial state and the institution of slavery, laws—and the paper they were written on—took on new significance.

While the missionaries relied on legal paperwork during the rebellion, enslaved people had no legal recourse. Black members of the Moravian church had to make difficult decisions about how to respond to the rebellion. At least some of them fought against the rebels and continued to attend Moravian worship meetings. Mathew, an enslaved man and a leader in the congregation at Mesopotamia, was a regular presence in the meeting house throughout the rebellion. When the revolt first broke out in Westmoreland, Mathew visited in the evening "and had a lot to tell." As fighting intensified in early June, the remaining whites relied on Mathew. He sent "loads of mules with provisions . . . to the Soldiers," and when a local white family sought refuge at Mesopotamia estate, he was asked to guard "the big house."[14] Mathew's growing responsibilities during the rebellion meant that he turned to the missionaries to help him protect his own belongings. On June 10, the missionaries wrote that Mathew "brought his money and his best things so we could watch them in the house."[15]

Mathew was not the only member of the congregation to support the plantocracy. On June 22, the missionaries wrote that Black Moravians at Mesopotamia plantation "caught one of the rebels on the plantation while he was sharpening his killing knife." After his capture, the Afro-Moravians "kept [the rebel] in the stocks until they could give him over to Mr. Macfarlane." The missionaries, who were clearly proud, concluded that their congregants "have now legitimated themselves in the neighborhood."[16] Meanwhile, at the Bogue plantation in St. Elizabeth Parish, when Afro-Moravians "Discover'd" the rebels "all round the plantation," they were "form'd in Companys & sent in p[u]rsuit of [the rebels]." In that case, they were not able to apprehend the rebel, but they did discover where he had "lodg'd."[17]

Why did so many enslaved people remain on plantations rather than joining the rebel forces? For some, like Mathew, the rebellion could be an opportunity to prove one's dedication to white colonials and possibly reap rewards. Others may have felt that it was too dangerous to join the rebellion, which would most likely fail.[18] Many simply tried to survive the ordeal. The historian Marjoleine Kars has called this "dodging rebellion," noting that some people "lived quietly on their plantations" and hid "in the bush" when rebels or soldiers appeared while others "migrated from plantation to plantation looking for food and safety."[19]

Some people of African descent sought to evade labels, appearing alternately as rebels or runaways. The slippage between categories is evident in the missionaries' occasional confusion about events. On November 6, for example, Nicholas Gandrup wrote that "there was a great uproar on this estate" when "one of the guards brought the message that the rebels were very close to the estate." In preparation, enslaved men and women "got as many weapons as could be obtained in a rush, and they went out against the rebels." When they did, they "found three Blacks who had robbed everything from the guard. They took them captive and put them immediately in the stocks." Later, however, they "found out that they weren't rebels, but were runaways who, on their telling, had made mischief against the rebels."[20]

The twists and turns in this story, and the missionaries' inability to distinguish between runaways and rebels, shows how Black men and women could utilize uncertainty to slip between categories, becoming rebels and then runaways depending on how events developed. Using stories about doing "mischief against the rebels," these three men not only performed as runaways but were able to convince other enslaved people, as well as local whites, that they had performed a service for the colonial state by making "mischief" against the rebels, undoubtedly saving their own lives in the process.

Still, ingenuity had its limits. Enslaved people were sometimes mistaken for rebels, as they were on November 4, when Brother Powell reported that "several innocent Slav[e]s" were killed by the colonial militia.[21] At other points, enslaved people were captured by rebel forces. On December 15, 1760, the missionaries at the Bogue noted that in a nearby plantation, some enslaved people were "kill'd," while "others [were] taken alive by the Rebbels [sic]."[22]

While some Afro-Moravians fought against the rebels or sought to avoid the conflict, others chose to join the rebel forces. In doing so, they may have been drawn to the rebels' use of Obeah to bind individuals together and prepare the community for battle. The missionaries never explicitly admitted that some of their congregants became rebels, but they did mention that several men and women disappeared during the first weeks of the rebellion. On June 26, for example, Mathew visited the missionaries and "complained that he has so few Black people at home to help him work the plantation; a few of them hadn't been home for four weeks."[23] That entry, on June 26, 1760, suggests that several of the men and women on the plantation had disappeared in late May—the same time that the rebels first appeared in Westmoreland. It is notable that the missionaries did not mention who these individuals were or make the connection that these men and women may have joined the revolt.

The missionaries wanted to believe that Christianity would make the enslaved less likely to rebel. In July 1760, Brother Powell noted that the enslaved who had "h[e]ard the Gospel" would "sooner be cut in pi[e]ces than have any part with the Rebel Murderers."[24] Yet the Moravian missionary diaries also reveal low rates of church attendance during Tacky's Revolt, particularly in the first months of the rebellion.[25] Over time, however, news about rebel forces declined while a famine spread across the island, changing the strategies for enslaved people and rebels alike. At Mesopotamia estate, Mathew told the missionaries on July 4 that there was a "great Hunger-emergency" and that many of the enslaved "had not had a bite to eat." The estate's attorney refused to provide any rice or flour, so the missionaries "loaned them our things and trusted them so much as our conscience allowed."[26] By July 11, the situation had gotten so bad that the attorney placed starving men and women in the stocks "because they had complained about their hunger," and the attorney "was afraid if they went out at night, they would steal."[27] The following day, when the missionaries visited the slave quarters they found men and women who were motionless with hunger.[28]

As the effects of the famine became more acute, the Moravian congregation began to grow once again. During this time, missionaries used Scripture to emphasize the importance of suffering. Powell spoke to the baptized and baptismal candidates on Luke 6:21, "Blessed are ye that hunger now," and Luke 6:25, "Woe unto you that are full! for ye shall hunger."[29] Powell believed that the desperate circumstances meant that the enslaved had "nothing left but our Saviour," and he thought this was a reason that "more attended the Meeting th[a]n usual."[30]

In the fall of 1760, after months of famine, rebel forces began to congregate again in St. Elizabeth Parish, close to the Bogue plantation.[31] In early November,

Powell noted that many of the baptized who had abandoned the mission at the beginning of the rebellion returned to the missionaries and sought support.[32] On November 19, Powell wrote that the meeting was very full, and it seemed to grow as the rebel force remained nearby.[33] The shifting rates of attendance suggest that while some congregants were initially drawn to the rebellion, over time, fatigue, fear, and famine led them to return to the Moravian congregation.

Still, even as the Moravian congregation grew in the fall of 1760, the missionaries—Christian Heinrich and Anna Rauch, Charles Schulz, Nicholas Gandrup, and Joseph Powell—often remained ignorant of the intentions of the enslaved men and women who congregated with them. On December 2, 1760, for example, Brother Powell noted that he "came on a Wicked company unawar[e]s, Assembel'd in Andrews a Baptis'd Negros Hous[e]." The group of people "immediately scatter'd," wrote Powell, "yet soon after assembil'd a gain."[34] Powell's entry, while short, can be read as an Africana irruption and expanded upon through critical fabulation. The fact that the secret meeting took place in the home of a baptized member of the Moravian congregation is significant. The purpose of the meeting is unclear, but the fact that the group assembled a second time suggests that it was important. It is notable that the meeting was in a house, rather than outdoors. Funerals, as well as other ritual events, were typically held outside, but the fact that this company was meeting in a house suggests a different purpose. Perhaps the congregated individuals were discussing their options for the future. Should they join the rebel forces? If not, how could they proceed? Maybe they were simply trying to find food or resolve an unrelated conflict. While we cannot be sure, Powell's diary entry is a reminder that enslaved people were frequently gathering together—with and without the missionaries.

For the enslaved members of the Moravian church, the evidence from archival sources suggests that some congregants sought out the rebels, even as others chose to demonstrate their allegiance to white colonial society and many chose to "dodge" rebellion. Over time, however, the famine and the decline of the rebel forces led many enslaved people to reintegrate the Moravian mission into their lives. Yet even as they did so, assemblies like the one at Andrew's house indicate that enslaved people often congregated outside the purview of the missionaries. For the missionaries, by contrast, the rebellion served as a reminder that the mission relied on colonial law—and legal paperwork—to legitimate its existence. Like the missionaries, enslavers would also turn to the law in the wake of the rebellion as they sought to reaffirm their authority and the reassert the brutal system of colonial slavery.

The Assembly House: Sacred Authority and Colonial Law

On December 13, 1760, the members of the Assembly of Jamaica entered a large, columned building in St. Jago de la Vega, or Spanish Town. The structure itself was not yet completed, but even in unfinished form, it dominated the urban landscape.[35] Once inside, the legislators finalized a new law that sought to prevent future rebellions like the one that had consumed the island for much of the previous year. The following section considers not only the effects of the act but also the *performance* of lawmaking and the *space* where the 1760 act was discussed and composed.

The title of the act—which highlighted "irregular Assemblies"—is a reminder of the importance of assembling and congregating to create political authority. Examining the "irregular Assemblies" of the rebels alongside the Assembly of Jamaica and the meeting house of the Moravians helps to illuminate the relationship between power, performance, and the sacred. It also demonstrates how the contours of legitimate religion, as defined in law, developed in conversation with—and opposition to—the sacred power of "irregular Assemblies."

Unlike the assemblies of the rebels, which were held in great secrecy in the interior of the island, the Jamaican Assembly had been meeting in St. Jago de la Vega since the English conquest of 1655.[36] In the first decades following the conquest, the Assembly met in the old Spanish Audencia, but in 1744, the Assembly passed a new act calling for "erecting a House or Edifice for the use of the Council and Assembly, and for the better preserving of the publick Records, and for the Reception of small Arms."[37] The fact that the Assembly met in the building that also held the "publick Records" and "small Arms" is a reminder that documents and weapons played a central role—alongside assembling—in sustaining empire. Written documents have had an especially lasting legacy in solidifying British imperial power. The very existence of written and printed laws has meant that historians often ignore the actual process of lawmaking, including the physical assemblies where these laws were debated and defined.

The new Assembly building boasted a neoclassical design with imposing columns and pediments.[38] While the majority of St. Jago de la Vega retained Spanish influences, including the city layout, the Assembly building reminded visitors of England. Built on a large public space called the Parade, it was "the only part which bears any resemblance to an English city," as one visitor commented.[39] Also on the Parade was the governor's house, known as the King's House. Together, the governor's mansion and the Assembly building formed the administrative core of the British Empire in Jamaica. In the next decades, the Jamaican government would add more neoclassical buildings along the Parade, thereby reinforcing imperial power and authority.[40]

The Jamaican colonial government consisted of three branches: the governor, the Upper House, and the Lower House. The Upper House, or Council, included twelve men appointed by the governor. The Lower House, or Assembly, was made up of representatives of the people, elected by the freeholders.[41] Upon appointment to the Council, all men were required to take an "oath of *secrecy* and *fidelity*."[42] The oaths did not create consensus—the Jamaican legislature was rife with factions—but they did conjure divine sanction. The oath of secrecy was especially significant. While the acts of the legislature, such as the creation of laws, were intended to be public, the legislature relied on secrecy to sacralize government. Their oaths, like the Obeah oaths taken by rebels, were intended to bind individuals together and to establish a sacred foundation for lawmaking.

Oaths were not the only sacred element of colonial politics in Jamaica. As in England, the Anglican church was deeply intertwined with the creation of state and imperial power—what Johnson, Sullivan, and Klassen have called "churchstatedness."[43] Just as the British monarch was the head of the Church of England, the governor of Jamaica oversaw the colonial church. As the enslaver-historian Edward Long wrote, the governor was not only "a vice-roy; a legislator; a general," he was also "a judge in equity and law, in ecclesiastical and in maritime affairs."[44] In fact, the absence of an Anglican bishop in the American colonies meant that the governor had outsized importance in the maintenance of the Anglican church on the island. As Bryan Edwards, another Jamaican enslaver-historian, wrote, "the governor or commander in chief, as supreme head of the provincial church, not only inducts into the several rectories . . . but he is likewise vested with the power of suspending a clergyman of lewd and disorderly life *ab officio*, upon application from his parishioners."[45]

While the colonial government was imbued with sacred authority stemming from the Church of England, lawmakers in Jamaica passed very few acts regarding religion. Still, religion was central to colonial governance, and especially the governance of enslaved men and women. When lawmakers referenced ministers or churches, it was primarily related to slave control, land settlements, and parish boundaries. Church wardens, lay officials who were chosen by the white male freeholders in each parish, were responsible for a diverse array of tasks related to slave governance, such as collecting penalties for such infractions as allowing an enslaved person to hire themselves out (1696: Act 38), posting printed copies of slave laws at the parish churches (1717: Act 64), and seizing illegal objects or property (1766: Act 40). Anglican ministers were responsible for announcing and distributing new laws, while parish churches doubled as community information boards, with postings about runaway slaves, missing items, and new laws about slavery.[46] As this makes clear, the Anglican Church was deeply implicated in the day-to-day practice of slavery in the Caribbean and elsewhere in the British Atlantic World.

Enslaved men and women were rarely included in Anglican congregations or baptized in the Anglican churches. This was a legacy of what I have called Protestant Supremacy, or the use of Christian status to distinguish between enslaved and free people.[47] Many Protestant slave owners feared that allowing enslaved people to become Protestants would challenge their claims of ownership. By the mid-eighteenth century, this fear had been mitigated by a variety of factors, including new laws that codified White Supremacy. Jamaican legislators, for example, specified in the 1696 "Act for the better Order and Government of Slaves" that "no Slave shall be free by becoming a Christian."[48] Despite legal assurances, however, the number of enslaved and free Black Anglicans remained a fraction of the Afro-Caribbean population, and the Anglican Church helped to uphold the brutal system of slavery throughout the British Caribbean.

Criminalizing Africana Religions: Reading for Irruptions in the Legal Archives

African diasporic religions went unmentioned in British colonial law until Tacky's Revolt. But their absence does not mean they were ignored. Scholars must read for irruptions to identify references to Africana religions in legal archives. In the British American colonies, lawmakers developed a legal tactic that targeted assemblies of people, especially those from different plantations. Every single English colonial slave code from Jamaica includes clauses on congregations of enslaved people, although they use the words *assembly* or *meeting*, rather than *congregation*. The slave codes also specify behaviors—such as drumming, feasting, or meeting together—as dangerous. The Jamaican Slave Code of 1696, for example, declared that "no Masters or Mistresses or Overseers, shall suffer any Drumming or Meeting of Slaves, not belonging to their own Plantation." The list of prohibited behaviors is informative: Gathered people were not to "rendezvous, feast, revel, beat Drums, or cause any other Disturbance."[49]

Similar regulations regarding assemblies are ubiquitous throughout the British Atlantic World. Virginia's Slave Code of 1680 notes that the "frequent meetings ... under pretense of feasts and burials is judged of dangerous consequence." One scholar has argued that the 1680 act's prohibition of enslaved meetings "under pretense of feast and burials" can be viewed as the first colonial restriction on African American religious assembly. However, there are earlier laws that restrict assembly without specifying burials.[50]

Rebellions often prompted lawmakers to pass new legislation restricting "religion" without using the word *religion*. In 1740, immediately following the Stono Rebellion, lawmakers in South Carolina reiterated legislation forbidding enslaved people "to beat drums, blow horns, or use any other loud instruments," and they threatened any enslaver who allowed "any public meeting or feastings" on their plantation. Again, "religion" is never specifically mentioned; instead, the legal wording targets a series of actions (beating drums, blowing horns, using loud instruments) as well as specific types of groupings (public meetings and feasts). Significantly, the actions and objects targeted by the act could all be connected to either religious practice or rebellion—a slippage that underscores the difficulty in distinguishing between the two categories.

Most slave laws included a provision for the "Prevention of the meeting of Slaves in great Numbers on Sunday and Holidays." The specification of Christian religious holidays revealed that state-sponsored religion could be a threat to the system of slavery. The days that were set aside for Christian worship—Sundays and holy days like Christmas, Easter, and Pentecost—were the days most feared by the white colonial authorities. With most enslaved people excluded from Christian congregations, religious holidays were transformed into days of danger, when enslaved people were under less supervision. Most slave rebellions in the Atlantic World occurred on religious holidays. In Jamaica, the 1831 Christmas Rebellion connected the holy day with the act of rebellion, and Tacky's Revolt, while not titled as such, was planned for Pentecost.[51]

The "Act to Remedy the Evils arising from irregular Assemblies of Slaves," passed in the wake of Tacky's Revolt, extended and transformed previous efforts to control religious life. Like the 1696 act, lawmakers specified a variety of instruments as being disruptive and dangerous. Yet while the 1696 act focused on drumming, the 1760 act was more specific: Enslaved people were forbidden from assembling to "beat their drums, Goards, Boards, Barrels, or other Instruments of Noise, or blow their Horns."[52] The reference to "drums" and "other Instruments" is significant because music played a central role for both rebellion and religion.

While the specification of instruments in the 1760 act was important, the greatest divergence from previous legislation related to Obeah, which had never before been named in a colonial law. Obeah was deemed a capital offense, punishable by execution or transportation. The severity of punishment suggests that Obeah was seen as a major threat to the colonial order. The specific language of the act is significant. It reads:

> And in order to prevent the many Mischiefs that may hereafter arise from the wicked Art of Negroes going under the appellation of Obeah Men and Women, pretending to have Communication with the Devil and other evil spirits, whereby the weak and superstitious are deluded into a Belief of their having full Power to exempt them whilst under their Protection from any Evils ... any Negro or other Slave who shall pretend to any Supernatural Power, and be detected in making use of any Blood, Feathers, Parrots Beaks, Dogs Teeth, Alligators Teeth, Broken Bottles, Grave Dirt, Rum, Egg-shells or any other Materials relative to the Practice of Obeah or Witchcraft in order to delude and impose on the Minds of others shall upon Conviction thereof before two Magistrates and three Freeholders suffer death or Transportation any thing in this Act or any other Law to the contrary notwithstanding.

In the act, colonial lawmakers identified a series of material objects that they associated with the illegal practice of Obeah. These included "Blood, Feathers, Parrots Beaks, Dogs Teeth, Alligators Teeth, Broken Bottles, Grave Dirt, Rum, [and] Egg-shells." Here, it is important to note that lawmakers were attempting to delegitimize Obeah by *materializing* it. By this, I mean that they broke Obeah into specific objects, which were easy to surveil and police. Within the context of Protestant theology, the decision to emphasize material object also contributed to the critique that Obeah practice was "superstitious."[53]

While it is important to recognize the lawmakers' intentions in breaking Obeah into a series of objects, the act also offers an opportunity to gain further insight into the meaning of Obeah. Notably, the first item on the list was "Blood," a reference that aligns with Moravians' blood and wounds theology as well as Africana religious traditions such as oath-swearing, which was often performed with blood. Similarly, "grave dirt" points to the powerful role of mortuary rites in African diasporic religious practice, even as it disregards the material as "superstitious" and "evil." In this way, the 1760 act confirms correlations that existed between Christianity and Obeah, even as the law aimed to criminalize the practice.

Aside from materializing Obeah, colonial lawmakers drew on English conceptions of witchcraft to criminalize Obeah. In 1736, the English Parliament had passed the Witchcraft Act, which reflected the increasingly skeptical attitude of elites toward claims of witchcraft. The 1736 act decriminalized witchcraft and it created a new crime: *pretending* to practice witchcraft. It also became illegal to accuse someone of witchcraft. In other words, the main goal of the Witchcraft Act of 1736 was to suppress the belief that witchcraft existed.[54] As Diana Paton has argued, lawmakers in Jamaica could not criminalize Obeah *as* witchcraft because it was against the law to believe that witchcraft was real. Instead, they wrote that "Obeah Men and Women" were "*pretending* to have Communication with the Devil and other evil spirits" and that "the weak and superstitious are deluded into a Belief."[55] As these lines suggest, lawmakers feared the practice of Obeah—even as they simultaneously stated their disbelief in its power.[56]

While the 1760 act intended to delegitimize Obeah, the text of the law can be read for Africana irruptions. References to Obeah-related objects such as blood and grave dirt affirm the importance of these materials, while the harsh punishments indicate that lawmakers feared the power of Obeah. Even as we can read for irruptions, however, we must remain vigilant about the narrative field of colonial slave law. The lawmakers who penned the 1760 act did so to reassert control over the enslaved population after the widespread uprisings of the previous year.

Reading the legal archives of slavery for irruptions, therefore, requires special attention to the formation of categories intended to surveil the enslaved. By identifying Obeah as a series of material objects, colonial lawmakers were trying break Obeah into parts that could be policed. The act also sought to individualize Obeah, referring only to "Obeah Men and Women" who were "*pretending* to have Communication with the Devil and other evil spirits." By focusing on individual practitioners, rather the religio-political collectivities that Obeah helped to create, lawmakers were seeking to undermine the power of Obeah as a force that bound people together. When we read the lawmakers' words, we must remind ourselves of their intentions as we seek to make sense of the archival irruptions in colonial lawbooks.

Re/formations of Religion and Rebellion

On January 26, 1761, one month after the Jamaican Assembly passed the "Act to Remedy the Evils arising from irregular Assemblies of Slaves," the Moravian missionaries at Mesopotamia estate heard that "Simeon the Captain of the rebels was taken captive, and lots of people rejoiced."[57] The Moravian missionaries hoped that Simeon's capture would mark a decisive end to the rebellion that had shaken the colonial government—and their mission—for nearly a year. But Simeon's very existence undermined the belief that the rebellion of 1760 was decisively over. In fact, Simeon was one of a series of rebel leaders identified by white colonials. As Vincent Brown and Maria Allessandra Bollettino have argued, the fact that the rebellion came to be known as Tacky's Revolt was, itself, an effort to historicize and limit the effect and duration of the rebellion.[58] Tacky was captured and killed in the early stages of the revolt, well before Simeon and other rebel leaders, many of whom went unnamed in the colonial records. The title "Tacky's Revolt" was, in fact, an invention of the enslaver-historian Edward Long, who wrote about the rebellion in his two-volume *History of Jamaica*, published in the 1770s.[59] Long's strategy of limiting the meaning of the revolt by attributing it to Tacky should be understood as a rhetorical strategy to contain and categorize Africana technologies of power.

Simeon the rebel was not the only Simeon to appear in the pages of the Moravian missionary diary. Eight months after Simeon's capture, missionaries were ready to perform their first baptism at Mesopotamia estate, the mission station founded in 1758. Jery, an enslaved man who had visited the missionaries regularly throughout the rebellion, was chosen to be the first person baptized. On August 24, Christian Heinrich Rauch informed Jery that he would be "buried in the death of Jesus through the holy baptism."[60] Jery was "taken with joy" and dressed in white for his baptism. At the ceremony, Afro-Moravian congregants sang verses and Rauch performed the baptism. The missionaries also chose a new name for Jery: Simeon.

Why was the name Simeon chosen for Jery? Did the Moravians remember Simeon the rebel when they chose the same name for their first baptismal candidate after the rebellion? Were they seeking to replace Simeon the rebel in their minds with one of their own congregants? Or was it just a coincidence? Alternatively, did Jery suggest the name Simeon? Any interpretation is possible. Regardless, it is significant that the first person baptized at Mesopotamia was given the same name as the last rebel captain.

Simeon, in the Gospel of Luke, is a devout and righteous man who was visited by the Holy Spirit and informed that he would live to see Christ. Inspired by the Spirit, Simeon entered the temple, where he came upon Mary, Joseph, and the baby Jesus. Upon meeting Jesus, Simeon asked for permission to die. The story of Simeon was undoubtedly significant in determining the missionaries' choice of name. Certainly, Jery's age ("old") was part of the reason they referenced the Simeon of Luke, who receives the Holy Spirit and meets Christ at the end of his life. Yet there were many other options, and Simeon was a relatively unusual name to choose. Joseph, Ludwig, John, Zacharias, Benjamin, Christian, and Thomas were more frequent choices for male converts. In the list of over five hundred baptismal names given to converts in Jamaica before 1770, only two were given the name Simeon, and only one—Jery—was at Mesopotamia plantation.[61]

The existence of two Simeons—one rebel and one Christian—is suggestive of the more elusive connections between rebellion and religion, as the two categories developed in the Atlantic World. The "Act to Remedy the Evils arising from irregular Assemblies of Slaves," passed after Tacky's Revolt, shows how lawmakers in Jamaica recognized the sacred power of "irregular Assemblies" and sought to eliminate them. In many ways, their strategy succeeded. Obeah remains a crime to this day, and the modern category of religion continues to exclude many African diasporic practices, as well as other religions.

In response to this legacy, I have argued that scholars must pay attention to the importance of assembling, congregating, and binding when examining how religion functioned during colonial slavery. While colonial lawmakers, like those who passed the act, aimed to exclude African diasporic religions from the realm of religion, they did so by targeting congregations of Black people without acknowledging their actions as religious. They used similar tactics in other colonial settings, including Native North America, where settler colonists refused to recognize indigenous religio-political formations as "religion."[62]

The 1760 act is notable because it came closest to legitimizing African diasporic religions as powerful by actually naming Obeah. Most slave codes, however, reduced all African practices to forms of "irregular Assemblies" and materialized their worship practices by criminalizing objects like parrot beaks and grave dirt. They did so even when the "irregular Assemblies" were Christian. In 1676, for example, lawmakers in Barbados had responded to a slave conspiracy by creating a new law that specifically banned enslaved people on the island from worshipping together with the Quakers.[63] In New York, after a slave rebellion in 1712, slave-owning whites cast blame on enslaved Christians gathering with the Anglican missionary Elias Neau.[64] Later rebellions, such as Denmark Vesey's conspiracy and Nat Turner's revolt, also led whites to criminalize aspects of Black Christian practice and placed suspicion on Black Christianity.[65]

In order to emphasize the importance of identifying religion through the lens of congregating and binding, I end by asking two questions:

1. How many people does one need to start a religion?
2. How many people does one need to start a rebellion?

The answers to both questions can vary considerably, but the answer to one is deeply intertwined with the other.[66] In Jamaica, legislators did not specify how many people were required to start either a religion or a rebellion, but in other colonies, they did. In South Carolina, for example, the 1669 Fundamental Constitutions of Carolina, coauthored by John Locke, declared that "any Seven or more" people "agreeing in any religion" could "constitute a church of profession."[67] In 1740, after the Stono Rebellion, another act specified that seven enslaved people traveling together would be assumed to be in rebellion. The connection between these two acts of legislation had the undeniable consequence of criminalizing any gathering of enslaved Black people that could be legally defined as a religion.

While not every definition of a "gathered church" or a potential rebellion used the number seven as its tipping point, the correlation is still revealing: It is a reminder that a gathering of people—an assembly—can easily slip between the perception of religion and the perception of rebellion based on who is gathered. If religion is defined as the gathering of seven people who are "of the same religion," then Black religion under slavery is literally a crime.

Re/membering Religion

Understanding religion through the lens of congregating and binding offers an important method for examining the history of religion during colonial slavery without reinscribing the anti-Black genealogy of religion. I am not suggesting that religion is, in essence, about assembling, but rather that we can see the category of religion in formation during colonial slavery by attending to the practices of assembling, congregating, and binding. White enslavers recognized that the power to bind people together was a threat to the system of slavery. This is why their laws were preoccupied with forbidding "illegal Assemblies." Obeah can be understood as a binding practice that drew people together through prophetic power, mentorship, and healing practices, as well as disciplinary practices. This power is what led colonial legislators to demarcate practices such as Obeah as criminal.

Today, the term *Obeah* has been indelibly marked by the negative associations that slave-owning lawmakers used to criminalize it. As a result, it is difficult to narrate a history of Obeah without reinscribing the same associations. This chapter has sought to attend to this issue by reading for Africana irruptions and writing about lawmaking, gatherings of rebels, and missionary worship meetings within the same framework of assembling, congregating, and binding. When we break the construct of religion into parts—into notions of sacred time, sacred space, communal bonds, and assembled people—we can recognize the strategies that white colonists used to deconstruct and delegitimize African diasporic practices such as Obeah. We can also recognize how Africans and their descendants responded to this epistemic violence by adopting new categories for their religio-political practices.[68]

Recognizing that religion was constructed in tandem with colonial slavery reveals the anti-Blackness embedded within the modern category of religion.

The category of religion, as it was constructed in missionary settings and in the legal codes of the early modern Atlantic World, excluded, policed, and criminalized Africana religio-political traditions that built community and challenged colonial power. Any accounting of religion must acknowledge these formative histories and reckon with the exclusion of Africana religions such as Obeah, as well as other marginalized traditions, from the modern category of religion.

Epilogue

LAND AND ARCHIVE: IDENTIFYING AND INTERPRETING IRRUPTIONS

The Moravian mission house where Cuffy, Titus, Elizabeth, and so many others were baptized is no longer standing. At the Bogue, the missionary cemetery is the most enduring physical reminder of the mission. Inscribed stone breaks through the surface of the ground, though some headstones have been subsumed by vines. At Carmel, by contrast, the mission station founded by Caries in 1756, the cemetery has been cleared and conserved by the local community and members of the Jamaican Moravian Church. A large historical plaque, researched and written by Dr. Abrilene Johnson-Scott, offers a history of the early mission and a list of missionaries buried at the site. According to the plaque, Christian Heinrich Rauch, who died in 1763, is buried in the cemetery. The graveyard for enslaved Moravians is—we know from the historical records—within view, but no one knows exactly where. The eighteenth-century Moravian missionaries did not create stone markers for the enslaved burials, even if they were church members—another example of silencing in both the archive and the built environment.

I began this book by arguing that scholars could read colonial and missionary records for irruptions to create alternative narrations based on Africana epistemologies that have been systematically oppressed. Visiting the old mission sites offered a different perspective on the idea of an irruption or, in Lisa Brooks's metaphor, the "weeds" that burst through a European-authored archival source. Certain materials—especially gravestones—break through the ground, reminding visitors of the existence of people who lived here before. Many of those physical reminders, however, highlight missionary or colonial stories.

Still, the histories of the eighteenth century are being resurrected and retold in important ways. Even when structures are destroyed, they are—in some cases—reintegrated into new structures. A few miles away from the Bogue cemetery, for example, is the Moravian church at New Eden. At the entrance to the grounds, about ten feet before the church doors, stands an unusual monument: a stone spiral, where visitors can walk through a small passageway into an enclosed area with a plaque in the center: "Not Far From This Spot," it reads, "The First Moravian Missionaries Began Their Work in 1754. The Church and Monument Are Erected With Stones From Their First Church Building." Below, a phrase from scripture: "Their Works Do Follow Them."—Rev. 14:13.

The verse, from Revelations, was the same one that Caries uttered during Sampson's burial in 1756 (chapter 1). At that time, Afro-Moravians had "formed a double circle" around *Gottes Acker*, the Moravian cemetery at the Bogue, where Sampson—who was dressed in white, with red ribbons on his hat and sleeves—was put to rest. Afterwards, Caries preached to the congregation in the mission house: "Blessed are the dead, which die in the Lord, from henceforth. Yea, says the Spirit, that they may rest from their labours; and their works do follow them."[1] The building where Caries spoke those words is no longer standing, but the stones have been picked up and carried from the Bogue to New Eden, where they were remade into the stone spiral that offers a new perspective on the past and a new experience for the present. The spiral reminded me of Lisa Brooks's description of history as "an inquiry into *pildowi ôjmowôgan*, the cyclical, spiraling process through which we (inclusive or exclusive) collectively participate in recovering and narrating 'a new history.'"[2]

I highlight these stories to ruminate on the evolving relationship between the past and present as well as the importance of creativity in building new structures from old materials. For me, visiting the site of archival creation—the mission house where Caries and Rauch composed their diaries and letters—allowed me to integrate new forms of evidence into my interpretation of the past. Just as the landscape offered a different way to think about archival production, archival texts helped me interpret the physical environment and to recognize the connections—like the verse from Revelations—between the eighteenth century and the present day.

There are always alternative narrations available; we just need to know how to look for them. In this book, I have argued that we can find alternative narratives in archival sources by identifying irruptions, moments when the narrative field of the archival producer is disrupted. Irruptions come in many forms: sometimes, as in the case of Obeah, a specific term breaks into a colonial or missionary archive in a surprising way. When I first saw Caries's reference to "Obea" as I sat in the Unitätsarchiv der Evangelischen Brüder-Unität in Herrnhut, Germany, I reacted with a start: As a historian of the Caribbean, I knew about Obeah, but I had never expected to see it in the Moravian missionary archive. Its existence was a jolt, and it forced me to rethink the categories I had imposed on my archival documents.

Over the years, as I sifted through missionary and colonial archives, I have realized that there are many types of archival irruptions: Some, like the nation designators I examined in chapter 2, are Africana irruptions that offer insight into Africana epistemologies, such as the religio-nations that Africans and their descendants used to re/form sacred communities throughout the Atlantic World. These irruptions must be read side by side with Africana scholarship; without that second step, the nation designators languish in the narrative field of the missionaries.

While some irruptions—like Obeah—are surprising, others require careful detective work. Reading for gendered irruptions, as I did in chapters 3 and 4, takes time and patience. Finding Margery's name was a laborious exercise that also required luck. Meanwhile, piecing together scattered references to enslaved women such as Elizabeth and Camilla is both painful and illuminating. Their lives are never fully available to us, but reading for irruptions allows us to imagine their lives. Drawing on Saidiya Hartman's call for "critical fabulation" along with Alexis Wells-Oghoghomeh's theorization of re/membrance, scholars can interpret gendered irruptions in patriarchal archives to center Black women's stories and experiences in slavery and freedom.

Irruptions can also be found in the disjunctures between colonial and missionary narrations. In chapter 5, I read missionary sources against each other to identify dissimulation in the archives. This method offered interpretive space in the archival field that is itself an irruption—an opportunity to identify alternative narrations. This is especially helpful for cases of censorship: In chapter 4, I asked why references to sexual violence were deleted, a question that offered insight into the production of archival knowledge. Paired with Trouillot's analysis of the four stages of archival production, scholars can read cases of censorship as irruptions to elucidate patterns in the creation of missionary and colonial archives.

In some cases, reading for irruptions means deconstructing colonial terminology. In the legal archives of slavery, for example, it is impossible to find evidence of Africana religions if one is looking for the word *religion*. Instead, scholars must recognize the tactics that lawmakers were using to delegitimize Africana religiopolitical power before it is possible to recognize the irruptions in the archive. Even then, interpreting legal archives for Africana irruptions is complicated and requires a vigilant reading of the sources alongside Africana scholarship.

An alternative narration is a story that the archival producer did not mean to tell. By reading for irruptions, we can tell new stories about the past. One story this book has emphasized is that Obeah was neither a crime nor a superstition, but rather a religio-political practice that bound people together through healing practices, rituals that emphasized the symbolic significance of blood, and prophetic power, including knowledge of the afterlife. Obeah was *not*, however, the opposite of Christianity. While later missionaries as well as Black Moravians would pit these categories against each other, the early Moravian missionary sources suggest a more nuanced picture.

Using Africana irruptions as our guide, it is possible to see how the Afro-Jamaicans who joined the Moravian church integrated Moravian rituals into their category of Obeah. Amos, the African-born man who was the sole person to fight back against white colonials in the violent episode described in chapter 4, offers an example of this. Two years after Caries landed in Jamaica, Amos explained how he first interpreted the rituals held in Christian churches, even before Caries's arrival: He explained that he had "heard word of Jesus's blood" and went to the church in Black River, where he "saw the white people... drink blood." He had been "thinking about it" even "before Br[other] Caries came to Jamaica." From that point, he narrated, "he has believed that drinking Jesus's blood must be something very great."[3] Amos's account, which highlights the significance of blood in Christian ritual, offers an Africana perspective on the sacrament of the Lord's Supper and shows how Afro-Jamaicans could interpret Jesus's blood as a powerful spiritual force.

By highlighting the spaces of correlation between Obeah and Moravian Christianity, *Archival Irruptions* has sought to tell a story about the criminalization of Obeah without allowing the oppressive aims of the colonial state to be the only lens for examining Africana religions under slavery. Learning about the lives of Afro-Moravians like Amos, Margery, Elizabeth, and Cuffy is an important reminder that the story of criminalization and oppression should be told alongside the individual experiences of men and women who saw power, meaning, and communal bonds in Obeah and Moravian Christianity. While archival sources like the Moravian missionary records cannot recover the full extent and meaning of Obeah as it existed in the mid-eighteenth century, they can help to identify Africana irruptions that burst through colonial narratives. My hope is that these irruptions can contribute to the efforts of so many others to break down the enduring legacies of anti-Blackness that still permeate the modern categories of religion, rebellion, and crime.

Appendix 1

FIGURE A.I. Afro-Caribbeans baptized in the Moravian church in Jamaica. Drawn by Bill Nelson for *Archival Irruptions*.

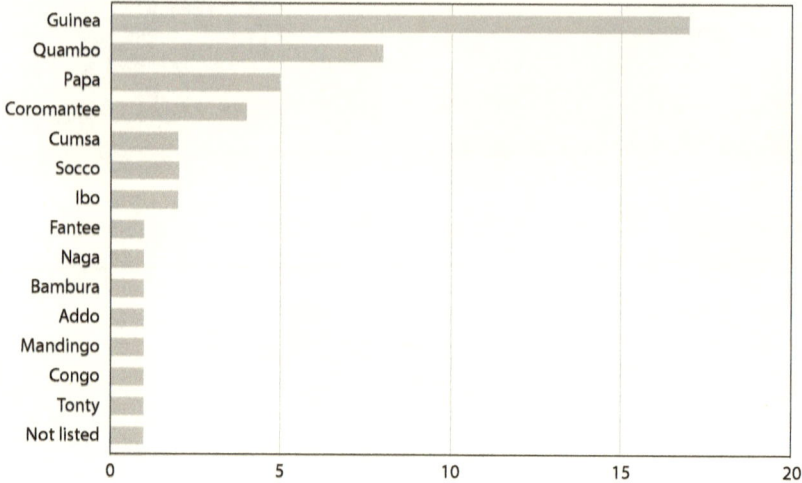

FIGURE A.2. African nations of Afro-Moravians, 1755–59. Drawn by Bill Nelson for *Archival Irruptions*.

Appendix 2

Excerpt from "Br Caries schreibt vom 17ten Marz [1755] aus Jamaica an Johannes" in the *Gemein Nachrichten* 5 (1755), GN 1755 5 A.44 (I–XL), Unitätsarchiv der Evangelischen Brüder-Unität.

German Transcription	English Translation
Es kommen immer mehrere in die Versammlung, so daß wir den Saal bald werden erwitern müßen. Sie heißen mich Obea, welches bedeuten soll einen Seher, oder einen der zukünftige dinge weis. Sie haben mich sehr lieb und ich sie. In der Candidaten 4telstunde ist ein unbeschreibliches Gefühl: Ihre Augen funkeln, und sie sehen so sünderhaft aus, daß es eine Freude ist. Mit den Candidaten so gegangen: Ich wurde mit 8 Negern bekant (alle Mannesleute, denn mit den Weibs leuten, unter denen auch welche angefaßt sind, kan ich mich nicht einlaßen) es sind 5 Männer u 3 ledige.	More and more come to the meeting, so that we will soon have to expand the hall. They call me Obea, which supposedly means a Seer, or one who knows things that will happen in the future. They like me a lot and I like them. In the meeting for [baptismal] candidates there is an indescribable feeling: Their eyes are sparkling and they look like poor sinners, that it is a joy. This is how it went with the candidates: I became acquainted with 8 Blacks (all men, since I cannot get involved with the women, although there are some who have been touched [i.e., by the Spirit]) there are 5 [married] men and 3 single men.
Weil ich vernahm, daß der l Geist an ihnen arbeitete, so find eine aparte 4tel Stunde mit ihnen an, da ich mit ihnen zusammen, oder mit jedem allein redete, und sie dem Heylde aus herz legte. Der heyld ließ sich fräftig nahe fühlen, sie krigten ein lebennis herz, und fingen an sich recht gefühlich von ihres Herzens Sehnen nach dem Heylde zu erklären.	Because I saw that the Spirit was working on them, I spent a separate quarter hour with them, when I talked to them together or to each one alone, and recommended them to the Lord. The Lord made himself feel close, they received a living heart, and they began to express their heart's longing for the Lord.

German Transcription	English Translation
Gottlieb hat etliche mal drauf getrieben, daß wir an die Taufe denken solten, weil die Neger wie brüder aussähen. Ich hatte an ihnen nicht auszusetzen sondern war nut über die Zeit bedencklich, und wolte lieber langsam als zu früh anfangen, schobs also auf bis den 28ten Febr, da 2 von ihnen ein besonders Verlangen nach der Taufe bezeugten; und weil Gottlieb darauf bestund, daß es Zeit sey anzufangen, so überlegten wirs wer dem Heylde, ob wir bald an Taufen gedenken solten. Der Heyld wieß uns dazu an und confirmirte uns die 8 Neger, die wir nur nach unsrer Überzeugung zur 4tel Stunde genommen, zu Candidaten der Taufe, doch nicht, daß sie alle auf einmal getauft werden sollen. Wir krigten außer denen noch 4 zu denen Candidaten, so daß ihrer nun 12 sind. Seitdem tractire ich mit ihnen die Materie von der Taufe, und ihr Sehnen darnach wird immer größer, daß sies kaum erwarten können. Der Heyland hat uns aber angewiesen, bis auf den 27ten Apr mit der ersten Taufe zu warten. Da haben wir auch gar schöne Texte. Nun sind wir verlegen, was wir mit den Weibs-leuten machen sollen, die uns so bald eine Taufe geschehen, sehr überlaufen werden. Mr Robertson will mich auch zu den 5 wilden Neger-Städten bringen, und mich bey ihren Obersten, die er kennt, introduciren.	Gottlieb several times pushed the idea that we should think about baptism because the Blacks looked like brothers. I didn't have any complaints about that, but was just concerned about the time, and would rather start slowly than too early, so I postponed it until February 28, as two of them testified that they had a special desire to be baptized; and because Gottlieb insisted that it was time to begin, we considered it with the Lord whether we should soon think about baptism. The Lord instructed us to do this and confirmed the 8 Blacks, whom, according to our conviction, we had accepted at the quarter hour [meeting] as candidates for baptism, but not that they should all be baptized at once. In addition to them, we got 4 more [baptismal] candidates, so that there are now 12 of them. Since then I have been going over the matter of baptism with them, and their longing for it is growing so much that they can hardly wait. However, the Lord instructed us to wait until April 27 for the first baptism. We also have some really nice texts. Now we have no idea what we will do with the women, who will overrun us as soon as they see a baptism take place. Mr. Robertson will also take me to the 5 wild [Maroon] towns and introduce me to their chiefs, whom he knows.
Nota; Die wilden Negers sind nicht native Einwohner (das waren die Caryben, die alle von den Spanier ausgerottet sind) sondern den Europäern entlaufene Sclaven, die sich in das Gebürge, das die länge des Eylandes durchneidet, retirirt, verschanzt, ihre eigene Republic aufgerühret, denen Engeländern vielen Schaden zugefüget, von diesen aber niemals haben bezwungen und aus den Bergen verjagt werden können. Daher das	Note: The Maroons are not native inhabitants (those were the Caribs, who were killed by the Spanish), but rather slaves who ran away from the Europeans and went into the mountains that span the interior of the island, where they barricaded themselves and created their own Republic. The English tried to destroy it, but they were never able to, nor could they chase [the Maroons] out of the mountains.

German Transcription	English Translation
Gouvernement einen Frieden mit ihnen gescholoßen und zur condition ihrer freyheit gemacht, daß sie keine neue Deserterirs aufnehmen, sondern gleich ausliefern sollen.	As a result, the government signed a peace treaty with them and on the condition of their freedom, they agreed to surrender any new runaways.

Notes

INTRODUCTION

1. "An Act to Remedy the Evils arising from irregular Assemblies of Slaves," Jamaica, 1760, in Colonial Office 139/21, National Archives (Kew), London (hereafter cited as CO). Historical background and Obeah-related sections of the act are available on the Obeah Histories blog, accessed November 18, 2024, https://Obeahhistories.org/1760-jamaica-law/.

2. Zacharias George Caries to Johannes Watteville, March 17, 1755, *Gemein Nachrichten* 5 (1755), GN 1755 5 A.44 (I–XL), 743–47, Unitätsarchiv der Evangelischen Brüder-Unität, Herrnhut, Germany (hereafter cited as UA). The original German reads, "Sie heißen mich Obea, welches bedeuten soll einen Seher, oder einen der zukünftige dinge weis." See appendix 2 for a longer excerpt of the letter.

3. See, for example, Boaz, *Banning Black Gods*; Paton, *The Cultural Politics of Obeah*; Paton and Forde, eds., *Obeah and Other Powers*; Ramsey, *The Spirits and the Law*; Beliso-De Jesús, *Excited Delirium*.

4. Aside from Brooks, I draw most explicitly on Michel-Rolph Trouillot's analysis of archival "silences"; Ann Stoler's approach to the archive as ethnography; Marisa Fuentes' concept of reading "along the bias grain," and Zeb Tortorici's concept of "visceral archives." Stoler, *Along the Archival Grain*; Trouillot, *Silencing the Past*; Fuentes, *Dispossessed Lives*; Tortorici, *Sins Against Nature*; Tortorici, "Visceral Archives of the Body." In critical archival studies, see especially Caswell, Punzalan, and Sangwand, "Critical Archival Studies"; Caswell, "'The Archive' Is Not an Archives"; Sutherland, "Disrupting Carceral Narratives"; Lowry, "Displaced Archives"; Lowry, *Disputed Archival Heritage*; Hughes-Watkins, "Moving Toward a Reparative Archive." On Caribbean archives, see Aarons, Bastian, and Griffin, *Archiving Caribbean Identity*; Bastian, Aarons, and Griffin, *Decolonizing the Caribbean Record;* Griffin, "Value Displaced, Value Re/Claimed." For decolonial methods and Indigenous studies, see especially Smith, *Decolonizing Methodologies*. On Religious Studies and archives, see especially Greene-Hayes, "Hair, Roots, and Crystal Balls."

5. Brooks, "Awikhigawôgan Ta Pildowi Ôjmowôgan," 259–94; Brooks, *Our Beloved Kin*.

6. "Irrupt, v.," and "Irruption, n.," *OED Online*. Accessed February 2, 2025.

7. The Moravian Archives in Bethlehem, PA, offers one of the only courses in the United States on German Script. For more information, see https://doi.org/10.1093/OED/2847251598.

8. Stoler, *Along the Archival Grain*; Trouillot, *Silencing the Past*; Fuentes, *Dispossessed Lives*.

9. On "spaces of correlation," see Fromont, *The Art of Conversion*.

10. The Moravians trace their lineage to the followers of Jan Hus in the fifteenth century, but they renewed their church in 1727, after Moravian refugees settled on the estate of Count Ludwig von Zinzendorf, a Pietist who became the leader of the Renewed Unitas Fratrum. For more on Zinzendorf and his theology, see Vogt, "Nicholas Ludwig von Zinzendorf"; Geiger, "Zinzendorf Stellung zum Halleschen Busskampf und zum Bekehrungserlebnis"; Beyreuther, *Die große Zinzendorf Trilogie*; Brecht and Peucker, *Neue Aspekte der Zinzendorf-Forschung*. For more on the early period of the Renewed Moravian Church, see Peucker, *Herrnhut*; Meyer, "Zinzendorf und Herrnhut."

11. On the Moravian global missions in the eighteenth-century, see Beck, *Brüder in Vielen Völkern*; Sensbach, *Rebecca's Revival*; Sensbach, *A Separate Canaan*; Fogleman, *Two Troubled Souls*; Fogleman, "A Moravian Mission"; Mettele, *Weltbürgertum oder Gottesreich;* Gerbner, *Christian Slavery*, chaps. 7–8; Kaelin, "To Be Proposed As Useful"; Wheeler, *To Live upon Hope*; Wheeler and Eyerly, "Singing Box 331"; Merritt, "Dreaming of the Savior's Blood"; Catron, *Embracing Protestantism*; Peucker, "Aus allen Nationen."

12. For the role of Moravians in the eighteenth-century Atlantic World, including the transatlantic Great Awakening, see Ward, *The Protestant Evangelical Awakening*; Gillespie and Beachy, *Pious Pursuits*; Roeber, "The Waters of Rebirth"; Engel, *Religion and Profit*; Atwood, *Community of the Cross*; Fogleman, *Jesus Is Female*.

13. On the rise of Black Protestantism in the eighteenth-century Atlantic World, see Frey and Wood, *Come Shouting to Zion*; Gerbner, *Christian Slavery;* Seeman, "'Justise Must Take Plase'"; Sobel, *Trabelin' On*; Sensbach, *Rebecca's Revival*; Sensbach, "'Don't Teach My Negroes to Be Pietists'"; Raboteau, *Slave Religion*; Butler, "Africans' Religions in British America"; Andrews, *Native Apostles*; Catron, *Embracing Protestantism*; Catron, "Evangelical Networks"; Dickerson, *African Methodist Episcopal Church*, chap. 1.

14. For the foundation of the debate on African retentions, see Frazier, "The Negro Family in Bahia," 465–78; Herskovits, "The Negro in Bahia, Brazil," 394–404; Herskovits, *The Myth of the Negro Past*; Raboteau, *Slave Religion*. For a helpful survey of the debate and its impact, see Stewart Diakité and Hucks, "Africana Religious Studies," 31–36.

15. See, for example, Matory, *Black Atlantic Religion*; Matory, "From 'Survival' to 'Dialogue'"; Palmié, *Africas of the Americas;* Stewart Diakité and Hucks, "Africana Religious Studies"; Beliso-De Jesús, *Electric Santería*; Wells-Oghoghomeh, *The Souls of Womenfolk*; Hucks, *Obeah, Orisa, and Religious Identity*; Stewart, *Obeah, Orisa and Religious Identity*.

16. In Jonathan Z. Smith's now-classic article, "Religion, Religions, Religious," he argued that religion was used by colonizers to describe the religion (or non-religion) of colonial "others." Smith, "Religion, Religions, Religious," 269–84. On the construction of religion and colonialism, see also Chidester, *Empire of Religion*; Chidester, *Savage Systems*; Masuzawa, *The Invention of World Religions*.

17. Schiebinger, "Agnotology and Exotic Abortifacients"; Schiebinger, *Plants and Empire*.

18. See, for example, Paton and Forde, *Obeah and Other Powers*; Paton, *The Cultural Politics of Obeah*; Ramsey, *The Spirits and the Law*; Boaz, *Banning Black Gods*.

19. "An Act to Remedy the Evils," CO 139/21.

20. On the evolving relationship between religion and race in the Atlantic World, see Harvey and Lum, eds., *The Oxford Handbook of Religion and Race*; Khan, *The Deepest Dye*; Lum, *Heathen*; Goetz, *The Baptism of Early Virginia*; Kopelson, *Faithful Bodies*; Bailey, *Race and Redemption*; Brewer-García, *Beyond Babel*; Rowe, *Black Saints*; Martínez, *Genealogical Fictions*; Weisenfeld, *New World A-Coming*.

21. McGeary, "On Fanaticism and Funding."

22. Aisha Khan has argued that "racial and religious identities necessarily and always work in some kind of conjunction," so the "racialization of religion and the 'religionization of race' define, substantiate, and justify identities and the hierarchies that rank them." Khan, *The Deepest Dye*, 15 and 27.

23. On the term *recovery*, see especially the special issue of *Social Text* edited by Helton et al., "The Question of Recovery," 1–18.

24. For the metaphor of reading "along the archival grain," see especially Stoler, *Along the Archival Grain*. For reading "along the bias grain," see Fuentes, *Dispossessed Lives*. Other texts that have influenced my thinking about archives include Tortorici, *Sins Against Nature*; Tortorici, "Visceral Archives of the Body"; Farge, *The Allure of the Archives*; Hartman, "Venus in Two Acts"; Trouillot, *Silencing the Past*.

25. On "silences," see especially Trouillot, *Silencing the Past*.

26. This is partially due to my reading of NAIS scholarship, but also thanks to the network of colleagues and graduate students that I have been fortunate to be in conversation with at the University of Minnesota. I am especially grateful to David Chang, Jeani O'Brien, and Sarah Pawlicki. For NAIS methods and early American studies, see the joint issue of *William and Mary Quarterly* and *Early American Literature*, coedited by Pleasant et al., "Materials and Methods in Native American and Indigenous Studies."

27. Brooks, "Awikhigawôgan Ta Pildowi Ôjmowôgan," 264.

28. Brooks, *Our Beloved Kin*, 10.

29. Brooks, *Our Beloved Kin*, 10.

30. Stewart Diakité and Hucks, "Africana Religious Studies," 42.

31. Trouillot, *Silencing the Past*, 26; Stoler, *Along the Archival Grain*, 20.

32. Tortorici, *Sins Against Nature*; Tortorici, "Visceral Archives of the Body."

33. The majority of archival sources from the Moravian mission to Jamaica are located in Herrnhut, Germany, at the Unitätsarchiv der Evangelischen Brüder-Unität and the Moravian Archives in Bethlehem, Pennsylvania (hereafter MAB). There are also important sources available at the Moravian Church House in London (hereafter MCH) that are not available in either Bethlehem or Herrnhut. The archival material related to Jamaica at the Moravian Archives in Bethlehem was recently digitized and is now available at Moravian Archives, Digital Resources, https://www.moravianchurcharchives.findbuch.net/php/main.php#4d6973734a6d63. The sources in Herrnhut have not been digitized, but there is a finding aid available online. For the most up-to-date information about how to access Moravian sources globally, see https://moravianarchives.net/find-out-whats-in-our-archival-collections/.

34. In recent years, more scholars have begun to integrate Moravian records about the Danish West Indies into research on the Caribbean and Atlantic history, but the Moravian records remain a largely untapped resource, particularly for the study of African diasporic history. One of the problems is that very few Caribbean scholars are trained in German, and those who do know German still have to learn how to read German Script. For some of the recent research that draws on the Moravian archives in the Caribbean, see especially Sensbach, *Rebecca's Revival*; Catron, *Embracing Protestantism*; Kaelin, "To Be Proposed as Useful." There are also important studies being published in German that use the Moravian archives from the Caribbean. See, for example, Hüsgen, *Mission und Sklaverei*.

35. I have benefited from the aid of graduate research assistants who have helped with the unwieldy transcription and translation process. Many thanks to Adam Blackler, Tanner Deeds, and Stephan Knott.

36. Additional transcriptions and translations are available on my website, www.katharinegerbner.com.

37. Here, I draw especially on J. Lorand Matory's analysis of paradigms of interpretation and the underlying logics of religion within a transatlantic framework. In *Black Atlantic Religion*, Matory situates Candomblé within a "supralocal geographical context" and shows how local traditions in Brazil and West Africa were developing in relationship to each other and in relation to other systems, traditions, and practices, including European and Native American. For Matory, "Afro-Atlantic dialogue" is an essential paradigm to understand Black Atlantic religion. Matory, *Black Atlantic Religion*, 34–35.

38. Thomas Shallecross died soon after his arrival in Jamaica, so he did not produce archival documents.

39. Wells-Oghoghomeh, *The Souls of Womenfolk*.

INTRODUCTION TO PART I

1. Caries, December 24, 1756, "Diary of Jamaica [Bogue estate]," MAB Miss Jmc 3.
2. Caries, December 31, 1756, "Diary of Jamaica [Bogue estate]," MAB Miss Jmc 3.
3. Caries, November 21, 1756, "Diary of Jamaica [Bogue estate]," MAB Miss Jmc 3; "Katalog der Getauften in Jamaica," UA R.15.C.a.02.9.a. Caries only baptized men. No women were baptized until Anna Rauch, the first female missionary to Jamaica, arrived in December 1756. I discuss this gender dynamic at greater length in chapter 4.
4. Gerbner, *Christian Slavery*, chaps. 7–8.
5. Glasson, "Missionaries, Slavery, and Race," 307; Glasson, *Mastering Christianity*.
6. Haberecht, December 24, 1756, "Diary of Jamaica [Bogue estate]," MAB Miss Jmc 2.

1. AFRICANA IRRUPTIONS

Parts of this chapter are drawn from my article "'They Call Me Obea': German Moravian Missionaries and Afro-Caribbean Religion in Jamaica, 1754–1760," *Atlantic Studies: Global Currents* 12, no. 2 (2015): 160–78. I am grateful to *Atlantic Studies* for permission to reprint portions of my article.

1. Caries, April 27, 1755, "Diary of Brother Caries' Voyage to Jamaica and Jamaica Diary, Oct 17–Dec 1755," MCH [uncatalogued]. See also "Beschreibung der ersten N*taufe, 27. April 1755," UA R.15.C.a.01.3.a.

2. Caries, April 27, 1755, "Diary of Brother Caries' Voyage," MCH [uncatalogued].

3. Caries, April 27, 1755, "Diary of Brother Caries' Voyage," MCH [uncatalogued]. The version of Caries's diary in the Moravian Church House in London, England, is in English, suggesting that Caries wanted his English benefactors to know about the state of his mission. German versions of Caries's diaries from these years can be found in the Unitätsarchiv der Evangelischen Brüder-Unität in Herrnhut, Germany. See UA R.15.C.a.05. Several of Caries's diaries are also available in the Moravian Archives in Bethlehem, PA.

4. Caries to Watteville, March 17, 1755, in *Gemein Nachrichten* (1755), vol. 5. UA GN.A.44, 743–47.

5. While Obeah has negative connotations in the modern Caribbean, Jerome Handler and Kenneth Bilby have argued that it had positive connotations among Afro-Caribbeans in the eighteenth-century British Caribbean. Handler and Bilby, "On the Early Use and Origin"; Bilby and Handler, "Obeah"; Handler and Bilby, *Enacting Power*.

6. His definition aligns with the one offered by Dianne Stewart, who has suggested that "in the pre-emancipation period, Obeah encompassed ... a priesthood of sorts, religious offices such as mediums, diviners, and other gifted or trained spiritualists." Stewart, *Three Eyes for the Journey*, 41. It also corresponds with Diana Paton's analysis of divination in some early references to Obeah. See Paton, *The Cultural Politics of Obeah*, 37–38.

7. Fromont, *The Art of Conversion*, 15.

8. Stewart, *Three Eyes for the Journey*, 43.

9. Olupona, *City of 201 Gods*, 1.

10. For this view, see especially Paton, "Obeah Acts"; Paton and Forde, *Obeah and Other Powers*, introduction; Wisecup, "Knowing Obeah."

11. For a careful analysis of the disputed etymology of the term *Obeah*, see Paton, *The Cultural Politics of Obeah*, 27–31. For the argument that Obeah had Akan roots, see Konadu, *The Akan Diaspora*, 140. For the argument that it derives from the Ibo word *dibia*, see Chambers, "My Own Nation," 88–90; Handler and Bilby, "On the Early Use and Origin," 90–92. See also Edmonds and Gonzalez, *Caribbean Religious History*, 122–23; Rucker, "Earth from a Dead Negro's Grave," 66–70. On the relationship between Obeah and Myal, see Stewart, *Three Eyes for the Journey*, chap. 1.

12. Thomas Walduck, "Letter to Mr. James Petiver," 1710, reprinted in *Journal of the Barbados Museum and Historical Society* (JBMHS) 15, no. 3 (1948): 137–49.

13. Hughes, *The Natural History of Barbados*, 14–17; Handler and Bilby, "On the Early Use and Origin," 88.

14. Cited in Paton, *The Cultural Politics of Obeah*, 36–37 and Gaspar, *Bondmen and Rebels*, 246–7. See also Rucker, "Earth from a Dead Negro's Grave," 63–65.

15. Paton, *The Cultural Politics of Obeah*, 35–38. See also Gaspar, *Bondmen and Rebels*, 246–47.

16. *Journals of the Assembly of Jamaica* 3:121, March 29, 1733. See also Sharpe, *Ghosts of Slavery*, 25; Kopytoff, "Early Political Development," 298–301; Paton, *The Cultural Politics of Obeah*, 34–35.

17. I. Lewis to James Knight, December 20, 1743, BL Add Ms 12431, f. 99; cited in Paton, *The Cultural Politics of Obeah*, 34.

18. Diary of Thomas Thistlewood, April 25, 1753, in Hall, *In Miserable Slavery*, 56; see also Brown, *The Reaper's Garden*, 145. For more on Thistlewood, see Burnard, *Mastery, Tyranny, and Desire*.

19. Diary of Thomas Thistlewood, January 6, 1754, in Hall, *In Miserable Slavery*, 61; Brown, *The Reaper's Garden*, 145.

20. Brown, *The Reaper's Garden*, 148–49; Brown, *Tacky's Revolt*, 138; Paton, *The Cultural Politics of Obeah*, 35–36, On binding oaths in Akan culture, see Rucker, *Gold Coast Diasporas*, 90–92.

21. Long, *The History of Jamaica*, 416; Edwards, *The History, Civil and Commercial*, 2:82–85.

22. Earle and Aravamudan, *Obi*; Paton et al., "Three-Fingered Jack."

23. Wisecup, "Knowing Obeah."

24. Brown, *The Reaper's Garden*, 149.

25. Bryson, "The Art of Power," 65. On poison and Obeah in comparative perspective, see Paton, "Witchcraft, Poison, Law and Atlantic Slavery."

26. Paton, *The Cultural Politics of Obeah*, chaps. 4–5. See also Handler and Bilby, *Enacting Power*.

27. Paton, "Obeah Acts." For an overview of Obeah laws in the British Caribbean, see Handler and Bilby, *Enacting Power*. For an examination of how laws against Obeah informed British theories about the relationship between the mind and the body, see Ramsey, "Powers of Imagination and Legal Regimes."

28. Paton, "The Racist History"; US Department of State, "2019 Report on International Religious Freedom," sec. 2. While Obeah remains a crime in Jamaica, it was decriminalized in Anguilla in 1980, in Barbados in 1998, in the Republic of Trinidad and Tobago in 2000, and in St. Lucia in 2004. In Jamaica the last conviction for Obeah was in 1964 and the last arrest for Obeah in 1977. Khan, *The Deepest Dye*, 18.

29. Crosson, *Experiments with Power*, x–xi, 3; Crosson, "What Obeah Does Do."

30. Khan, *The Deepest Dye*, 18.

31. Hucks, *Obeah, Orisa, and Religious Identity*, xi; Stewart, *Obeah, Orisa, and Religious Identity*, xi.

32. The Moravian Church, also known as the Unitas Fratrum or Brüdergemeine, was a small but influential Protestant group headquartered in Herrnhut, Saxony. Known for their radical views on gender, community, and worship, the Moravians were also the first Protestant group to actively evangelize enslaved Africans in the Caribbean. For their radical views on gender and community, see Fogleman, *Jesus Is Female*; Atwood, *Community of the Cross*. For their role as missionaries in the eighteenth-century Caribbean, see Sensbach, *Rebecca's Revival*; Gerbner, *Christian Slavery*.

33. Caries spoke English, but it was likely accented. He wrote primarily in German, and his English writing contains minor errors typical of a German speaker.

34. In 1753, Barham wrote to Cennick, "[I would like to] communicate my thoughts to you upon a point in which you cannot with myself but be deeply interested, I mean the enlightening [of] those poor souls, the Negroes in that part of the World where Providence has cast my show of temporal Blessing." MCH AB 75, Missions Box.

35. "Barham Brothers Proposal to the Brethren," May 23, 1754, UA R.15.C.a.01.1a.
36. "Zur 16ten Woche," *Gemein Nachrichten* 5 (1755), UA GN A.44 (I–XL), 352–55.
37. Watteville to Caries, Gottlieb and Shallecross, 5 Oct 1754, UA R.15.C.a.01.1b.
38. For more on the mission in Saint Thomas, see Sensbach, *Rebecca's Revival*; Gerbner, *Christian Slavery*, chaps. 7–8; Kaelin, "To Be Proposed as Useful."
39. Caries, October 12, 1754, "Diary of Brother Caries' Voyage," MCH [uncatalogued].
40. Caries, October 12, 1754, "Diary of Brother Caries' Voyage," MCH [uncatalogued].
41. Ward, *The Protestant Evangelical Awakening*; Fogleman, *Jesus Is Female*.
42. Podmore, *The Moravian Church in England*, chap. 8.
43. Caries, January 1, 1755 and January 13, 1755, "Diary of Brother Caries' Voyage," MCH [uncatalogued].
44. Caries, January 13, 1755, "Diary of Brother Caries' Voyage," MCH [uncatalogued].
45. Caries, September 15, 1755, "Diary of Brother Caries' Voyage," MCH [uncatalogued].
46. Gerbner, *Christian Slavery*; Dayfoot, *The Shaping of the West Indian Church*; Beasley, *Christian Ritual and the Creation*.
47. Peucker, "Pink, White, and Blue," 181.
48. For female Moravian dress, see Sommer, "Fashion Passion." Until the mid-1750s, single Moravian men and boys sometimes wore a ribbon around their neck or tied in their shirt. This practice began to subside after 1750. After 1760, colored ribbons became associated exclusively with female Moravian dress. For more on the meaning of the Moravian ribbons, see Peucker, "Pink, White, and Blue." In 1749, the Moravian painter Johann Valentin Haidt depicted two Black Moravian boys from the island of Saint Thomas wearing pink ribbons around their necks, suggesting that the ribbons may have been worn in the Caribbean. Johann Valentin Haidt, *Erstlingsbild* (ca. 1749), UA GS.391.
49. Cited in Peucker, "Pink, White, and Blue," 196.
50. Peucker, "Pink, White, and Blue," 181.
51. March 29, 1760, *Diarien von Mesopotamia*, UA R.15.C.b.01.3.
52. Caries, December 23, 1754, "Diary of Brother Caries' Voyage," MCH [uncatalogued].
53. Caries, January 21, 1755, "Diary of Brother Caries' Voyage," MCH [uncatalogued].
54. Caries, January 26, 1755, "Diary of Brother Caries' Voyage," MCH [uncatalogued].
55. Quoted in Handler and Bilby, "On the Early Use and Origin," 88.
56. Bilby and Handler, "Obeah," 155. See also Handler, "Slave Medicine and Obeah."
57. Caries, January 17, 1755, "Diary of Brother Caries' Voyage," MCH [uncatalogued].
58. Caries, December 17, 1754, "Diary of Brother Caries' Voyage," MCH [uncatalogued].
59. Caries, March 9, 1755, "Diary of Brother Caries' Voyage," MCH [uncatalogued].
60. Caries, in his preface to the letters, wrote that he transcribed the letters of each man "in the same order as they have been baptized, one after another." He was also careful to note that he listened to each individual alone, "one at a Time," so that they "might not use anothers Expressions." Caries's gestures toward authenticity suggest that he was concerned that his imagined reader—William Foster—would doubt the reliability of the enslaved converts' words.
61. Caries, July 8, 1755, "Diary of Brother Caries' Voyage," MCH [uncatalogued].
62. Caries, July 8, 1755, "Diary of Brother Caries' Voyage," MCH [uncatalogued].

63. Atwood, *Community of the Cross*; Fogleman, *Jesus Is Female*; Peucker, *A Time of Sifting*.

64. Fromont, *The Art of Conversion*, 67. On power objects, see also Fromont, "Paper, Ink, Vodun, and the Inquisition," which discusses *bolsas de mandinga*.

65. Rucker, *Gold Coast Diasporas*; Rucker, "Earth from a Dead Negro's Grave," 63–65.

66. Caries, April 29, 1755, "Diary of Brother Caries' Voyage," MCH [uncatalogued].

67. Caries to Zinzendorf, April 25, 1755, UA R.15.C.a.01.2.

68. Caries to Zinzendorf, April 25, 1755, UA R.15.C.a.01.2.

69. Caries to Zinzendorf, June 2, 1755, UA R.15.C.a.01.2.

70. "Candidaten zur Tauffe at the Bogue Im Monath Aug: 1756"; Also "A List of Negroes Belonging to Wm Foster Esq Taken the First of May 1756," UA R.15.C.a.02.4.

71. Caries only baptized men because he was not accompanied by a female missionary. No women were baptized until Anna Rauch, the first female missionary in Jamaica, arrived in December 1756.

72. Caries, March 14, 1755, "Diary of Brother Caries' Voyage," MCH [uncatalogued].

73. Caries to Watteville, March 17, 1755, *Gemein Nachrichten* 5 (1755), UA GN.A.44 (I–XL), 743–47.

74. Caries to Zinzendorf, July 19, 1756, UA R.15.C.a.01.2.

75. Oldendorp, *Historie der caribischen Inseln*, 1: 366–465. For background on Oldendorp, see Meier et al., *Christian Georg Andreas Oldendorp*, especially Jones, "Oldendorps Beitrag zur Afrika-Forschung des radikalen Pietismus"; Palmié, "Oldendorps Bedeutung für die Afroamerikanistik," and Baldauf, "Oldendorp als Historiker." Oldendorp's manuscripts are one of the most important sources for Danish West Indian and African diasporic histories. Oldendorp originally wrote about six thousand pages based on extensive research in the 1760s and 170s. However, the Moravian Church decided to publish only a fraction of his research. The abridged version of Oldendorp's *Historie*, edited by Johann Jakob Bossart, was translated into English in 1987 by Arnold Highfield under the title *A Caribbean Mission*. Oldendorp's full manuscript was published for the first time in 2000 and 2002 in German, but there is no English translation available. All English translations of Oldendorp are my own.

76. Oldendorp, *Historie der caribischen Inseln*, 1: 448–49.

77. Caries, June 2, 1756, "Bro. Caries Diary of the little Congregation in Jamaica for 1756," MCH [uncatalogued].

78. Rucker, *Gold Coast Diasporas*, 88–89.

79. On Nzambi Mpungu, see Thornton, "Religious and Ceremonial Life," 75–77; on Chukwu, see Ilogu, *Christianity and Igbo Culture*, 34.

80. Stewart, *Three Eyes for the Journey*, 41–43.

81. Paton, *The Cultural Politics of Obeah*, 38.

82. Caries, May 13, 1755, "Diary of Brother Caries' Voyage," MCH [uncatalogued].

83. Caries, November 12, 1755, "Diary of Brother Caries' Voyage," MCH [uncatalogued].

84. Caries, December 14, 1755, "Diary of Brother Caries' Voyage," MCH [uncatalogued].

85. Caries, March 23, 1755, "Diary of Brother Caries' Voyage," MCH [uncatalogued].

86. Caries, February 15, 1756, "Bro. Caries Diary of the little Congregation in Jamaica for 1756," MCH [uncatalogued]; Sensbach, *Rebecca's Revival*, 94–96.

87. On this point, the Moravian congregation could be fruitfully compared to Catholic confraternities in the Atlantic World. See especially, Dewulf, *Afro-Atlantic Catholics*; Monroe, "Black Brotherhoods."

88. "Candidaten zur Tauffe at the Bogue Im Monath Aug: 1756," UA R.15.C.A.02.4.

89. Sensbach, *Rebecca's Revival*; Kaelin, *Women, Race, and the Moravian Church*.

90. "Candidaten zur Tauffe at the Bogue Im Monath Aug: 1756," UA R.15.C.A.02.4. For Silva's desire to be baptized, see Caries, November 12, 1755, "Diary of Brother Caries' Voyage," MCH [uncatalogued]. For references to Barbara (Salome), see February 14, 1757; April 4–26, 1757; June 7, 1757, "Diary of Jamaica [Bogue estate]," MAB Miss Jmc 4.

91. Rucker "Earth from a Dead Negro's Grave," 66.

92. Brown, *The Reaper's Garden*.

93. Caries, October 4, 1756, "Diary of Jamaica [Bogue estate]," MAB Miss Jmc 3.

94. Caries, October 4, 1756, "Diary of Jamaica [Bogue estate]," MAB Miss Jmc 3.

95. Brown, *The Reaper's Garden*, 132–33; see also Rucker, *Gold Coast Diasporas*, 86.

96. Caries to Spangenberg, January 23, 1757, MAB Miss Jmc 32.2.

97. Caries, October 4, 1756, "Diary of Jamaica [Bogue estate]," MAB Miss Jmc 3.

98. Haberecht, October 4, 1756, "Diary of Jamaica [Bogue estate]," MAB Miss Jmc 2.

99. Oldendorp, *Historie der caribischen Inseln*, vol. 1, 485. See also Thorp, "New Wine in Old Bottles," 5–6.

100. Oldendorp, *Historie der caribischen Inseln*, vol. 1, 432.

101. Oldendorp, *Historie der caribischen Inseln*, vol. 1, 442.

102. Caries, October 5, 1756, "Diary of Jamaica [Bogue estate]," MAB Miss Jmc 3.

103. Oldendorp, *Historie der Caribischen Inseln*, 1: 448–49.

104. Caries, October 5, 1756, "Diary of Jamaica [Bogue estate]," MAB Miss Jmc 3.

105. Caries, October 5, 1756, "Diary of Jamaica [Bogue estate]," MAB Miss Jmc 3.

106. Caries, October 5, 1756, "Diary of Jamaica [Bogue estate]," MAB Miss Jmc 3.

107. On the significance of salt in Jamaica and its relationship with beliefs in Kongo, see Schuler, *Alas, Alas, Kongo*, 77, 80, 93–96. Schuler notes that while "the full cosmological significance of salt is not clear ... spirits do not eat salt, and abstention from it was believed to confer special powers, making people 'come like a witch,' 'interpret all things,' and powerful enough to fly back to Africa," 96.

108. On the significance of divine justice in Christian eschatology for the enslaved in Jamaica, see also Turner, "The Nameless and the Forgotten," 241.

2. RELIGIO-NATIONS IN THE ARCHIVES

1. "Catalogus von den Getaufften Negern in Jamaica vor Br. George Caries den 12ten Oct 1759," UA R.15.C.a.02.5.

2. "Catalog of members on St. Thomas and St. Croix," MAB Miss WI 185; "Apendix zum Kirchen Buch der Evangelischen Bruder Gemeine in St. Thomas, Crux, u. Jan bis 6. Sept 1750," MAB Miss WI.

3. Hucks, *Obeah, Orisa, and Religious Identity*; Stewart, *Obeah, Orisa and Religious Identity*; Weisenfeld, *New World A-Coming*.

4. Byrd, "Eboe, Country, Nation," 123–48; Matory, *Black Atlantic Religion*.

5. Following Dianne Stewart and Tracey Hucks, I do not emphasize the term *ethnicity*, though there are several works of scholarship that have utilized this category effectively. Stewart, *Obeah, Orisa and Religious Identity*, 19.

6. There have been three major areas of controversy in the scholarship on African nations or ethnicities: First, there has been—and continues to be—some confusion about the relationship between ethnic identity and geographic region. Second, there is disagreement about what an ethnic designation really means and whether it was a fixed or evolving category. Finally, some scholars have argued that African ethnic designations should be disregarded because they were usually recorded by Europeans who could not reliably identify ethnicities. They point out, among other things, that enslavers sought to utilize ethnic divisions to undermine communal identity among the enslaved population, and that Europeans favored some ethnicities over others, meaning that the records we have about African ethnicities are deeply suspect. For a summary of the debates about African ethnicities in the Atlantic World, see Mann, "Shifting Paradigms in the Study"; Hall, *Slavery and African Ethnicities*; Chambers, "Ethnicity in the Diaspora."

7. Matory, *Black Atlantic Religion*, 73.

8. Stewart, *Obeah, Orisa and Religious Identity*, 51.

9. On the co-constitution of race and religion, see especially, Weisenfeld, *New World A-Coming*; Khan, *The Deepest Dye*; Harvey and Lum, *The Oxford Handbook of Religion and Race*.

10. Gerbner, *Christian Slavery*.

11. Weisenfeld, *New World A-Coming*, 6.

12. Weisenfeld acknowledges that the phrase "religio-racial" could be used widely to characterize "all religious groups in the United States," but she employs the term "in a more specific sense . . . to designate a set of early twentieth-century black religious movements." Weisenfeld, *New World A-Coming*, 5–6.

13. Weisenfeld, *New World A-Coming*, 7.

14. Gerbner, "Theorizing Conversion."

15. Brown, *Tacky's Revolt*, 101.

16. Many of the men and women who arrived from the Gold Coast were enslaved as a result of warfare that accompanied the rapid expansion of the Asante kingdom. During that decade, some of those individuals would have participated in the same battles and campaigns, and some knew each other. Yet even those individuals who did not share memories of specific events would have been able to draw on other areas of communal understanding. Coalition-building strategies such as oath-taking could secure bonds of political and social alliance. Brown, *Tacky's Revolt*, 102–7.

17. On Anomabu in the Atlantic World, see Sparks, *Where the Negroes Are Masters*; Shumway, *The Fante and the Transatlantic Slave Trade*. See also Rucker, *Gold Coast Diasporas*, 62–64.

18. Before the era of the slave trade, the Fante had migrated from the Akan hinterland to the coast of Ghana. Shumway, *The Fante and the Transatlantic Slave Trade*, 15. On the Akan influence in Jamaica and elsewhere in the Atlantic World, see also Rucker, *Gold Coast Diasporas*; Konadu, *The Akan Diaspora*; Schuler, *Alas, Alas, Kongo*.

19. Shumway, *The Fante and the Transatlantic Slave Trade*, 142; Shumway, "The Fante Shrine of Nananom Mpow"; Rucker, *Gold Coast Diasporas*, 64.

20. The missionaries did not describe Dumbarton as "old," which they did with other congregants. This suggests that Dumbarton was in his twenties or thirties.

21. Shumway, *The Fante and the Transatlantic Slave Trade*, 14. The Borbor Fante, who had controlled about twelve miles of coastline in the seventeenth century, gradually expanded their influence. Rebecca Shumway has argued that the Borbor Fante, along with other coastal groups, developed a decentralized system of governance based on treaties that she calls the Coastal Coalition. The Coastal Coalition controlled commerce in much of southern Ghana. See also Kea, *Settlements, Trade, and Polities in the Seventeenth-Century Gold Coast*, 286; Brown, *Tacky's Revolt*, 40–43.

22. Shumway, *The Fante and the Transatlantic Slave Trade*, chaps. 2–3.

23. Agorsah, "Spiritual Vibrations of Historic Kormantse," 90. For historical and archaeological maps for historic Kormantse, see Kormantse Archaeological Research Project, "Maps," accessed February 4, 2021, http://www.kormantse.org/historical-kormantse/maps.

24. Agorsah, "Spiritual Vibrations of Historic Kormantse," 90; Brown, *Tacky's Revolt*, 92; Chambers, "Ethnicity in the Diaspora," 29–30. Coromantee could be spelled in various ways—Calamante, Cormantine, and Calamantine—but spelling eventually stabilized around Coromantee in the mid-eighteenth century. Brown, *Tacky's Revolt*, 91. Caries, in fact, spelled Coromantee five different ways in the church register.

25. Behn, *Oroonoko*.

26. Brown, *Tacky's Revolt*, 102–3.

27. See, for example, Christopher Codrington's comments on the Coromantees, whom he considered to be "not only the best and most faithful of our slaves" but "all born Heroes . . . grateful and obedient to a kind master, but implacably revengeful when ill-treated." CSP 19 (1701): no. 1132.

28. Brown, *Tacky's Revolt*, chap. 3; Agorsah, "Spiritual Vibrations of Historic Kormantse"; Hanserd, *Identity, Spirit and Freedom*; Rucker, *Gold Coast Diasporas*, 126–40.

29. Brown, *Tacky's Revolt*, 90. Yet as Vincent Brown writes, common heritage or shared ethnicities did not necessarily result in solidarity. Men and women who shared ethnic identities could develop opposing allegiances in the Americas, due to a variety of cultural, political, economic, and social factors. In other words, politics and political allegiance are messy and contingent, and historians must recognize this complexity when they draw upon terms such as Coromantee in order to postulate a hypothesis about allegiance and African ethnic heritage.

30. Rucker, *Gold Coast Diasporas*, chaps. 2–3.

31. Caries, June 2, 1756, "Bro. Caries Diary of the little Congregation in Jamaica for 1756," MCH [uncatalogued]. For Oldendorp's description of "Jankombum" see Oldendorp, *Historie der caribischen Inseln*, vol. 1, 408. Oldendorp referred to Jankombum as the "God of the Amina," and he interviewed at least three Africans from the Gold Coast who offered slightly different descriptions of Jancómpon's place in the cosmos. For more on Oldendorp's use of the term *Amina*, see Kelley and Lovejoy, "Oldendorp's 'Amina.'"

According to Oldendorp, "some say that the God in heaven, who made the world and its nations, is named Borriborri. This God has a wife, Jankomaago, and a son, Jankombum, who speaks for the great God and to whom everyone directs their prayers with their concerns/requests. Another attested to the fact that they had three Gods, but that in his region they called the father Quereampum, the mother Krieampum and the son Jankombum. They stand by the son and call him Father as well. During war they sing to Jankombum in the midst of the shooting: He helps us, he is the father, we are his children and can't help ourselves. Every morning, after they've washed themselves, they call to him to protect them, give them good food and let them be happy." Translation by the author. Oldendorp's full manuscript has been translated into modern German but is not yet translated into English. The only English translation is heavily excerpted and contains only a fraction of Oldendorp's original manuscript.

32. Rucker, *Gold Coast Diasporas*, 86.

33. Law, "Religion, Trade and Politics," 42; Law, *The Slave Coast of West Africa*; Asiwaju and Law, "From the Volta to the Niger."

34. Asiwaju and Law, "From the Volta to the Niger"; Strickrodt, *Afro-European Trade in the Atlantic World*, 109; Brown, *Tacky's Revolt*, 26.

35. The first reference to Popo in European sources came from a 1561 Portuguese map, where it appears as Poupous. Law, "Problems of Plagiarism, Harmonization and Misunderstanding," 342. By the end of the seventeenth century, European sources referred to two Popos: Grand Popo, in modern day Benin, and Little Popo, which is now known as Aného, Togo. There has been some confusion between the two. Before 1680, Popo generally referred to Grand Popo. When Little Popo entered the European trade in the 1680s, it was called a variety of names, including Abree, Abrow, Poccahonna, and Little Paw Paw or Little Po Po. Strickrodt, *Afro-European Trade in the Atlantic World*, 2–6.

36. Law, "Problems of Plagiarism, Harmonization and Misunderstanding," 347–48. The Jesuit missionary Alonso de Sandoval used the term *Popo* to refer to both the state of Popo and its king ("el Popo").

37. Contemporary scholarship uses the term *Hula* to refer to this group, but that is actually a Fon term, meaning "sea people." Strickrodt, *Afro-European Trade in the Atlantic World*, 41–44. See also Parés, "The Hula 'Problem.'"

38. While the exact date of their migration is unknown, historical sources and oral histories connect the settlement of Grand Popo with other Aja migrations, including the founding of Allada, Nuatja (Notsie), and Ouidah (Whydah). Asiwaju and Law, "From the Volta to the Niger," 429. At times, Grand Popo fell under the control of Allada (Ardra), the major power in the region during the seventeenth century, while at other times it maintained its independence. In the early eighteenth century, Little Popo was attacked multiple times by Akwamu forces. Strickrodt, *Afro-European Trade in the Atlantic World*, 102–3.

39. Strickrodt, *Afro-European Trade in the Atlantic World*, 77–78, 95; Asiwaju and Law, "From the Volta to the Niger," 415.

40. For an in-depth analysis of the migration, see Strickrodt, *Afro-European Trade in the Atlantic World*, 78–79.

41. On Christian Protten, see Sensbach, *Rebecca's Revival*, chap. 8; Simonsen, "Belonging in Africa"; Kea, "Crossroads and Exchanges in the Scandinavian Atlantic"; Sebro, *Mellem afrikaner og kreol*, chap. 1.

42. Strickrodt, *Afro-European Trade in the Atlantic World*, 5; Sensbach, *Rebecca's Revival*.

43. Protten, *En nyttig grammaticalsk Indledelse*; Sensbach, *Rebecca's Revival*, 218–19; Sebro, *Mellem afrikaner og kreol*, chap. 1.

44. "Draft of a letter from Marotta/Magdalena to the Queen of Denmark," UA R.15.Ba.03.61_a-b. For the translation of "adga Tome" as "Aja country," see Kea, "From Catholicism to Moravian Pietism," 116. However, as Louise Sebro has pointed out, Kea misinterprets the Moravian records and mistakenly confuses Madlena/Damma with another woman named Magdalena, so much of his article falsely presumes a Catholic African identity for Madlena/Damma. See Sebro, *Mellem afrikaner og kreol*, chap. 1. I am grateful to Louise Sebro for sharing an English translation of her Danish-language thesis with me.

45. The distinction between "adga Tome" and "Poppo op Africa" is an important one. Significantly, in the original draft, either Madlena/Damma or the missionary scribe crossed out the words "Poppo lande" in Gbe, and replaced them with "adga Tome," suggesting they considered these two terms as meaningfully distinct from each other.

46. My argument here draws on my collaborative research with Enoch Aboh, James Essegbey, Felix Ameka, Peter Stein, Cefas Van Rossen, and Louise Sebro. Together, we have been developing a translation of the Gbe-language portion of Damma/Madlena's letter for the first time. Our work is forthcoming and will be accessible through a link on my website, www.katharinegerbner.com.

47. Asiwaju and Law, "From the Volta to the Niger," 414.

48. Matory, *Black Atlantic Religion*, 54; Law, "Ethnicity and the Slave Trade," 206.

49. Murphy, "Yoruba Religions in Diaspora," 400–409.

50. Robin Law has suggested that the more generic usage of *Nago* to refer to Yoruba speakers in West Africa was a "feedback loop" from the diaspora, as Africans in the diaspora expanded and redefined the term *Nago*. Law, "Ethnicity and the Slave Trade." For more on the Yoruba diaspora, see Falola and Childs, *The Yoruba Diaspora in the Atlantic World*.

51. Cortes de Oliviera, "The Reconstruction of Ethnicity in Bahia"; Murphy, "Yoruba Religions in Diaspora," 401–2.

52. Law, "Ethnicity and the Slave Trade," 209–10.

53. The missionaries spelled the nation *Naga*, but this is almost certainly an alternative spelling of *Nago*.

54. Murphy, "Yoruba Religions in Diaspora," 400.

55. Murphy, "Yoruba Religions in Diaspora"; Eltis, "The Diaspora of Yoruba Speakers," 26.

56. Law, "Ethnicity and the Slave Trade."

57. Caries, September 21, 1755, "Diary of Brother Caries' Voyage," MCH [uncatalogued].

58. Lovejoy, *Slavery in the Global Diaspora*, 229.

59. Curtin, *Economic Change in Precolonial Africa*, 3–5; Diouf, *Servants of Allah*, 20. In the eleventh century, Takrur, in northern Senegal, adopted Islam as the state religion, and the religion continued to spread through Senegambia—mostly through the influence of indigenous traders, clerics, and rulers. Diouf, *Servants of Allah*, 21.

60. This is in part due to Alex Haley's *Roots*, in which Haley's ancestor Kunta Kinte is Mandinka. Haley, *Roots*; see also the 1975 film *Mandingo*, based on a book of the same name.

61. As R. A. Spears has written, "The basic problem with the term Mandingo is that no one—not even the specialist—can be sure of what it means. It may refer to all the Mande people or only the Northern Mande people—namely the Bambara, Malinke, and Djula." Cited in "Mandingo, n. and adj.," in *OED Online* (Oxford University Press), accessed March 1, 2021, http://www.oed.com/view/Entry/113325.

62. *Sape* was used to refer to southern Upper Guinea and *Jalof* for the northern part of the region. In the sixteenth century, Europeans also used the term *Mandinga* to refer to the region of Senegambia that was under the influence of Mali. Bühnen, "Ethnic Origins of Peruvian Slaves," 76.

63. Bühnen, "Ethnic Origins of Peruvian Slaves," 75.

64. Curtin, *The Atlantic Slave Trade*, 184–85. On the Mandingo people, see also Barry, *Senegambia and the Atlantic Slave Trade*.

65. Hall, *Slavery and African Ethnicities*, 82.

66. In the fourteenth century, the king of the Mali Empire, Kankan Musa (r. 1312–37), made a pilgrimage to Mecca. Gall and Hobby, "Malinke." Most Mandingos did not drink wine or eat pork, though there were also non-Muslim Mandingos. Hall, *Africans in Colonial Louisiana*, 38.

67. Fromont, "Paper, Ink, Vodun, and the Inquisition," 465.

68. Some Portuguese writers used the word *Mandingo* interchangeably with *feitiçaria*, or "fetish." Johnson, *African American Religions*, 62; Fromont, "Paper, Ink, Vodun, and the Inquisition." See also Pietz, "The Problem of the Fetish."

69. Oldendorp distinguished the Mandinga from the Mandongo. Oldendorp, *Historie der caribischen Inseln*, vol. 1, 376 §395.

70. Oldendorp, *Historie der caribischen Inseln*, vol. 1, 376 §395.

71. Oldendorp, *Historie der caribischen Inseln*, vol. 1, 376 §396.

72. Diouf, *Servants of Allah*, 25.

73. Oldendorp, *Historie der caribischen Inseln*, vol. 1, 376–77.

74. Bücher-Katalog für Carmel, 1759, UA R.15.Ca.01.3.c.

75. Caron, "'Of a Nation Which the Others Do Not Understand.'" This history has led to debate about whether scholars today should use the term *Bambara* or *Bamana*. Gwendolyn Midlo Hall notes that during her own visits to Francophone Africa in the 1980s, she was told numerous times that *Bambara* is an insulting term that "twists this ethnic name to mean 'barbarian' (*barbar*)." Hall, *Slavery and African Ethnicities*, 97.

76. Curtin, *Economic Change in Precolonial Africa*, 178–79.

77. On the evolving meaning of the terms *slav* and *slave*, see Karras, *Slavery and Society in Medieval Scandinavia*; Blackburn, "The Old World Background." On the term *Bambara*, see also Johnson, *Wicked Flesh*, 38–39.

78. Hall, *Africans in Colonial Louisiana*, 42.
79. Caron, "'Of a Nation Which the Others Do Not Understand,'" 102–7.
80. Curtin, *Economic Change in Precolonial Africa*, 179.
81. Chambers, "Ethnicity in the Diaspora," 28.
82. On the founding of the Kingdom of Kongo, see Fromont, *The Art of Conversion*, 2–3; Bosteen and Brinkman, introduction to *The Kongo Kingdom*, 2; Thornton, "The Origins of Kongo."
83. On the history of Christianity in the Kingdom of Kongo, see Fromont, *The Art of Conversion*; Thornton, "The Development of an African Catholic Church"; Thornton, "Afro-Christian Syncretism." The establishment of Christianity in West Central Africa, therefore, occurred on very different terms than in other regions in Africa, where it was associated with colonization. See also Bennett, *African Kings*.
84. Fromont, *The Art of Conversion*, 6–7; Thornton, *The Kingdom of Kongo*.
85. Thornton, *The Kingdom of Kongo*; Thornton, "Soyo and Kongo."
86. Thornton, *The Kongolese Saint Anthony*; Fromont, *The Art of Conversion* 206–7.
87. Fromont, *The Art of Conversion*, 14–15.
88. See, for example, Dewulf, *Afro-Atlantic Catholics;* Fromont, *Afro-Catholic Festivals*. On the connection between Kongolese religion and South Carolina, see Young, *Rituals of Resistance*; Brown, *African-Atlantic Cultures and the South Carolina Lowcountry*.
89. Byrd, *Captives and Voyagers*, 20–21.
90. Koelle, *Polyglotta Africana*; Byrd, *Captives and Voyagers*, 20. See also Chambers, "'My Own Nation.'"
91. Byrd, *Captives and Voyagers*, 32.
92. Equiano, *Interesting Narrative*; Byrd, "Eboe, Country, Nation," 124. While some scholars have used this observation to suggest that Vassa was not actually African, Alexander Byrd has argued that Vassa's deployment of the term *Eboe* is "profoundly African" and that it demonstrates how ethnic terms like *Eboe* developed new meanings within an Atlantic context. Byrd, "Eboe, Country, Nation," 125. On Equiano's identity, see Carretta, "Olaudah Equiano or Gustavus Vassa?"; Caretta, *Equiano, The African;* Lovejoy, "Autobiography and Memory"; Carretta, "Response"; Lovejoy, "Olaudah Equiano or Gustavus Vassa." For an excellent digital project including several essays on Equiano, see https://www.equianosworld.org/.
93. Byrd, "Eboe, Country, Nation," 130.
94. Equiano distinguished his nation from "different nations" in the Biafran interior, even those who spoke the same language.
95. Byrd, "Eboe, Country, Nation," 134.
96. Catron, "Slavery, Ethnic Identity, and Christianity in Eighteenth-Century Moravian Antigua," 176.
97. Hall, *Slavery and African Ethnicities*, chap. 5.
98. Law, *The Slave Coast of West Africa*, 246. This possibility is supported by recent research by Africanists, who argue that "Aquambo" was a Danish spelling of Akwamu. Kelley and Lovejoy, "Oldendorp's 'Amina,'" 308; Kea, "'When I Die, I Shall Return to My Own Land.'"
99. Shumway, *The Fante and the Transatlantic Slave Trade*, 52–58.

100. Kea, "Akwamu-Anlo Relations, c. 1750–1813," 33; Shumway, *The Fante and the Transatlantic Slave Trade*, 52–58.

101. Kea, "'When I Die, I Shall Return to My Own Land.'"

102. Brown, *Tacky's Revolt*; Rucker, *Gold Coast Diasporas*.

3. MAROONS, BLOOD OATHS, AND GENDERED IRRUPTIONS

1. Parts of this chapter and chapter 6 are drawn from my article "Maroon Science," in Sheldon, Ragab, and Keel, eds., *Critical Approaches to Science and Religion* (Columbia University Press, 2023), 325–47. I am grateful for permission to reprint portions of my article.

2. Brown, *Tacky's Revolt*, 111; Paton, *The Cultural Politics of Obeah*, 34.

3. Caries, March 27, 1755, "Diary of Brother Caries' Voyage," MCH [uncatalogued].

4. Caries, August 7, 1755, "Diary of Brother Caries' Voyage," MCH [uncatalogued].

5. For histories of the Maroons in Jamaica, see Campbell, *The Maroons of Jamaica*; Kopytoff, "Jamaican Maroon Political Organization"; Kopytoff, "Early Political Development"; Kopytoff, "Colonial Treaty as Sacred Charter"; Kopytoff, "Religious Change"; Sheridan, "The Maroons of Jamaica"; Bilby, "Swearing by the Past"; Carey, *The Maroon Story*; Wilson, "The Performance of Freedom"; McKee, "From Violence to Alliance"; Sivapragasam, "After the Treaties"; Brown, *Tacky's Revolt*, 108–19; Craig, "Oathbound"; Scott, "Women on the 'Fringes.'"

6. McKittrick, *Demonic Grounds*.

7. For a contemporary Jamaican oral history about Maroon origins, see Melville Curry, November 14, 1999, in Bilby, *True-Born Maroons*, 87. For colonial English narratives about Maroon origins, see Dallas, *The History of the Maroons*, 24–26; Knight, *The Natural, Moral, and Political History*, 498–500. The anthropologist Barbara Kopytoff writes that the "nucleus" of the Windward Maroons was a group of Spanish Maroons who were alternately called "Varmahaly," "Carmahalay," "Vermaxales," or "Vermahallis" Negroes. The Leeward Maroons were escaped slaves who fled to the interior of the island following a rebellion in 1673. More rebels joined them following a revolt in 1690. In the 1720s, Leeward Maroons under the leadership of Captain Cudjoe defeated a rival Maroon group led by a man from Madagascar. Kopytoff, "The Early Political Development," 290–93. See also Campbell, *The Maroons of Jamaica*, 14–43; Craton, *Testing the Chains*, 67–77; Craig, "Oathbound," chap. 2.

8. Kopytoff, "The Early Political Development," 293–94; Campbell, *The Maroons of Jamaica*, chap. 1; Brown, *Tacky's Revolt*, 108–11.

9. Brown, *Tacky's Revolt*, 111.

10. Kopytoff, "The Early Political Development," 296.

11. When these two towns were abandoned in the 1730s due to clashes with the English, two new towns—New Nanny Town and Crawford Town—developed a similar cooperative federation. Kopytoff, "The Early Political Development," 298–99.

12. Bilby, *True-Born Maroons*, 483. Kopytoff, "The Early Political Development," 300.

13. On the First Maroon War, see Kopytoff, "The Early Political Development," 294; Brown, *Tacky's Revolt*, 108–17.

14. Kopytoff, "The Early Political Development"; Bilby, *True-Born Maroons*; Paton, *The Cultural Politics of Obeah*, 34–35.

15. For Maroon military tactics and the siege of Nanny Town, see Knight, *The Natural, Moral, and Political History*, 502–3; Brown, *Tacky's Revolt*, 110–14.

16. Nanny is now a national hero, and Jamaican currency portrays her image on the $500 bill. Bilby, *True-Born Maroons*, 193. See also Sharpe, *Ghosts of Slavery*, chap. 1.

17. It is unclear whether there was a single woman named Nanny or whether "Nanny" was a title. While one colonial record described her death, another one from the following year records her as being alive. Sharpe, *Ghosts of Slavery*, chap. 1; Scott, "Women on the 'Fringes.'" 92–102.

18. *Journals of the Assembly of Jamaica* 3:121, March 29, 1733. Sharpe, *Ghosts of Slavery*, 25.

19. "Ayscough to the Council of Trade and Plantation," February 27, 1735. CO 137/21, folio 207. See also Sharpe, *Ghosts of Slavery*, chap. 1.

20. Thicknesse, *Memoirs and Anecdotes*, 74.

21. *Journals of the Assembly of Jamaica*, 3: 458. For an English slave owner's narrative of the treaty signing written in 1746, see Knight, *The Natural, Moral, and Political History*, 502–10. For contemporary Maroon narratives about the treaty signing, see the oral histories in Bilby, *True-Born Maroons*, 261–88. For an overview and analysis of the historical sources, see Kopytoff, "Jamaican Maroon Political Organization," 90.

22. The Windward Maroons were resistant to signing a treaty with the British and only did so once Kojo (Cudjoe) promised to hunt down Maroons who did not make peace with the British. In Windward Maroon oral histories, reluctance to accept peace with whites is a persistent theme. See Bilby, *True-Born Maroons*, 261–73. See also Kopytoff, "Jamaican Maroon Political Organization," 90.

23. According to Thicknesse, when Quao, the Windward Maroon leader, consulted their "obea woman," about whether the Maroons should sign a treaty with the British, she "opposed the measure." Thicknesse, *Memoirs and Anecdotes*, 74. Shavagne Scott has argued that "colonial officials refused to negotiate with [Nanny] via the treaty process because she was a woman," but that they did issue a land grant to a woman named "Nanny" in 1740, one year after the treaty. Scott, "Women on the 'Fringes,'" 110. Michael Sivapragasam has similarly noted that Nanny reappeared later in British colonial records as a leader of a Windward Maroon town. Sivapragasam, "After the Treaties," 65–67.

24. Sydney McDonald (February 4, 1991), cited in Bilby, *True-Born Maroons*, 286–88.

25. Geretius McKenzie (January 9, 1991) notes that the treaty was signed in the "Peace Cave." Cited in Bilby, *True-Born Maroons*, 277. Peace Cave is also known as Ambush Cave because it was used to ambush British forces during the First Maroon War. For oral histories about the Peace Cave, see Bilby, *True-Born Maroons*, 171–74.

26. Thomas Rowe to Kenneth Bilby, Accompong, Jamaica, 1991. Cited in Bilby, "Swearing by the Past," 659.

27. Kopytoff, "Colonial Treaty as Sacred Charter," 45–64; Bilby, *True-Born Maroons*, 274–88. For the historical significance of the blood oath within Akan political culture, see Bilby, "Swearing by the Past."

28. Rucker, "'Earth from a Dead Negro's Grave,'" 62–84; Rucker, *Gold Coast Diasporas*; Craig, "Oathbound." See also Brown, *Tacky's Revolt*, 105–7.

29. Kopytoff, "Colonial Treaty as Sacred Charter."

30. Cited in Bilby, "Swearing by the Past," 659. See also Archibald Cooper, "Papers Relating to the Maroons, 1938–1939," UWI Mona Library, WISC.

31. Bilby, "Swearing by the Past"; Bilby, *True-Born Maroons*.

32. Visit by the author to Accompong Town museum, March 12, 2022. Edwards, "Preserving Maroon Heritage."

33. Richard Currie, Instagram post: @chiefrichardcurrie, March 22, 2022. Currie uses 1738 as the treaty date because the Maroon and British representatives met on March 1. In the old style of dating, the new year began on March 15, so archival sources label the treaty as happening on March 1, 1738. However, according to modern dating, it occurred on March 1, 1739. See also "Chief Currie Wants Peace."

34. Kopytoff, "Colonial Treaty as Sacred Charter"; Bilby, *True-Born Maroons*, 274–88. For the historical significance of the blood oath within Akan political culture, see Bilby, "Swearing by the Past."

35. Cited in Bilby, "Swearing by the Past," 659.

36. British imperial tactics with the Maroons paralleled their treaty-making with indigenous nations in North America. See, for example, Calloway, *Pen and Ink Witchcraft*.

37. Kopytoff, "Jamaican Maroon Political Organization," 95–96.

38. Kopytoff, "Colonial Treaty as Sacred Charter."

39. Craig, "Oathbound."

40. See, for example, Craig, "Oathbound"; Calloway, *Pen and Ink Witchcraft*; Pietz, "The Problem of the Fetish," 23–45; Buck-Morss, *Hegel, Haiti, and Universal History*.

41. Craig, "Oathbound," 124. See also Calloway, *Pen and Ink Witchcraft*.

42. Accompong's silver medal may have been similar to the medals that represent the sacred treaties made between indigenous nations and the British Crown. See Klassen, "Spiritual Jurisdictions," 153; Corbiere, "Anishinaabe Treaty-Making"; Klassen, "Medals, Memory, and Findspots."

43. Caries, March 27, 1755, "Diary of Brother Caries' Voyage."

44. For more on Maroon efforts to assert their political autonomy through sartorial strategies, see Wilson, "The Performance of Freedom."

45. For a description of Accompong, see Thomas Thistlewood, January 8, 1751, "Diary," 1, BLY. https://collections.library.yale.edu/catalog/10187105.

46. Thomas Thistlewood, May 24, 1753, "Diary," [p. 51], BLY. https://collections.library.yale.edu/catalog/11871649.

47. The page is titled, "Im Vorschlag für Candidaten aus dem weiblischen Geschlecht," Katalog mit Getauften und Taufkandidaten, 1756. UA R.15.C.a.02.04_08. The line reads, "Titus, sr. Margery," i.e., "Titus, seiner Margery," which can be translated as "Titus's Margery."

48. As the historian Jane Landers writes, "Women have remained largely invisible in the literature about maroons." Landers, "Maroon Women in Colonial Spanish America." Some scholars have suggested that Maroon communities were generally hostile environments for women. For a critique of this argument, see Thompson, "Gender and Marronage in the Caribbean."

49. Scott, "Women on the 'Fringes.'" Exceptions include Groot, "Maroon Women as Ancestors"; Landers, "Maroon Women in Colonial Spanish America;" McKnight, "Gendered Declarations"; Price, *Co-Wives and Calabashes*.

50. McKittrick, *Demonic Grounds*; Camp, *Closer to Freedom*; Morgan, *Reckoning with Slavery*; Scott, "Women on the 'Fringes.'"

51. Caries, May 13, 1755, "Diary of Brother Caries' Voyage," MCH.

52. "Titus went to St Criux [sic] to have the Inspection there," Caries, July 28, 1755, "Diary of Brother Caries' Voyage," MCH. On the role of drivers in the British Caribbean, see Browne, *The Driver's Story*.

53. Caries, May 13, 1755, "Diary of Brother Caries' Voyage," MCH.

54. Caries, March 11, 1755. "Diary of Brother Caries' Voyage," MCH.

55. Caries, March 23, 1755. "Diary of Brother Caries' Voyage," MCH.

56. "Louis & Titus were chosen to be servants, their office was explained to them and was very weighty to them." Caries, May 25, 1755, "Diary of Brother Caries' Voyage," MCH.

57. Caries, July 8, 1755, "Diary of Brother Caries' Voyage," MCH.

58. Caries, March 11, 1755, "Diary of Brother Caries' Voyage," MCH.

59. Caries, March 23, 1755, "Diary of Brother Caries' Voyage," MCH.

60. Caries, May 13, 1755, "Diary of Brother Caries' Voyage," MCH.

61. Caries, May 20, 1755, "Diary of Brother Caries' Voyage," MCH.

62. Caries to Watteville, March 17, 1755, *Gemein Nachrichten* 5 (1755), UA GN.A.44 (I–XL), 743–47.

63. On Maroon landscapes, see especially Moulton, "Towards the Arboreal Side-Effects of Marronage." On "rival geographies," see Camp, *Closer to Freedom*. On fugitivity, see the special issue co-edited by Gross-Wyrtzen and Moulton, "Toward 'Fugitivity as Method.'"

64. "An Act for the better Order and Government of the Negroes belonging to the several Negroe Towns," *Acts of Assembly, passed in the island of Jamaica; from 1681, to 1754, inclusive*. Jamaica, 1756, 332–33. I am grateful to Shavagne Scott for alerting me to the significance of this act and for offering helpful feedback on an earlier draft of this chapter.

65. "An Act for the better Order and Government of the Negroes belonging to the several Negroe Towns," *Acts of Assembly, passed in the island of Jamaica; from 1681, to 1754, inclusive*. Jamaica, 1756, 33.

66. Caries, November 6, 1755, "Diary of Brother Caries' Voyage," MCH.

67. Caries, July 8, 1755, "Diary of Brother Caries' Voyage," MCH.

68. Caries, August 7, 1755, "Diary of Brother Caries' Voyage," MCH.

69. Caries, August 7, 1755, "Diary of Brother Caries' Voyage," MCH.

70. Caries, August 7, 1755, "Diary of Brother Caries' Voyage," MCH.

71. Caries, November 6, 1755, "Diary of Brother Caries' Voyage," MCH.

72. The full line reads, "Having spoken w[i]th Titus, I found he mistrusted one of our bapt[ized] who some years ago had by Titus own consent & approbation liv'd w[i]th his wife, w[hi]ch is the custom here among the best friend, tho God be praised it begins to leave off at the Bogue entirely." Caries, November 6, 1755, "Diary of Brother Caries' Voyage," MCH.

73. Polyandry, which refers to a woman with multiple partners, is considered to be less common than polygyny, a man with multiple wives, according to most scholarship on African and African-diasporic practices. See, for example, Wells-Oghoghomeh, *The Souls of Womenfolk* 124, "An Act for the better Order and Government of the Negroes belonging to the several Negroe Towns," *Acts of Assembly, passed in the island of Jamaica; from 1681,*

to 1754, inclusive, 332–35; Bush, *Slave Women*, 1, 20–21, 97–98, 126; Price, *Alabi's World*, 169; Kars, *Blood on the River*, 68–69; Price, *Maroon Societies*, 19.

74. Caries, November 6, 1755, "Diary of Brother Caries' Voyage," MCH.

75. Wells-Oghoghomeh, *The Souls of Womenfolk*, 123.

76. Caries, November 6, 1755, "Diary of Brother Caries' Voyage," MCH. Margery's story complicates the narrative that the Jamaica Maroons had a "shortage of women" and practiced polygyny. It may be that both practices were common. On the prevalence of polygyny among the Maroons, see Price, *Maroon Societies*, 19; Craig, "Oathbound," 93–94.

77. February 7, 1757, "Jamaica Diary [Bogue Estate]," MAB Miss Jmc 4.

INTRODUCTION TO PART II

1. Caries, December 31, 1756, "Diary of Jamaica [Bogue estate]," MAB Miss Jmc 3.
2. Caries, December 31, 1756, "Diary of Jamaica [Bogue estate]," MAB Miss Jmc 3.
3. Wells-Oghoghomeh, *The Souls of Womenfolk*.

4. ARCHIVAL SILENCE, SEXUAL VIOLENCE

A few lines in this chapter are drawn from my article "Archival Violence Archival Capital," *William & Mary Quarterly* 79, no. 2 (2022), 595–624. I am grateful to *William & Mary Quarterly* for permission to reprint portions of my article.

1. July 14, 1758, "Das Diarium von der Bogue in Jamaica vom Monath July vor Bethlehem," *Diarien von der Bogue*, UA R.15.C.b.02.1. Some portions of the diary were written by other missionaries, but the entries from July 1758 were written by Christian Heinrich Rauch. The original German reads: "Ab[end]s hatten wir besuch, mit der Elizabeth u ihrer Tochter Camilla sprach die Schw Anna sehr gründl. u ausführl. die Tochter bekannte alles, wie sie als ein kind wäre zur Hurerey anfängl. gezwungen worden; auch das wer u wie usw." The full journal entry also includes information about a young Black woman named Grace, who was subjected to the sexual predations of a different white man. This reference was also deleted from the edited version of the diary.

2. July 15, 1758, "Das Diarium von der Bogue in Jamaica vom Monath July vor Bethlehem," *Diarien von der Bogue*, UA R.15.C.b.02.1.

3. July 15, 1758, "Diary of Jamaica [Bogue estate] June–Oct 1758," MAB Miss Jmc 7.

4. On the metaphor of "silences" and enslaved women in Black feminist scholarship, see Owens, *Consent in the Presence of Force*, 4–5.

5. While most references to sexual assault and violence related to enslaved women and girls, I did find one reference to the assault of an enslaved man named George, which occurred in 1761 at the Carmel estate in Jamaica. See May 11, 1761 and July 20, 1761, *Diarien von Carmel*, UA R.15.C.b.02.2.

6. Trouillot, *Silencing the Past*; Hartman, "Venus in Two Acts"; Hartman, *Lose Your Mother*; Fuentes, *Dispossessed Lives*; Turner, *Contested Bodies*; Turner, "The Nameless and the Forgotten"; Wells-Oghoghomeh, *The Souls of Womenfolk*. This chapter also draws on scholarship about gender and slavery, especially Morgan, *Laboring Women*, Morgan, *Reck-*

oning with Slavery; Spillers, "Mama's Baby, Papa's Maybe"; Jones, *Labor of Love*; White, *Ar'n't I a Woman?*; Johnson, *Wicked Flesh*; Davis, *Women, Race, and Class*; Berry, *The Price for Their Pound of Flesh*; Camp, *Closer to Freedom*; Owens, *Consent in the Presence of Force*.

7. As Lisa Sowle Cahill has written, "For humans, 'sexuality' is 'morality.' It is part of our expressing, for good or ill, relationship to the material world, to other life forms, to the self, and to other persons, including God." Cahill, "Sexuality and Christian Ethics," 19.

8. Wells-Oghoghomeh, *The Souls of Womenfolk*.

9. Trouillot, *Silencing the Past*, 26.

10. July 15, 1758, "Diary of Jamaica [Bogue estate]," MAB Miss Jmc 6.

11. On the use of the *Gemein Nachrichten* in Moravian worship services, see Beachy, "Manuscript Missions in the Age of Print." As Beachy writes, "the manuscript functioned primarily as a communal devotional organ, circulating reports from Moravian missionaries and communities," 34–35.

12. This version of the journal is now located in the Moravian Archives in Bethlehem, PA. "Diary of Jamaica [Bogue estate], June–Oct 1758," MAB Miss Jmc 7.

13. Maria Schulz, another female missionary, arrived at the same time as Anna Rauch, but she died in December 1757, after one year on the island.

14. On the tense relationship between white and Black women under slavery, see Jones-Rogers, *They Were Her Property*; Glymph, *Out of the House of Bondage*.

15. Fuentes, *Dispossessed Lives*, 5–6.

16. Fuentes, *Dispossessed Lives*, 6.

17. Fuentes, *Dispossessed Lives*, 78, 142.

18. Hartman, "Venus in Two Acts"; Hartman, *Lose Your Mother*.

19. Under slavery, where Black women's parental authority was constantly questioned and undermined by whites, the difficulties of raising a daughter were especially acute. On motherhood and slavery, see especially Morgan, *Laboring Women*; Schwartz, *Born in Bondage*; Turner, *Contested Bodies*; Wells-Oghoghomeh, *The Souls of Womenfolk*.

20. December 23, 1757, "Diary of Jamaica [Bogue estate]," MAB Misc Jmc 4.

21. May 12, 1758, "Caries' Diarium vom Monath May 1758 in Jamaica," *Diarien von Jamaica*, UA R.15.C.b.01.1.

22. May 15, 1758, "Caries' Diarium vom Monath May 1758 in Jamaica," *Diarien von Jamaica*, UA R.15.C.b.01.1.

23. "Catalogus von den Getaufften Negern in Jamaica vor Br. George Caries," October 12, 1759, UA R.15.C.a.02.5.

24. July 3, 1758, "das Diarium von der Bogue in Jamaica vom Monath July 1758 vor Bethlehem," *Diarien von Jamaica*, UA R.15.C.b.02.1. The original reads, "die Schw Anna gab der Elizabeth einen guten rath, wenn die Blancken sie etwa zwingen wolten mit gewalt ihnen ihre Tochter zu geben vor ihre H. (die noch ein hures Kind ist) wie sie sich dabey zu verhalten habe. Sie nahm es mit danch an u versprach treue darinnen zu beweisen. Eine andere negerinnen hatte eben denselbe rath nötig; die es der Anna mit thränen klagte."

25. October 17, 1761, *Diarien von der Bogue*, UA R.15.C.b.02.1.24. The 1761 portion of the diary is written by the missionary Joseph Powell, who arrived at the Bogue in 1759. Powell's entries are in English, while Rauch wrote in German.

26. October 17, 1761, *Diarien von der Bogue*, UA R.15.C.b.02.1.24.

27. October 27, 1761, *Diarien von der Bogue*, UA R.15.C.b.02.1.24. Together, these two incidents suggest that it was common for white men to alert parents of their intentions. This pervasive threat of violence is evidence of what Emily Owens has called "sexual terror." Owens, *Consent in the Presence of Force*, 73–79.

28. October 3, 1758. *Diarien von der Bogue*, UA R.15.C.b.02.1. On marriage and slavery, see especially Hunter, *Bound in Wedlock*.

29. On the complicated social dynamics of plantation slavery, see especially Glymph, *Out of the House of Bondage*; Wells-Oghoghomeh, *The Souls of Womenfolk*; Turner, *Contested Bodies*.

30. Catalogus von den Getaufften Negern in Jamaica vor Br. George Caries," 1759. UA R.15.Ca.2.5. For a description of the family, see the entry for June 2, 1757: "er ist ein sohn unsers alten Isaac der mit seiner Frau u Kindern eine Ausserwählte famillie ausmacht. Er u 3 von seinen Söhnen viz Joseph, Ignatius u Daniel sind getaufft, u die übrige 4 Kinder die noch June, sind kinder guter Hofnung, die v. uns allen geliebt werden. das 8te Kind von der Famillie wurde von Caries auf worlangen der Eltern noch ehe es aus der Zeit ging (da es etwa 2 Jahr alt war) eingesegnet." "Diary of Jamaica [Bogue estate] 1757," MAB Miss Jmc 4.

31. For scholarship that emphasizes sexual choice, see Wells-Oghoghomeh, *The Souls of Womenfolk*; for the importance of love and courtship under slavery, see Fraser, *Courtship and Love Among the Enslaved in North Carolina*; Hunter, *Bound in Wedlock*; Foster, *'Till Death or Distance Do Us Part*. Many scholars have written excellent analyses of Jacobs's *Incidents*. See especially Hine, "Rape and the Inner Lives of Black Women"; Owens, *Consent in the Presence of Force*, 71–83. Owens argues that the "omnipresent nonphysicalized threat of sexual violence" that Jacobs experiences amounts to "sexual terrorism," and that Jacobs's narrative structure "asks readers to de-exceptionalize physical sexual violence," 74.

32. Jacobs, *Incidents in the Life of a Slave Girl*, 47.

33. Jacobs, *Incidents in the Life of a Slave Girl*, 59.

34. Jacobs, *Incidents in the Life of a Slave Girl*, 86.

35. Jacobs, *Incidents in the Life of a Slave Girl*, 22.

36. July 30, 1758, "Caries Diarium vom Monath Jul: 1758," *Diarien von Jamaica*, UA R.15.C.b.01.1.

37. July 30, 1758, "Caries Diarium vom Monath Jul: 1758," *Diarien von Jamaica*. UA R.15.C.b.01.1. Original German transcription reads: "Nachher hielt ich alle gewohnliche Sontags gelegenheiten im Segen, in der letzten viz der Negers abends wurden wir durch weisse Leute gestört, welche beyn fenster u bey der Thüre stunden, daran der eine seine Hand durchs Gitter steckte, u eine Negerin die er zu seiner Hure gezwungen, wincktе daß sie herrauß aus der Versammlung kommen solte, u wie sie nicht wolte, so steckte er die Hand zur Thüre hinnein u zog sie bey Rock usw. Es störte mich aben nicht weil ich die Versamlung hielt u in meiner Materie ganz drinne war aber m. l. Geschw. sahen den Spectacle u wie sehr unser l. Schwarzen zuhörern, die nicht gerne wollten gestört wurden. Wir Geschw. waren nachher noch bis spät in gesegneten Unterredungen beysammen."

38. July 30, 1758, "Diarium von der Bogue in Jamaica vom Monath July 1758 vor Bethlehem," *Diarien von der Bogue*, UA R.15.C.b.02.1.

39. See the entries for December 20, 1757, "Diary of Jamaica [Bogue estate], 1757." MAB Miss Jmc 4; February 13, 1758, "Diarium der kleinen Gemeine in Jamaica vom Monath

Feb 1758," *Diarien von Jamaica*, UA R.15.C.b.01.1; for his whipping, see December 25, 1758, "Das Diarium von der Bogue in Jamaica, vom Monath December 1758 vor Bethlehem," *Diarien von der Bogue*, UA R.15.C.b.02.1.

40. Vermeulen, "Thomas Thistlewood's Libidinal Linnaean Project," 19. For a material history of the Thistlewood manuscripts and their prominence for historical scholarship, see Gerbner, "Archival Violence, Archival Capital."

41. Thistlewood's diaries are available online at Yale's Beinecke Library: Thomas Thistlewood papers, https://beinecke.library.yale.edu/collections/highlights/thomas-thistlewood-papers.

42. See, for example, Chenoweth, *The 18th Century Climate of Jamaica*; Sheridan, "Slave Medicine in Jamaica," 1; Morgan, "Slaves and Livestock." For a full examination of the scholarship on Thistlewood, see Gerbner, "Archival Violence Archival Capital."

43. Burnard, *Mastery, Tyranny, and Desire*.

44. Burnard, *Mastery, Tyranny, and Desire*, 157.

45. Vermeulen, "Thomas Thistlewood's Libidinal Linnaean Project," 19. See also Hartman, "Venus in Two Acts."

46. Hartman, "Venus in Two Acts," 6.

47. Aside from the entries for July 14–15, 1758, see the entries for July 3, 1758, and August 13, 1758, *Diarien von der Bogue*, UA R.15.C.b.02.1.

48. Thomas Thistlewood, *Diary*, July 15, 1758, BLY. https://collections.library.yale.edu/catalog/11874015. I am grateful to Trevor Burnard for allowing me to use his transcriptions of the Thistlewood diaries.

49. Wells-Oghoghomeh, *The Souls of Womenfolk*, 5.

50. Wells-Oghoghomeh, *The Souls of Womenfolk*, 5–6, 94–97. On dealing with maternal grief and loss, see also Turner, "The Nameless and the Forgotten."

51. Wells-Oghoghomeh, *The Souls of Womenfolk*, 123.

52. Wells-Oghoghomeh, *The Souls of Womenfolk*, 124–27.

53. Wells-Oghoghomeh, *The Souls of Womenfolk*, 122.

54. While Moravians were radical in many of their beliefs about sexuality, by the 1750s, they believed that sex should be confined to marital relationships. On Moravian sexual practices and ideas about gender, see Fogleman, *Jesus Is Female*. For the "sifting time" in Moravian history, see Peucker, *A Time of Sifting*.

55. One Black Christian man named Alexander challenged the missionaries on this point, explaining to them that neither whites nor Blacks on the island maintained monogamous marriages. West African family structures were often polygamous, while whites took advantage of their power to rape enslaved people with regularity. Aside from these issues, the missionaries also acknowledged that even when a man and a woman sought to maintain a monogamous marriage, one partner could be sold off the island at any point. Gerbner, *Christian Slavery*, chaps. 7–8.

56. In 1749, during a set of conferences on Saint Thomas, the Moravians concluded that men with multiple wives could join the congregation, but they were not allowed to divorce any of their spouses after their baptism. Congregants with multiple spouses were also prevented from holding leadership positions within the church. The flexible policy was mostly a concession to Black men with authority. For more on this, see Gerbner, *Christian Slavery*, chap. 8.

57. See, for example, July 22, 1759, *Diarien von Carmel,* UA R.15.C.b.02.2: "Die Elisabeth eine getauffte Negerinnen welche gestern von der Bogue zum besuch zu uns gekommen und an welcher wir freude haben, auch die Schwestern sich sehr viel mit ihr zu thun machten, ging nachmittags gestärckt u sel. wieder nach hause."

58. July 25, 1761, *Diarien von der Bogue,* UA R.15.C.b.02.1.21.

5. POLICING BODIES, SAVING SOULS

1. Christian Heinrich to Brethren, June 27, 1758, UA R.15.C.a.01.29. Rauch also criticized Caries for preaching to white people too frequently, for mishandling funds, and on several other counts. In this chapter, I focus on Rauch's complaints about baptism and the Maroons because those were more important for Afro-Moravians.

2. "Catalogus von den Getaufften Negern in Jamaica vor Br. George Caries," October 12, 1759, UA R.15.Ca.02.5.

3. Caries to Spangenberg, October 14, 1757. MAB Miss Jmc 32.4. The fact that women outnumbered men in the baptismal ceremonies during these years is not surprising. Black women played an important role in building the "religio-nation" of the congregation, but Caries refused to baptize women until a female missionary arrived. Moreover, as we saw in chapter 4, enslaved women—and especially enslaved mothers—sought out Anna Rauch in the hopes that she could use her influence to protect their families. Still, the low baptismal numbers are striking.

4. The few histories of the early mission that exist have drawn from J. H. Buchner's 1854 account, which uses Caries's and Rauch's diaries as its sources. Buchner, *The Moravians in Jamaica*; Hastings and MacLeavy, *Seedtime and Harvest*; Dunn, *Moravian Missionaries at Work*.

5. On spaces of correlation, see Fromont, *The Art of Conversion*.

6. Rauch biography, MAB. Sources: *Lebenslauf* in R.22.1b.128; *Gemein Nachrichten* 1764, Bd. 6, S. 500ff.

7. Loskiel and Latrobe, *History of the Mission,* pt. 2, 7.

8. Loskiel and Latrobe, *History of the Mission,* pt. 2, 8–9.

9. Loskiel and Latrobe, *History of the Mission,* pt. 2, 9–13; Wheeler, *To Live upon Hope,* 70–72.

10. Wheeler, *To Live upon Hope,* 72–73, 80–82.

11. Loskiel and Latrobe, *History of the Mission,* pt. 2, 10–14; Wheeler, *To Live upon Hope,* 72–73.

12. Loskiel and Latrobe, *History of the Mission,* pt. 2, 20–21. Tschoop was unable to make the journey due to a lame leg. Wheeler, *To Live upon Hope,* 72–73.

13. Loskiel and Latrobe, *History of the Mission,* pt. 2, 26–27. For the Moravians, the baptism of the first Mohicans was a momentous event. It took on special significance in 1742 because by that point, it had become clear that Count Ludwig von Zinzendorf's effort to establish a broad ecumenical "Church of God in the Spirit," a nondenominational union of different groups of German Protestants, was failing. In Oley, Zinzendorf and the Moravians had planned a third ecumenical synod to build support for their "Church of God in the Spirit," but several groups—disillusioned after the first

two synods—had already dropped out. As the Moravians' ecumenical vision collapsed, their "heathen" missions took on increased importance. Wheeler, *To Live upon Hope*, 73–74. See also Atwood, *Community of the Cross*; Vogt, "Zinzendorf und die Pennsylvanischen Synoden."

14. Loskiel and Latrobe, *History of the Mission*, pt. 2, 29. It is notable that Zinzendorf did not seem opposed to the conversion of entire nations on principle but rather believed that it currently did "not... appear to be at hand." As a result, as he wrote in Article 2, "great attention and faithful care should be bestowed upon the few who are converted." Article 3 reiterated the sparing approach to baptism: While the gospel should be "preached to all who will hear it," baptism should be bestowed only on those "in whom true life from God, and a living faith in Jesus Christ, is perceptible."

15. Loskiel and Latrobe, *History of the Mission*, pt. 2, 29.

16. Loskiel and Latrobe, *History of the Mission*, pt. 2, 29–30.

17. Wheeler, *To Live upon Hope*, 76–77. English colonists were also suspicious of the Mohican Christians—a suspicion that helped to facilitate settler colonial dispossession of Mohican lands. Tschoop, who refused to leave Shekomeko with the group of Mohicans who moved to the Moravian community at Bethlehem, died of smallpox in 1746. Shabash also refused to leave Shekomeko and continued to preach even after the ban against Moravian preaching in 1744. By 1747, however, white creditors forced him and other Mohicans off their land, and he and his wife, who was pregnant, moved to the Moravian community of Gnadenhütten. Wheeler, *To Live upon Hope*, 77–78.

18. Rauch was chosen in order to assess the state of Saint Thomas and to strengthen the connection between Saint Thomas and Bethlehem, the newly founded Moravian community in Pennsylvania. Oldendorp, *Historie der caribischen Inseln*, 2: 625–26. For more on Rauch's 1745 visit to Saint Thomas, see Kaelin, *Women, Race, and the Moravian Church*, chap 6. I am grateful to Kelly Kaelin for sharing her manuscript draft with me.

19. On the early history of the Moravian mission in Saint Thomas, including the precarious relationship between the Moravian missionaries and the colonial government, see Sensbach, *Rebecca's Revival*; Gerbner, *Christian Slavery*, chaps. 7–8.

20. Rauch, July 19, 1745, *Journal from New York to Saint Thomas, June 13–October 2, 1745*, MAB JD V 1.

21. Oldendorp, *Historie der caribischen Inseln*, 2: 1122.

22. January 15, 1757, "Diary of Jamaica [Bogue estate]," MAB Miss Jmc 3.

23. January 18–22, 1757, "Diary of Jamaica [Bogue estate]," MAB Miss Jmc 3.

24. January 23, 1757, "Diary of Jamaica [Bogue estate]," MAB Miss Jmc 3.

25. February 5, 1757, "Diary of Jamaica [Bogue estate], 1757," MAB Miss Jmc 4.

26. February 6, 1757, "Diary of Jamaica [Bogue estate], 1757," MAB Miss Jmc 4.

27. April 28–30, 1757, "Diary of Jamaica [Bogue estate], 1757," MAB Miss Jmc 4.

28. March 30, 1757, "Diary of Jamaica [Bogue estate], 1757," MAB Miss Jmc 4.

29. February 14, 1757, "Diary of Jamaica [Bogue estate], 1757," MAB Miss Jmc 4.

30. April 4, 1757, and April 7, 1757, "Diary of Jamaica [Bogue estate], 1757," MAB Miss Jmc 4.

31. April 24, 1757, "Diary of Jamaica [Bogue estate], 1757," MAB Miss Jmc 4.

32. April 26, 1757, and June 7, 1757, "Diary of Jamaica [Bogue estate]", 1757, MAB Miss Jmc 4.

33. Caries to Spangenberg, January 23, 1757, MAB Miss Jmc 32.2.

34. "Von Br Christian Henrich," *Gemein Nachrichten* 8 (1757) UA GN.A.60 (XXXVI–LII), 123–24.

35. Von Br Carl Schulzens d.d. February 2, 1757, *Gemein Nachrichten* 8 (1757), UA GN.A.60 (XXXVI-LII), 124–26.

36. Spangenberg to Rauch, July 9, 1757, MAB Miss Jmc 33.2.

37. Spangenberg to Caries, July 9, 1757, MAB Miss Jmc 33.3.

38. Spangenberg to Rauch, July 9, 1757, MAB Miss Jmc 33.2.

39. July 20, 1757, *Jamaica Diary [Bogue estate] 1757*, MAB Miss Jmc 4.

40. Caries to Böhler, August 17, 1757, *Zacharias George Caries Diarium, Oktober 1754-Dezember 1757*. UA R.15.C.a.05. Note: The letter is inside the 1757 diary.

41. Caries to Böhler, August 17, 1757, *Zacharias George Caries Diarium, Oktober 1754–Dezember 1757*. UA R.15.C.a.05. Note: The letter is inside the 1757 diary.

42. Caries to Spangenberg, October 14, 1757. MAB Miss Jmc 32.4.

43. Rauch to Spangenberg, October 19, 1757, MAB Miss Jmc 32.5. Rauch's letter to Spangenberg also went into detail about English laws about religion and slavery. Rauch noted that he had been researching English law books and had found a 1696 Jamaica act to encourage slave conversion. Rauch was very pleased with this discovery and hoped he could use it to support their mission.

44. Caries to Spangenberg, October 14, 1757. MAB Miss Jmc 32.4.

45. Caries to Spangenberg, December 13, 1757, MAB Miss Jmc 32.6.

46. Oldendorp, *Historie der caribischen Inseln*, 1: 462.

47. Oldendorp, *Historie der caribischen Inseln*, 1: 462–64.

48. Oldendorp, *Historie der caribischen Inseln*, 1: 462–64.

49. "Catalogus von den Getaufften Negern in Jamaica vor Br. George Caries," UA R.15.Ca.02.5.

50. Christian Heinrich to Brethren, June 27, 1758, UA R.15.Ca.2.29.

51. Conference 5, #6, Minutes from the Conferences on Jamaica, September 28, 1759. West Indies Visits and Visitation 1740–1785, MAB WI 177.4. Note that the Herrnhut version (UA R.15.C.a.01.3.e) is mostly identical but has one extra conference.

52. Conference 5, #7, Minutes from the Conferences on Jamaica, September 28, 1759. MAB WI 177.4.

53. For a full elaboration of this point, see Gerbner, *Christian Slavery*, chap. 8.

54. Conference 5, #17–20, Minutes from the Conferences on Jamaica, September 28, 1759. MAB WI 177.4.

55. Conference 1, #3, Minutes from the Conferences on Jamaica, August 30, 1759. MAB WI 177.4.

56. Conference 5, #12, Minutes from the Conferences on Jamaica, September 28, 1759. MAB WI 177.4.

57. Wells-Oghoghomeh, *The Souls of Womenfolk*.

58. Conference 4, #4, Minutes from the Conferences on Jamaica, September 27, 1759. MAB WI 177.4.

59. Conference 1, #8 and #9, Minutes from the Conferences on Jamaica, August 30, 1759. MAB WI 177.4.

60. Conference 5, #18, Minutes from the Conferences on Jamaica, September 28, 1759. MAB WI 177.4.

6. CONSTRUCTING RELIGION, DEFINING CRIME

Parts of this chapter are drawn from my chapter "Rebellion and Religion," in Johnson and Wenger, eds., *Religion and US Empire* (NYU Press, 2022), 19–40. I am grateful for permission to reprint portions of my chapter.

1. May 26, 1760, *Diarien von Mesopotamia 1759–1761, 1763 and 1765*, UA R.15.C.b.01.3.

2. The best history of the rebellion is Brown, *Tacky's Revolt*. See also Brown, "Slave Revolt in Jamaica, 1760–1761: A Cartographic Narrative," http://revolt.axismaps.com/, which visualizes the movement of rebels on the island. For a study that places Tacky's Revolt in the framework of imperial warfare, see Bollettino, "Slavery, War, and Britain's Atlantic Empire."

3. On policing and Obeah, see especially Paton, "'Obeah Acts'"; Bryson, "The Art of Power"; Paton, "The Trials of Inspector Thomas." For the criminalization of Obeah and other African diasporic religions in the Caribbean, see Handler and Bilby, *Enacting Power*, chap. 4; Stewart, *Three Eyes for the Journey*; Boaz, *Banning Black Gods*, chap. 7; Hucks and Stewart, *Obeah, Orisa and Religious Identity*. For additional resources and information on the history of policing and religious freedom in the Caribbean from the eighteenth century to the present, see "Obeah Histories" at https://obeahhistories.org/ and "Caribbean Religious Trials" at https://www.caribbeanreligioustrials.org/.

4. The literature on this subject is vast. My analysis draws especially from Smith, "Religion, Religions, Religious"; Chidester, *Empire of Religion*; Chidester, *Savage Systems*; Boaz, *Banning Black Gods*; Wenger, *We Have a Religion*; McNally, *Defend the Sacred*; Johnson et al., *Ekklesia*.

5. Klassen, "Spiritual Jurisdictions," in Johnson et al., *Ekklesia*, 110.

6. On the disputed etymology of the word *religion*, see Smith, "Religion, Religions, Religious," 269.

7. Johnson et al., *Ekklesia*, 4–7.

8. On "lived religion," see especially the essays in Hall, *Lived Religion in America*.

9. Hucks, *Obeah, Orisa, and Religious Identity*, xi. See also Hucks, "Perspectives in Lived History."

10. *Diarien von Mesopotamien*, UA R.15.C.b.01.3. For more on the Mesopotamia mission, see Dunn, *A Tale of Two Plantations*, chap. 6.

11. May 27, 1760, *Diarien von Mesopotamien*, UA R.15.C.b.01.3.

12. May 27, 1760, *Diarien von Mesopotamien*, UA R.15.C.b.01.3.

13. May 28 and June 3, 1760, *Diarien von Mesopotamien*, UA R.15.C.b.01.3.

14. June 1 and June 10, 1760, *Diarien von Mesopotamien*, UA R.15.C.b.01.3.

15. June 10, 1760, *Diarien von Mesopotamien*, UA R.15.C.b.01.3.

16. June 22, 1760, *Diarien von Mesopotamien*, UA R.15.C.b.01.3. Original German: "Unser neger haben heute in ihren Plantagen einen von den Rebellen gefangen; der eben geschäfftig war, sich seine Mord-Meßer Scharff zu machen. Sie verwahrten ihn in dem

Stock bis sie ihn dem Mr. Macfarlane überantworten konten. Unser negers haben sich dadurch in der nachbarschafft sehr Legitimirt." By "ihren Plantagen," the missionaries were referring to the small gardens where the enslaved grew their own food. The following day, the rebel was found guilty of "murdering 2 children" and burned alive. June 23, 1760, *Diarien von Mesopotamien*, UA R.15.C.b.01.3.

17. January 5, 1761, *Diarien von der Bogue, 1758–1761*, UA R.15.C.b.02.1.21. "Had been this Night of the Rebbels all round the plantation, who early in the morning w[e]re Discover'd by several of our Negros who immediatly w[e]re form'd in Companys & sent in p[e]rsuit of them but found nothing except whare they had lodg'd near [?] from whence brack'd them into the River."

18. Kars, "Dodging Rebellion."

19. Kars, "Dodging Rebellion," 41; Kars, *Blood on the River*, 90–92.

20. November 6, 1760, *Diarien von Mesopotamien*, UA R.15.C.b.01.3.

21. November 4, 1760, *Diarien von der Bogue*, UA R.15.C.b.02.1.20. "Br & Sister Returne'd to Carmel had account of part of a Company of the Rebbel Negros being taken, as also of several innocent Slav[e]s being killed by the Company sent against the Rebbels."

22. December 15, 1760, *Diarien von der Bogue*, UA R.15.C.b.02.1.20. December 15, 1760: "had Accounts from an Adjacent Neighbourhood of Som[e] Slav[e]s being kill'd, others taken alive by the Rebbels after which the Company here went in p[u]rsuit."

23. June 26, 1760, *Diarien von Mesopotamien*, UA R.15.C.b.01.3.

24. July 2, 1760, *Diarien von der Bogue*, UA R.15.C.b.02.1.18.

25. June 26, 1760, *Diarien von Mesopotamien*, UA R.15.C.b.01.3. See also July 22, 1760, and September 3, 1760, *Diarien von der Bogue, 1758–1761*, UA R.15.C.b.02.1.

26. July 4, 1760, *Diarien von Mesopotamien*, UA R.15.C.b.01.3.

27. July 11 and 12, 1760, *Diarien von Mesopotamien*, UA R.15.C.b.01.3.

28. July 13, 1760, *Diarien von Mesopotamien*, UA R.15.C.b.01.3.

29. Luke 6:21 and 25, King James Version; October 12, 1760, *Diarien von der Bogue*, UA R.15.C.b.02.1.19.

30. October 12, 1760, *Diarien von der Bogue*, UA R.15.C.b.02.1.19.

31. On October 21, Powell wrote that an estate about five miles from Island estate was destroyed. *Diarien von der Bogue*, UA R.15.C.b.02.1.19.

32. November 7, 1760, *Diarien von der Bogue*, UA R.15.C.b.02.1.20. "Nov 7—In Evening came several of the Baptiz'd who hitherto have liv'd like other Heathen, they seem'd under som consern; said they w[e]re too much Convinst that we w[e]re thare only & best friends, who earnest & truly sought thare Happyness, hoping time to com, better to emprove, each Opportunity."

33. November 19, 1760, *Diarien von der Bogue*, UA R.15.C.b.02.1.20.

34. December 2, 1760, *Diarien von der Bogue*, UA R.15.C.b.02.1.20: "In Evening about 10 O Clock I came on a Wicked company unawars, Assembel'd in Andrews a Baptis'd Negros Hous. who tho immediatly scatter'd yet soon after assembil'd a gain, Disturb'd the Overseear who sharply chastis'd & Rebuk't them."

35. Robertson, "Giving Directions in Spanish Town"; Robertson, "Architectures of Confidence?"

36. With the exception of a three-year stint in Kingston, 1755–58. Robertson, "Giving Directions in Spanish Town." See also Robertson, "Architectures of Confidence?"

37. Act 134, 1744, *Acts of Assembly*, vol. 1.
38. Robertson, "Architectures of Confidence?," 239.
39. Robertson, "Architectures of Confidence?," 250.
40. Robertson, "Architectures of Confidence?," 239.
41. Long, *The History of Jamaica*, 1:10.
42. Long, *The History of Jamaica*, 1:49. On the importance of oath-taking practice in the British Caribbean, see Ogborn, "The Power of Speech."
43. Johnson et al., *Ekklesia*.
44. Long, *The History of Jamaica*, 1:26.
45. Edwards, *The History, Civil and Commercial*, 1:206–7. For the role of the bishop of London in the American colonies, see Yeo, "A Case Without Parallel"; Bennett, "English Bishops"; Hunte, "Protestantism and Slavery," 87–89.
46. *Acts of Assembly*, 1787, vol. 2. See also Beasley, *Christian Ritual*.
47. Gerbner, *Christian Slavery*, chap 2.
48. "An Act for the better Order and Government of Slaves," 1696, *Acts of Assembly*, 1787, vol. 2.
49. "An Act for the better Order and Government of Slaves," 1696, *Acts of Assembly*, 1787, vol. 2.
50. May, "Holy Rebellion."
51. Rebels in St. Mary's Parish started the revolt early—on Easter—thereby weakening the impact of the rebellion. It is unclear why the St. Mary's rebels chose Easter. It may have been a miscommunication, or there could have been another precipitating factor.
52. "An Act to Remedy the Evils arising from irregular Assemblies of Slaves," Jamaica 1760, in CO 139/21. Historical background and Obeah-related sections of the act are available at "Obeah Histories" (blog), accessed November 27, 2024, https://Obeahhistories.org/1760-jamaica-law/.
53. The language of "superstition" and the 1760 act's focus on specific material objects can also be connected to European discourse about the "fetish" in Africa and the Atlantic World. On the history of the "fetish," see Pietz, "The Problem of the Fetish"; Johnson, *African American Religions*, chap. 2.
54. Paton, *The Cultural Politics of Obeah*, 40–41.
55. "An Act to Remedy the Evils," 1760, emphasis added.
56. Paton, *The Cultural Politics of Obeah*, 40–41.
57. January 26, 1761, *Diarien von Mesopotamien*, UA R.15.C.b.01.3.
58. Brown, *Tacky's Revolt*, 131; Bollettino, "Slavery, War, and Britain's Atlantic Empire," 21.
59. Long, *The History of Jamaica*, 2:447–72; Brown, *Tacky's Revolt*, 160–61.
60. August 24, 1761, *Diarien von Mesopotamien*, UA R.15.C.b.01.3. Jery was known as "Sharry" in the archival documents kept by the attorneys at the Mesopotamia estate. He was born in West Africa and arrived at Mesopotamia sometime between 1744–1751. Richard Dunn has noted that he worked in the boiling house during the harvest and as a rat catcher the rest of the year. See Dunn, *A Tale of Two Plantations*, 237. The Foster Barhams have one of the most extensive account books in the eighteenth century, and it can be fruitfully compared to the Moravian records. The Barham papers are available at the Bodleian Library at Oxford University. For the year 1760, see BLO MS. Clar. dep. b. 37/1.
61. "Katalog der Getauften in Jamaica," UA R.15.C.a.2.9.a.

62. Wenger, *We Have a Religion*; McNally, *Defend the Sacred*.

63. For the 1676 Barbados conspiracy, see Gerbner, "The Ultimate Sin."

64. For the 1712 rebellion in New York, see Glasson, *Mastering Christianity*; Gerbner, *Christian Slavery*, chap. 6.

65. Gerbner, *Christian Slavery*, chap. 3; Gerbner, "Rebellion and Religion." On Vesey's conspiracy, see Egerton, *He Shall Go Out Free*; Egerton and Paquette, *The Denmark Vesey Affair*; Schipper, "On Such Texts Comment Is Unnecessary." For Nat Turner's rebellion, see Tomlins, *In the Matter of Nat Turner*.

66. I elaborate upon this point in Gerbner, "Rebellion and Religion." Some sections of this conclusion are revised from that article.

67. Fundamental Constitutions of Carolina, 1669, clause 97. The full text of the act is available at https://avalon.law.yale.edu/17th_century/nc05.asp. See also Wenger, *Religious Freedom*, introduction. I write more extensively about this in Gerbner, "Rebellion and Religion."

68. For example, Jamaican Maroons now use the term "Science" rather than "Obeah." For an analysis of this shift, see Gerbner, "Maroon Science."

EPILOGUE

1. Caries, October 5, 1756, "Diary of Jamaica [Bogue estate]," MAB Miss Jmc 3.
2. Brooks, "Awikhigawôgan Ta Pildowi Ôjmowôgan," 264.
3. October 17, 1757, "Diary of Jamaica [Bogue estate]," MAB Miss Jmc 4.

Bibliography

ARCHIVAL SOURCES

BL   British Library
BLO   Bodleian Library, Oxford, England
BLY   Beinecke Library, Yale University, New Haven, Connecticut
CO   Colonial Office, National Archives (Kew), London, England
CSP   Calendar of State Papers, Colonial Series
MAB   Moravian Archives, Bethlehem, Pennsylvania*
MCH   Moravian Church House, London, England
UA   Unitätsarchiv der Evangelischen Brüder-Unität, Herrnhut, Germany
WISC   West Indies Special Collections, University of the West Indies, Mona, Jamaica

*The archival records at the Moravian Archives in Bethlehem, Pennsylvania, have been digitized at https://www.moravianchurcharchives.findbuch.net/php/main.php#4d6973734a6d63.

PUBLISHED PRIMARY SOURCES

Acts of Assembly, Passed in the Island of Jamaica; from 1681, to 1754, inclusive. Jamaica: Curtis Brett and Company, 1756.
Acts of Assembly, Passed in the Island of Jamaica, from the Year 1681 to the Year 1769 Inclusive. 2 vols. Kingston, Jamaica: Printed by Alexander Aikman, 1787.
Acts of Assembly, Passed in the Island of Jamaica, from the Year 1681 to the Year 1769 Inclusive. Vol. 2. 2 vols. Kingston, Jamaica: Printed by Alexander Aikman, 1787.
Behn, Aphra. *Oroonoko.* Edited by Janet Todd. London: Penguin Classics, 2004.
Bosman, Willem. *A New and Accurate Description of the Coast of Guinea.* London: J. Knapton, 1721.
Buchner, J. H. *The Moravians in Jamaica: History of the Mission of the United Brethren's Church to the Negroes in the Island of Jamaica from the Year 1754 to 1854.* London: Longman, Brown, 1854.

Cranz, David. *The Ancient and Modern History of the Brethren: Or, a Succinct Narrative of the Protestant Church of the United Brethren, or, Unitas Fratrum, in the Remoter Ages, and Particularly in the Present Century*. London: W. and A. Strahan, 1780.

Cranz, David. *The History of Greenland: Containing a Description of the Country, and Its Inhabitants: And Particularly, a Relation of the Mission, Carried on for Above These Thirty Years by the Unitas Fratrum, at New Herrnhuth and Lichtenfels, in That Country*. 2 vols. London: Brethren's Society for the Furtherance of the Gospel Among the Heathen, 1767.

Dallas, Robert Charles. *The History of the Maroons: From Their Origin to the Establishment of Their Chief Tribe at Sierra Leone, Including the Expedition to Cuba, for the Purpose of Procuring Spanish Chasseurs, and the State of the Island of Jamaica for the Last Ten Years, with a Succinct History of the Island Previous to That Period*. Vol. 1. London: A. Strahan, 1803.

Edwards, Bryan. *The History, Civil and Commercial, of the British Colonies in the West Indies*. 2 vols. Dublin: Luke White, 1793.

Equiano, Olaudah. *The Interesting Narrative of the Life of Olaudah Equiano, or Gustavus Vassa, the African. Written by Himself*. London: Printed for the author, 1789.

Hall, Richard. *Acts, Passed in the Island of Barbados. From 1643, to 1762, Inclusive*. London: Printed for Richard Hall, 1764.

Hughes, Griffith. *The Natural History of Barbados*. London: Printed for the author, 1750.

Jacobs, Harriet. *Incidents in the Life of a Slave Girl*. Boston: Published for the author, 1861.

Jamaica Assembly and Bryan Edwards. *The Proceedings of the Governor and Assembly of Jamaica, in Regard to the Maroon Negroes*. London: J. Stockdale, 1796. https://catalog.hathitrust.org/Record/001465229.

Journals of the Assembly of Jamaica. Vol. 3. Jamaica: Alexander Aikman, 1797. https://dds.crl.edu/crldelivery/19317.

Journals of the Assembly of Jamaica. Vol. 5. Jamaica: Alexander Aikman, 1709. https://dds.crl.edu/crldelivery/19317.

Knight, James. *The Natural, Moral, and Political History of Jamaica and the Territories Thereon Depending: From the First Discovery of the Island by Christopher Columbus, to the Year 1746*. Edited by Jack P. Greene and Taylor Stoermer. Charlottesville: University of Virginia Press, 2021.

Koelle, S. W. *Polyglotta Africana: Or, a Comparative Vocabulary of Nearly Three Hundred Words and Phrases in More Than One Hundred Distinct African Languages*. London: Church Missionary House, 1854.

Leslie, Charles. *A New and Exact Account of Jamaica*. Edinburgh: R. Fleming, 1739.

Long, Edward. *The History of Jamaica. Or, General Survey of the Antient and Modern State of That Island with Reflections on Its Situation, Settlements, Inhabitants, Climate, Products, Commerce, Laws, and Government*. 3 vols. London: T. Lowndes, 1774.

Loskiel, George Henry, and Christian Ignatius Latrobe. *History of the Mission of the United Brethren among the Indians in North America*. . . . London: Brethren's Society for the Furtherance of the Gospel, 1794. https://catalog.hathitrust.org/Record/000559376.

McCord, David J., and Thomas Cooper, eds. *The Statutes at Large of South Carolina*. Vol. 7. Columbia, SC: Johnston, 1840. https://babel.hathitrust.org/cgi/pt?id=nyp.33433090745146&seq=7.

Moreton, J. B. *West India Customs and Manners: Containing Strictures on the Soil, Cultivation, Produce, Trade, Officers, and Inhabitants: With the Method of Establishing, and Conducting a Sugar Plantation. To Which Is Added, the Practice of Training New Slaves. A New Edition.* London: Printed for J. Parsons, Paternoster Row; W. Richardson, Royal Exchange; H. Gardner, Strand; and J. Walter, Piccadilly, 1793.

Oldendorp, C. G. A. *A Caribbean Mission.* Edited by Johann Jakob Bossart. Translated by Arnold R. Highfield and Vladimir Barac. Ann Arbor, MI: Karoma, 1987.

Oldendorp, C. G. A. *Historie der Caribischen Inseln Sanct Thomas, Sanct Crux und Sanct Jan: insbesondere der dasigen Neger und der Mission der evangelischen Brüder unter denselben.* Edited by Gudrun Meier, Stephan Palmié, Peter Stein, and Horst Ulbricht. Vol. 1. Berlin: Verlag für Wissenschaft und Bildung, 2000.

Oldendorp, C. G. A. *Historie der Caribischen Inseln Sanct Thomas, Sanct Crux und Sanct Jan, insbesondere der dasigen Neger und der Mission der evangelischen Brüder unter denselben.* Edited by Gudrun Meier, Hartmut Beck, Stephan Palmié, Aart H. van Soest, Peter Stein, and Horst Ulbricht. Vol. 2. Berlin: Verlag für Wissenschaft und Bildung, 2002.

Protten, Christian. *En nyttig grammaticalsk Indledelse til tvende hidintil gandske ubekiendte Sprog, Fanteisk og Acraisk, (paa Guldküsten udi Guinea), efter den danske Pronunciation og Udtale.* Copenhagen: Gottmann Friderich Kisel, 1764.

Spangenberg, August Gottlieb. *An Exposition of Christian Doctrine, as Taught in the Protestant Church of the United Brethren, or, Unitas Fratrum.* London: W. and A. Strahan, 1784.

Thicknesse, Philip. *Memoirs and Anecdotes of Philip Thicknesse, Late Lieutenant Governor of Land Guard Fort, and Unfortunately Father to George Touchet, Baron Audley.* Dublin: Printed by Graisberry and Campbell for William Jones, 1790.

SECONDARY SOURCES

Aarons, John A., Jeannette A. Bastian, and Stanley H. Griffin, eds. *Archiving Caribbean Identity: Records, Community, and Memory.* London: Routledge, 2022.

Aarons, John A., and Helena Leonce. "Diasporic, Displaced, Alienated or Shared: Caribbean Literary Archives." In Lowry, *Disputed Archival Heritage.* London: Routledge, 2022.

Achebe, Nwando. "Igbo Goddesses and the Priests and Male Priestesses Who Serve Them." In *Igbo in the Atlantic World*, edited by Toyin Falola and Raphael Chijioke Njoku, 28–45. African Origins and Diasporic Destinations. Bloomington: Indiana University Press, 2016.

Agorsah, E. Kofi, ed. *Maroon Heritage: Archaeological. Ethnographic and Historical Perspectives.* Kingston, Jamaica: Canoe, 1994.

Agorsah, E. Kofi. "Spiritual Vibrations of Historic Kormantse and the Search for African Diaspora Identity and Freedom." In *Materialities of Ritual in the Black Atlantic*, edited by Akinwumi Ogundiran and Paula Saunders, 87–107. Bloomington: Indiana University Press, 2014.

Akinjogbin, I. A. *Dahomey and Its Neighbours, 1708–1818.* Cambridge: Cambridge University Press, 1967.

Akyeampong, Emmanuel. *Between the Sea and the Lagoon: An Eco-Social History of the Anlo of Southeastern Ghana c. 1850 to Recent Times.* Athens: Ohio University Press, 2001.

Akyeampong, Emmanuel. "Sexuality and Prostitution Among the Akan of the Gold Coast c. 1650–1950." *Past & Present* 156 (1997): 144–73.

Amussen, Susan Dwyer. *Caribbean Exchanges: Slavery and the Transformation of English Society, 1640–1700.* Chapel Hill: University of North Carolina Press, 2007.

Andrews, Edward E. *Native Apostles: Black and Indian Missionaries in the British Atlantic World.* Cambridge, MA: Harvard University Press, 2013.

Asad, Talal. *Formations of the Secular: Christianity, Islam, Modernity.* Stanford, CA: Stanford University Press, 2003.

Asad, Talal. *Genealogies of Religion: Discipline and Reasons of Power in Christianity and Islam.* Baltimore MD: Johns Hopkins University Press, 2009.

Asiwaju, A. I., and Robin Law. "From the Volta to the Niger, 1600–1800." In *History of West Africa*, edited by J. F. A. Ajayi and Michael Crowder. 3rd ed., 1:412–64. New York: Longman, 1985.

Atwood, Craig D. *Community of the Cross: Moravian Piety in Colonial Bethlehem.* University Park: Pennsylvania State University Press, 2012.

Atwood, Craig D. "Understanding Zinzendorf's blood and wounds theology." *Journal of Moravian History* 1 (2006), 31–47.

Bailey, Richard A. *Race and Redemption in Puritan New England.* 1st ed. Oxford: Oxford University Press, 2011.

Baldauf, Ingeborg. "Christian Georg Andreas Oldendorp als Historiker." In Meier et al., *Christian Georg Andreas Oldendorp*, 81–140.

Barry, Boubacar. *Senegambia and the Atlantic Slave Trade.* Translated by Ayi Kwei Armah. Cambridge: Cambridge University Press, 1998.

Bascom, William. *Sixteen Cowries: Yoruba Divination from Africa to the New World.* Bloomington: Indiana University Press, 1980.

Bastian, Jeannette A., John A. Aarons, and Stanley H. Griffin, eds., *Decolonizing the Caribbean Record: An Archives Reader.* Sacramento, CA:Littwin Books, 2018.

Bayne, Brandon. *Missions Begin with Blood: Suffering and Salvation in the Borderlands of New Spain.* New York: Fordham University Press, 2022.

Bayne, Brandon. "Willy-Nilly Baptisms and Chichimeca Freedoms: Missionary Disputes, Indigenous Desires and the 1695 O'odham Revolt." *Journal of Early Modern History* 21, nos. 1–2 (2017): 9–37.

Beachy, Robert. "Manuscript Missions in the Age of Print: Moravian Community in the Atlantic World." In *Pious Pursuits*, edited by Robert Beachy and Michele Gillespie, 33–49. German Moravians in the Atlantic World. New York: Berghahn Books, 2007.

Beasley, Nicholas M. *Christian Ritual and the Creation of British Slave Societies, 1650–1780.* Athens: University of Georgia Press, 2010.

Beck, Hartmut. *Brüder in Vielen Völkern: 250 Jahre Mission der Brüdergemeine.* Erlangen: Verlag der Evangelischen-Lutherischen Mission, 1981.

Beliso-De Jesús, Aisha M. *Electric Santería: Racial and Sexual Assemblages of Transnational Religion.* New York: Columbia University Press, 2015.

Beliso-De Jesús, Aisha M. *Excited Delirium: Race, Police Violence, and the Invention of a Disease*. Durham, NC: Duke University Press, 2024.
Bennett, Herman L. *African Kings and Black Slaves: Sovereignty and Dispossession in the Early Modern Atlantic*. Philadelphia: University of Pennsylvania Press, 2018.
Bennett, J. H. "English Bishops and Imperial Jurisdiction 1660–1725." *Historical Magazine of the Protestant Episcopal Church* 32, no. 3 (1964): 175–88.
Berry, Daina Ramey. *The Price for Their Pound of Flesh: The Value of the Enslaved, from Womb to Grave, in the Building of a Nation*. Boston: Beacon Press, 2017.
Besson, Jean. "The Creolization of African-American Slave Kinship in Jamaican Free Village and Maroon Communities." In *Slave Cultures and the Cultures of Slavery*, edited by Stephan Palmié. Knoxville: University of Tennessee Press, 1995.
Besson, Jean. "Empowering and Engendering Hidden Histories in Caribbean Peasant Communities." *History and Histories in the Caribbean* 70 (2001): 69–113.
Besson, Jean. "Euro-Creole, Afro-Creole, Meso-Creole: Creolization and Ethnic Identity in West-Central Jamaica." *Matatu* 27–28 (2003): 169–88.
Besson, Jean. "Folk Law and Legal Pluralism in Jamaica." *Journal of Legal Pluralism and Unofficial Law* 31, no. 43 (1999): 31–56.
Besson, Jean. "Sacred Sites, Shifting Histories: Narratives of Belonging, Land and Globalisation in the Cockpit Country, Jamaica." In *Caribbean Narratives of Belonging: Fields of Relations, Sites of Identity*, edited by Jean Besson and Karen Fog Olwig, 17–43. London: Macmillan Caribbean, 2005.
Besson, Jean. *Transformations of Freedom in the Land of the Maroons: Creolization in the Cockpits of Jamaica*. Kingston, Jamaica: Ian Randle, 2016.
Beyreuther, Erich. *Die große Zinzendorf Trilogie*. Marburg an der Lahn, Germany: Verlag der Francke-Buchhandlung, 1988.
Bilby, Kenneth M. "Swearing by the Past, Swearing to the Future: Sacred Oaths, Alliances, and Treaties Among the Guianese and Jamaican Maroons." *Ethnohistory* 44, no. 4 (1997): 655–89.
Bilby, Kenneth M. *True-Born Maroons*. Gainesville: University Press of Florida, 2005.
Bilby, Kenneth M. "'Two Sister Pikni': A Historical Tradition of Dual Ethnogenesis in Eastern Jamaica." *Caribbean Quarterly* 30, nos. 3–4 (1984): 10–25.
Bilby, Kenneth M., and Jerome S. Handler. "Obeah: Healing and Protection in West Indian Slave Life." *Journal of Caribbean History* 38, no. 2 (December 2004): 153–83.
Blackburn, Robin. "The Old World Background to European Colonial Slavery." *William & Mary Quarterly* 54, no. 1 (1997): 65–102.
Blier, Suzanne Preston. *African Vodun: Art, Psychology, and Power*. Chicago: University of Chicago Press, 1995.
Block, Sharon. *Rape and Sexual Power in Early America*. Chapel Hill: University of North Carolina Press, 2006.
Boaz, Danielle N. *Banning Black Gods: Law and Religions of the African Diaspora*. University Park: Pennsylvania State University Press, 2021.
Boaz, Danielle N. "'Instruments of Obeah': The Significance of Ritual Objects in the Jamaican Legal System, 1760 to the Present." In *Materialities of Ritual in the Black Atlantic*, edited by Akinwumi Ogundiran and Paula Saunders, 143–58. Bloomington: Indiana University Press, 2014.

Bohaker, Heidi, Alan Ojiig Corbiere, and Ruth B. Phillips. "Wampum Unites Us: Digital Access, Interdisciplinarity and Indigenous Knowledge—Situating the GRASAC Knowledge Sharing Database." In *Museum as Process: Translating Local and Global Knowledges*, edited by Raymond A. Silverman, 45–66. New York: Routledge, 2015.

Bollettino, Maria Alessandra. "Slavery, War, and Britain's Atlantic Empire: Black Soldiers, Sailors, and Rebels in the Seven Years' War." PhD diss., University of Texas at Austin, 2009.

Bonomi, Patricia U. "'Swarms of Negroes Comeing About My Door': Black Christianity in Early Dutch and English North America." *Journal of American History* 103, no. 1 (2016):34–58.

Bostoen, Koen, and Inge Brinkman, eds. *The Kongo Kingdom: The Origins, Dynamics and Cosmopolitan Culture of an African Polity*. Cambridge: Cambridge University Press, 2018.

Brathwaite, Edward Kamau. *Wars of Respect: Nanny, Sam Sharpe and the Struggle for People's Liberation*. Kingston, Jamaica: Agency for Public Information, 1977.

Brecht, Martin, and Paul Peucker, eds. *Neue Aspekte Der Zinzendorf-Forschung*. Göttingen: Vandenhoeck & Ruprecht, 2006.

Brewer, Holly. "Slavery, Sovereignty, and 'Inheritable Blood': Reconsidering John Locke and the Origins of American Slavery." *American Historical Review* 122, no. 4 (2017): 1038–78.

Brewer-García, Larissa. *Beyond Babel: Translations of Blackness in Colonial Peru and New Granada*. Cambridge: Cambridge University Press, 2020.

Brewer-García, Larissa. "Hierarchy and Holiness in the Earliest Colonial Black Hagiographies: Alonso de Sandoval and His Sources." *William & Mary Quarterly* 76, no. 3 (2019): 477–508.

Bristol, Joan Cameron. "From Curing to Witchcraft: Afro-Mexicans and the Mediation of Authority." *Journal of Colonialism and Colonial History* 7, no. 1 (2006): 1–37.

Brooks, Lisa T. "Awikhigawôgan Ta Pildowi Ôjmowôgan: Mapping a New History." *William & Mary Quarterly* 75, no. 2 (2018): 259–94.

Brooks, Lisa T. *Our Beloved Kin: A New History of King Philip's War*. Henry Roe Cloud Series on American Indians and Modernity. New Haven, CT: Yale University Press, 2018.

Brown, Ras Michael. *African-Atlantic Cultures and the South Carolina Lowcountry*. Cambridge: Cambridge University Press, 2012.

Brown, Vincent. "Eating the Dead: Consumption and Regeneration in the History of Sugar." *Food and Foodways* 16, no. 2 (2008): 117–26.

Brown, Vincent. *The Reaper's Garden: Death and Power in the World of Atlantic Slavery*. Cambridge, MA: Harvard University Press, 2008.

Brown, Vincent. "Social Death and Political Life in the Study of Slavery." *American Historical Review* 114, no. 5 (December 2009): 1231–49.

Brown, Vincent. *Tacky's Revolt: The Story of an Atlantic Slave War*. Cambridge, MA: Harvard University Press, 2020.

Browne, Randy M. "The 'Bad Business' of Obeah: Power, Authority, and the Politics of Slave Culture in the British Caribbean." *William & Mary Quarterly* 68, no. 3 (July 2011): 451–80.

Browne, Randy M. *The Driver's Story: Labor and Power in the World of Atlantic Slavery.* Philadelphia: University of Pennsylvania Press, 2024.

Browne, Randy M. *Surviving Slavery in the British Caribbean.* Philadelphia: University of Pennsylvania Press, 2017.

Browne, Randy M., and Trevor Burnard. "Husbands and Fathers: The Family Experience of Enslaved Men in Berbice, 1819–1834." *New West Indian Guide/Nieuwe West-Indische Gids* 91, nos. 3–4 (2017): 193–222.

Bryant, Sherwin K. *Rivers of Gold, Lives of Bondage: Governing Through Slavery in Colonial Quito.* Chapel Hill: University of North Carolina Press, 2014.

Bryson, Sasha Turner. "The Art of Power: Poison and Obeah Accusations and the Struggle for Dominance and Survival in Jamaica's Slave Society." *Caribbean Studies* 41, no. 2 (2013): 61–90.

Buchner, J. H. *The Moravians in Jamaica: History of the Mission of the United Brethren's Church to the Negroes in the Island of Jamaica from the Year 1754 to 1854.* London: Longman, Brown, 1854.

Buck-Morss, Susan. *Hegel, Haiti, and Universal History.* Pittsburgh, PA: University of Pittsburgh Press, 2009.

Buckridge, Steeve O., and Rex Nettleford. *The Language of Dress: Resistance and Accommodation in Jamaica, 1750–1890.* Mona, Kingston: University of the West Indies Press, 2009.

Bühnen, Stephan. "Ethnic Origins of Peruvian Slaves (1548–1650): Figures for Upper Guinea." *Paideuma* 39 (1993): 57–110.

Burkhart, Louise M. *The Slippery Earth: Nahua-Christian Moral Dialogue in Sixteenth-Century Mexico.* Tucson: University of Arizona Press, 1989.

Burnard, Trevor. *Mastery, Tyranny, and Desire: Thomas Thistlewood and His Slaves in the Anglo-Jamaican World.* Chapel Hill: University of North Carolina Press, 2004.

Bush, Barbara. *Slave Women in Caribbean Society, 1640–1832.* Bloomington: Indiana University Press, 1990.

Butler, Jon. "Africans' Religions in British America, 1650–1840." *Church History: Studies in Christianity and Culture* 68, no. 1 (1999): 118–27.

Bynum, Caroline Walker. *Christian Materiality: An Essay on Religion in Late Medieval Europe.* New York: Zone Books, 2015.

Byrd, Alexander X. *Captives and Voyagers: Black Migrants Across the Eighteenth-Century British Atlantic World.* Baton Rouge: Louisiana State University Press, 2010.

Byrd, Alexander X. "Eboe, Country, Nation, and Gustavus Vassa's 'Interesting Narrative.'" *William & Mary Quarterly* 63, no. 1 (2006): 123–48.

Cahill, Lisa Sowle. "Sexuality and Christian Ethics: How to Proceed." In *Sexuality and the Sacred: Sources for Theological Reflection*, edited by James B. Nelson and Sandra P. Longfellow, 19–27. Louisville, KY: Westminster John Knox Press, 1994.

Calloway, Colin G. *Pen and Ink Witchcraft: Treaties and Treaty Making in American Indian History.* New York: Oxford University Press, 2013.

Camp, Stephanie. *Closer to Freedom: Enslaved Women and Everyday Resistance in the Plantation South.* Chapel Hill: University of North Carolina Press, 2005.

Campbell, Mavis C. *The Maroons of Jamaica 1655–1796: A History of Resistance, Collaboration and Betrayal.* Granby, MA: Bergin and Garvey, 1988.

Capone, Stefania. *Transatlantic Dialogue: Roger Bastide and the African American Religions*. Africas of the Americas. Leiden: Brill, 2008.

Carey, Bev. *The Maroon Story: The Authentic and Original History of the Maroons in the History of Jamaica, 1490–1880*. Gordon Town, Jamaica: Agouti, 1997.

Caron, Peter. "'Of a Nation Which the Others Do Not Understand': Bambara Slaves and African Ethnicity in Colonial Louisiana, 1718–60." *Slavery & Abolition* 18, no. 1 (1997): 98–121.

Carretta, Vincent. *Equiano, the African: Biography of a Self-Made Man*. New York: Penguin Books, 2007.

Carretta, Vincent. "Olaudah Equiano or Gustavus Vassa? New Light on an Eighteenth-Century Question of Identity." *Slavery & Abolition* 20, no. 3 (December 1999): 96–105.

Carretta, Vincent. "Response to Paul Lovejoy's 'Autobiography and Memory: Gustavus Vassa, Alias Olaudah Equiano, the African.'" *Slavery & Abolition* 28, no. 1 (2007): 115–19.

Carter, J. Kameron. "Anarchē; or, the Matter of Charles Long and Black Feminism—Anarchē; o, La Materia de Charles Long y El Feminismo Negro." *American Religion* 2, no. 2 (2021): 103–35.

Carter, J. Kameron. *Race: A Theological Account*. Oxford and New York: Oxford University Press, 2008.

Caswell, Michelle "'The Archive' Is Not an Archives: On Acknowledging the Intellectual Contributions of Archival Studies." August 4, 2016. https://escholarship.org/uc/item/7bn4v1fk.

Caswell, Michelle. "'Owning Critical Archival Studies: A Plea." July 1, 2016. https://escholarship.org/uc/item/75x090df.

Caswell, Michelle, Ricardo Punzalan, and T.-Kay Sangwand. "Critical Archival Studies: An Introduction." *Journal of Critical Library and Information Studies* 1, no. 2 (2017). https://doi.org/10.24242/jclis.v1i2.50.

Catron, John W. "Across the Great Water: Religion and Diaspora in the Black Atlantic." PhD diss., University of Florida, 2008.

Catron, John W. *Embracing Protestantism: Black Identities in the Atlantic World*. Gainesville: University Press of Florida, 2016.

Catron, John W. "Evangelical Networks in the Greater Caribbean and the Origins of the Black Church." *Church History* 79, no. 1 (2010): 77–114.

Catron, John W. "Slavery, Ethnic Identity, and Christianity in Eighteenth-Century Moravian Antigua." *Journal of Moravian History* 14, no. 2 (2014): 153–78.

Chambers, Douglas B. "Ethnicity in the Diaspora: The Slave-Trade and the Creation of African 'Nations' in the Americas." *Slavery & Abolition* 22, no. 3 (December 2001): 25–39.

Chambers, Douglas B. "'My Own Nation': Igbo Exiles in the Diaspora." *Slavery & Abolition* 18, no. 1 (April 1997): 72–97.

Chambers, Douglas B. "Rejoinder—The Significance of Igbo in the Bight of Biafra Slave-Trade: A Rejoinder to Northrup's 'Myth Igbo.'" *Slavery & Abolition* 23, no. 1 (2002): 101–20.

Chang, David A. "The Good Written Word of Life: The Native Hawaiian Appropriation of Textuality." *William & Mary Quarterly* 75, no. 2 (2018): 237–58.

Chang, David A. *The World and All the Things upon It: Native Hawaiian Geographies of Exploration*. Minneapolis: University of Minnesota Press, 2016.

Chaudhuri, Nupur, Sherry J. Katz, and Mary Elizabeth Perry. *Contesting Archives: Finding Women in the Sources*. Urbana: University of Illinois Press, 2010.

Chenoweth, Michael. *The 18th Century Climate of Jamaica: Derived from the Journals of Thomas Thistlewood, 1750–1786*. Transactions of the American Philosophical Society, vol. 93, pt. 2. Philadelphia: American Philosophical Society, 2003.

Chidester, David. *Empire of Religion: Imperialism and Comparative Religion*. Chicago: University of Chicago Press, 2014.

Chidester, David. *Religion: Material Dynamics*. Oakland: University of California Press, 2018.

Chidester, David. *Savage Systems: Colonialism and Comparative Religion in Southern Africa*. Charlottesville: University of Virginia Press, 1996.

"Chief Currie Wants Peace, but Prepared to Fight." *The Gleaner*. August 13, 2021. https://jamaica-gleaner.com/article/news/20210813/chief-currie-wants-peace-prepared-fight.

Chireau, Yvonne P. *Black Magic: Religion and the African American Conjuring Tradition*. Oakland: University of California Press, 2006.

Conroy-Krutz, Emily. *Christian Imperialism: Converting the World in the Early American Republic*. Ithaca, NY: Cornell University Press, 2015.

Corbiere, Alan Ojiig. "Anishinaabe Treaty-Making in the 18th- and 19th-Century," PhD diss., York University, 2020.

Cortes de Oliviera, Maria Ines. "The Reconstruction of Ethnicity in Bahia: The Case of the Nago in the Nineteenth Century." In *Trans-Atlantic Dimensions of Ethnicity in the African Diaspora*, edited by Paul E. Lovejoy and David V. Trotman, 158–80. New York: Continuum, 2003.

Covington-Ward, Yolanda, and Jeanette S. Jouili, eds. *Embodying Black Religions in Africa and Its Diasporas*. Durham, NC: Duke University Press, 2021.

Craig, Bradley. "Oathbound: The Trelawny Maroons of Jamaica in the Revolutionary Atlantic World." PhD diss., Harvard University, 2020.

Craton, Michael. *Testing the Chains: Resistance to Slavery in the British West Indies*. Ithaca, NY: Cornell University Press, 2009.

Crawford, Matthew James, and Joseph M. Gabriel. *Drugs on the Page: Pharmacopoeias and Healing Knowledge in the Early Modern Atlantic World*. Pittsburgh, PA: University of Pittsburgh Press, 2019.

Crosson, J. Brent. *Experiments with Power: Obeah and the Remaking of Religion in Trinidad*. Chicago: University of Chicago Press, 2020.

Crosson, J. Brent. "Oil, Obeah and Science." *Cosmologics Magazine*, July 2016.

Crosson, J. Brent. "What Obeah Does Do: Healing, Harm, and the Limits of Religion." *Journal of Africana Religions* 3, no. 2 (2015): 151–76.

Cummings, Ronald. "Jamaican Female Masculinities: Nanny of the Maroons and the Genealogy of the Man-Royal." *Journal of West Indian Literature* 21, nos. 1–2 (2012): 129–54.

Cummings, Ronald. "Maroon In/Securities." *Small Axe: A Caribbean Journal of Criticism* 22, no. 3 (2018): 47–55.

Curtin, Philip D. *Economic Change in Precolonial Africa: Senegambia in the Era of the Slave Trade*. Madison: University of Wisconsin Press, 1975.

Darr, Orna Alyagon. "Experiments in the Courtroom: Social Dynamics and Spectacles of Proof in Early Modern English Witch Trials." *Law & Social Inquiry* 39 (2014): 152–75.

Davis, Angela. *Women, Race, and Class*. New York: Random House, 1982.

Davis, Natalie Zemon. "Judges, Masters, Diviners: Slaves' Experience of Criminal Justice in Colonial Suriname." *Law and History Review* 29, no. 4 (2011): 925–84.

Dayan, Colin. *The Law Is a White Dog: How Legal Rituals Make and Unmake Persons*. Princeton, NJ: Princeton University Press, 2013.

Dayan, Joan. *Haiti, History, and the Gods*. Oakland: University of California Press, 1998.

Dayfoot, Arthur Charles. *The Shaping of the West Indian Church, 1492–1962*. Gainesville: University Press of Florida, 1999.

De Barros, Juanita. "'Setting Things Right': Medicine and Magic in British Guiana." *Slavery & Abolition* 25, no. 1 (2004): 28–50.

Delgado, Jessica, and Kelsey Moss. "Race and Religion in the Early Modern Iberian Atlantic." In *The Oxford Handbook of Religion and Race in American History*, edited by Kathryn Gin Lum and Paul Harvey. Oxford: Oxford University Press, 2018.

Dewulf, Jeroen. *Afro-Atlantic Catholics: America's First Black Christians*. Notre Dame, IN: University of Notre Dame Press, 2022.

Dickerson, Dennis C. *The African Methodist Episcopal Church: A History*. Cambridge: Cambridge University Press, 2020.

Din, Gilbert C. "'Cimarrones' and the San Malo Band in Spanish Louisiana." *Louisiana History: The Journal of the Louisiana Historical Association* 21, no. 3 (1980): 237–62.

Diouf, Sylviane A. *Servants of Allah: African Muslims Enslaved in the Americas*. New York: NYU Press, 2013.

Diouf, Sylviane A. *Slavery's Exiles: The Story of the American Maroons*. New York: NYU Press, 2016.

Dorlin, Elsa. *Self-Defense: A Philosophy of Violence*. New York: Verso Books, 2022.

Douma-Kaelin, Kelly. "Interchangeable Bodies: International Marriage and Migration in the Eighteenth-Century Moravian Church." *Church History* 90, no. 2 (2021): 348–66.

Drexler-Dreis, Joseph. "Theological Thinking and Eurocentric Epistemologies: A Challenge to Theologians from Within Africana Religious Studies." *Journal of Africana Religions* 6, no. 1 (2018): 27–49.

Dunham, Katherine. *Journey to Accompong*. New York: Henry Holt and Company, 1946.

Dunn, Richard S. *Moravian Missionaries at Work in a Jamaican Slave Community: 1754–1835*. Minneapolis: James Ford Bell Library, University of Minnesota, 1994.

Dunn, Richard S. *Sugar and Slaves: The Rise of the Planter Class in the English West Indies, 1624–1713*. Chapel Hill: University of North Carolina Press, 2000.

Dunn, Richard S. *A Tale of Two Plantations: Slave Life and Labor in Jamaica and Virginia*. Cambridge, MA: Harvard University Press, 2014.

Earle, William, and Srinivas Aravamudan. *Obi, or, the History of Three-Fingered Jack*. Peterborough, ON: Broadview Press, 2005.

Eddins, Crystal. "'Rejoice! Your Wombs Will Not Beget Slaves!' Marronnage as Reproductive Justice in Colonial Haiti." *Gender & History* 32, no. 3 (2020): 562–80.

Edmonds, Ennis, and Michelle A. Gonzalez. *Caribbean Religious History: An Introduction*. New York: NYU Press, 2010.

Edwards, Kassie M. "Preserving Maroon Heritage: The Accompong Museum." National Museum of African American History and Culture, 2017. http://repository.si.edu/xmlui/handle/10088/116340.

Egerton, Douglas R. *He Shall Go Out Free: The Lives of Denmark Vesey*. Lanham, MD: Rowman & Littlefield, 1999.

Egerton, Douglas R., and Robert L. Paquette, eds. *The Denmark Vesey Affair: A Documentary History*. Gainesville: University Press of Florida, 2017.

Eltis, David. "The Diaspora of Yoruba Speakers, 1650–1865: Dimensions and Implications." In Falola and Childs, *The Yoruba Diaspora in the Atlantic World*, 17–39.

Engel, Katherine Carte. *Religion and Profit: Moravians in Early America*. Philadelphia: University of Pennsylvania Press, 2011.

Falola, Toyin, and Matt D. Childs, eds. *The Yoruba Diaspora in the Atlantic World*. Bloomington: Indiana University Press, 2005.

Farge, Arlette. *The Allure of the Archives*. Translated by Thomas Scott-Railton. New Haven, CT: Yale University Press, 2013.

Fett, Sharla. *Working Cures: Healing, Health, and Power on Southern Slave Plantations*. Chapel Hill: University of North Carolina Press, 2002.

Finch, Aisha. "'What Looks Like a Revolution': Enslaved Women and the Gendered Terrain of Slave Insurgencies in Cuba, 1843–1844." *Journal of Women's History* 26, no. 1 (2014): 112–34.

Fogleman, Aaron Spencer. *Jesus Is Female: Moravians and Radical Religion in Early America*. Philadelphia: University of Pennsylvania Press, 2008.

Fogleman, Aaron Spencer. "A Moravian Mission and the Origins of Evangelical Protestantism Among Slaves in the Carolina Lowcountry." *Journal of Early Modern History* 21, nos. 1–2 (2017): 38–63.

Fogleman, Aaron Spencer. *Two Troubled Souls: An Eighteenth-Century Couple's Spiritual Journey in the Atlantic World*. Chapel Hill: University of North Carolina Press, 2013.

Foster, Francis Smith. *'Till Death or Distance Do Us Part: Love and Marriage in African America*. New York: Oxford University Press, 2010.

Fraser, Rebecca J. *Courtship and Love among the Enslaved in North Carolina*. Oxford: University Press of Mississippi, 2007.

Frazier, Franklin E. "The Negro Family in Bahia, Brazil." *American Sociological Review* 7, no. 4 (1942): 465–78.

Frey, Sylvia R. "The Visible Church: Historiography of African American Religion Since Raboteau." *Slavery & Abolition* 29, no. 1 (2008): 83–110.

Frey, Sylvia R., and Betty Wood. *Come Shouting to Zion: African American Protestantism in the American South and British Caribbean to 1830*. Chapel Hill: University of North Carolina Press, 1998.

Fromont, Cécile, ed. *Afro-Catholic Festivals in the Americas: Performance, Representation, and the Making of Black Atlantic Tradition*. University Park: Pennsylvania State University Press, 2019.

Fromont, Cécile. *The Art of Conversion: Christian Visual Culture in the Kingdom of Kongo*. Chapel Hill: University of North Carolina Press, 2014.

Fromont, Cécile. "Paper, Ink, Vodun, and the Inquisition: Tracing Power, Slavery, and Witchcraft in the Early Modern Portuguese Atlantic." *Journal of the American Academy of Religion* 88, no. 2 (2020): 460–504.

Fuentes, Marisa J. *Dispossessed Lives: Enslaved Women, Violence, and the Archive*. Philadelphia: University of Pennsylvania Press, 2016.

Fuentes, Marisa J. "Power and Historical Figuring: Rachael Pringle Polgreen's Troubled Archive." *Gender & History* 22, no. 3 (2010): 564–84.

Füllberg-Stolberg, Claus. "The Moravian Mission and the Emancipation of Slaves in the Caribbean." In *The End of Slavery in Africia and the Americas: A Comparative Approach*, edited by Ulrike Schmieder, Michael Zeuske, and Katja Füllberg-Stolberg, 81–102. Münster: LIT Verlag, 2011.

Fuller, Harcourt. "Maroon History, Music, and Sacred Sounds in the Americas: A Jamaican Case." *Journal of Africana Religions* 5, no. 2 (2017): 275–82.

Gall, Timothy L., and Jeneen Hobby, eds. "Malinke." In *Worldmark Encyclopedia of Cultures and Daily Life*, 2nd ed., 1:375–81. Detroit: Gale, 2009.

Gaspar, David Barry. *Bondmen and Rebels: A Study of Master-Slave Relations in Antigua*. Durham, NC: Duke University Press, 1993.

Gaspar, David Barry. "A Dangerous Spirit of Liberty: Slave Rebellion in the West Indies in the 1730s." In *Origins of the Black Atlantic*, edited by Laurent Dubois and Julius S. Scott, 11–25. London: Routledge, 2013.

Gaspar, David Barry. "With a Rod of Iron: Barbados Slave Laws as a Model for Jamaica, South Carolina, and Antigua, 1661–1697." In *Crossing Boundaries: Comparative History of Black People in Diaspora*, edited by Darlene Clark Hine and Jacqueline McLeod, 343–66. Bloomington: Indiana University Press, 1999.

Geiger, Erika. "Zinzendorf Stellung zum Halleschen Busskampf und zum Bekehrungserlebnis." *Unitas Fratrum: Zeitschrift für Geschichte und Gegenwartsfragen der Brudergemeine*, nos. 49–50 (2002): 12–22.

Gerbner, Katharine. "Archival Violence, Archival Capital: Ethics, Inheritance, and Reparations in the Thistlewood Diaries." *William & Mary Quarterly* 79, no. 4 (2022): 595–624.

Gerbner, Katharine. *Christian Slavery: Conversion and Race in the Protestant Atlantic World*. Philadelphia: University of Pennsylvania Press, 2018.

Gerbner, Katharine. "Maroon Science: Knowledge, Secrecy, and Crime in Jamaica." In Sheldon, Ragab, and Keel, *Critical Approaches to Science and Religion*, 325–47.

Gerbner, Katharine. "Rebellion and Religion: Slavery and Empire in Early America." In Wenger and Johnson, *Religion and US Empire: Critical New Histories*, 19–40.

Gerbner, Katharine. "Theorizing Conversion: Christianity, Colonization, and Consciousness in the Early Modern Atlantic World." *History Compass* 13, no. 3 (2015): 134–47.

Gerbner, Katharine. "'They Call Me Obea': German Moravian Missionaries and Afro-Caribbean Religion in Jamaica, 1754–1760." *Atlantic Studies: Global Currents* 12, no. 2 (2015): 160–78.

Gerbner, Katharine. "The Ultimate Sin: Christianising Slaves in Barbados in the Seventeenth Century." *Slavery & Abolition* 31, no. 1 (2010): 57–73.

Gillespie, Michele, and Robert Beachy, eds. *Pious Pursuits: German Moravians in the Atlantic World*. New York: Berghahn, 2007.

Glasson, Travis. *Mastering Christianity: Missionary Anglicanism and Slavery in the Atlantic World*. New York: Oxford University Press, 2011.

Glasson, Travis. "Missionaries, Slavery, and Race: The Society for the Propagation of the Gospel in Foreign Parts in the Eighteenth-Century British Atlantic World." PhD diss., Columbia University, 2005.

Glymph, Thavolia. *Out of the House of Bondage: The Transformation of the Plantation Household*. Cambridge: Cambridge University Press, 2008.

Goetz, Rebecca Anne. *The Baptism of Early Virginia: How Christianity Created Race*. Baltimore, MD: Johns Hopkins University Press, 2012.

Gomez, Michael A. *Exchanging Our Country Marks: The Transformation of African Identities in the Colonial and Antebellum South*. Chapel Hill: University of North Carolina Press, 1998.

Gómez, Pablo F. *The Experiential Caribbean*. Chapel Hill: University of North Carolina Press, 2017.

Gómez, Pablo F. "Incommensurable Epistemologies? The Atlantic Geography of Healing in the Early Modern Caribbean." *Small Axe: A Caribbean Journal of Criticism* 18, no. 2 (44) (2014): 95–107.

Gordon, Sarah Barringer. "The African Supplement: Religion, Race, and Corporate Law in Early National America." *William & Mary Quarterly* 72, no. 3 (2015): 385–422.

Gordon, Shirley C. *God Almighty, Make Me Free: Christianity in Preemancipation Jamaica*. Bloomington: Indiana University Press, 1996.

Greene-Hayes, Ahmad. "Hair, Roots, and Crystal Balls: Archival Viscerality, Black Conjuring Traditions, and the Study of American Religions." *Journal of the American Academy of Religion* 91, no. 4 (2023): 798–819.

Griffin, Stanley H. "Value Displaced, Value Re/Claimed: Reparations, Shared Heritage and Caribbean Archival Records." In Lowry, *Disputed Archival Heritage*.

Groot, Silvia W de. "Maroon Women as Ancestors, Priests and Mediums in Surinam." *Slavery & Abolition* 7, no. 2 (1986): 160–74.

Gross-Wyrtzen, Leslie, and Alex A. Moulton. "Toward 'Fugitivity as Method': An Introduction to the Special Issue." *ACME: An International Journal for Critical Geographies* 22, no. 5 (2023): 1258–72.

Haley, Alex. *Roots: The Saga of an American Family*. Boston: Da Capo Press, 2016.

Hall, Catherine. *Civilising Subjects: Metropole and Colony in the English Imagination 1830–1867*. Chicago: University of Chicago Press, 2002.

Hall, Catherine. "Doing Reparatory History: Bringing 'Race' and Slavery Home." *Race & Class* 60, no. 1 (2018): 3–21.

Hall, David D., ed. *Lived Religion in America: Toward a History of Practice*. Princeton, NJ: Princeton University Press, 1997.

Hall, Douglas. *In Miserable Slavery: Thomas Thistlewood in Jamaica, 1750–86*. Basingstoke, UK: Macmillan, 1989.

Hall, Gwendolyn Midlo. *Africans in Colonial Louisiana: The Development of Afro-Creole Culture in the Eighteenth Century*. Baton Rouge: Louisiana State University Press, 1995.

Hall, Gwendolyn Midlo. *Slavery and African Ethnicities in the Americas: Restoring the Links*. Chapel Hill: University of North Carolina Press, 2009.

Hamilton, John Taylor. *A History of the Missions of the Moravian Church: During the Eighteenth and Nineteenth Centuries.* Bethlehem, PA: Times, 1901.

Handler, Jerome. "Slave Medicine and Obeah in Barbados, Circa 1650 to 1834." *NWIG: New West Indian Guide/Nieuwe West-Indische Gids* 74, nos. 1–2 (2000): 57–90.

Handler, Jerome, and Kenneth M. Bilby. *Enacting Power: The Criminalization of Obeah in the Anglophone Caribbean, 1760–2011.* Mona, Jamaica: University of the West Indies Press, 2013.

Handler, Jerome, and Kenneth M. Bilby. "On the Early Use and Origin of the Term 'Obeah' in Barbados and the Anglophone Caribbean." *Slavery & Abolition* 22, no. 2 (2001): 87–100.

Hanserd, Robert. *Identity, Spirit and Freedom in the Atlantic World: The Gold Coast and the African Diaspora.* New York: Routledge, 2019.

Hanserd, Robert. "Okomfo Anokye Formed a Tree to Hide from the Akwamu: Priestly Power, Freedom, and Enslavement in the Afro-Atlantic." *Atlantic Studies* 12, no. 4 (2015): 522–44.

Harding, Rachel E. *A Refuge in Thunder: Candomblé and Alternative Spaces of Blackness.* Bloomington: Indiana University Press, 2000.

Hartman, Saidiya V. *Lose Your Mother: A Journey Along the Atlantic Slave Route.* New York: Farrar, Straus and Giroux, 2008.

Hartman, Saidiya V. *Scenes of Subjection: Terror, Slavery, and Self-Making in Nineteenth-Century America.* New York: Oxford University Press, 1997.

Hartman, Saidiya V. "Venus in Two Acts." *Small Axe: A Caribbean Journal of Criticism* 26 (2008): 1–14.

Harvey, Paul, and Kathryn Gin Lum. *The Oxford Handbook of Religion and Race in American History.* Oxford Handbooks. Oxford: Oxford University Press, 2018.

Hastings, S. U., and B. L. MacLeavy. *Seedtime and Harvest: A Brief History of the Moravian Church in Jamaica, 1754–1979.* Kingston, Jamaica: Moravian Church, 1979.

Helton, Laura, Justin Leroy, Max A. Mishler, Samantha Seeley, and Shauna Sweeney. "The Question of Recovery: An Introduction." *Social Text* 33, no. 4 (125) (2015): 1–18.

Herrmann, Rachel B. "Consider the Source: An 1800 Maroon Treaty." *Early American Studies: An Interdisciplinary Journal* 21, no. 1 (2023): 166–99.

Herskovits, Melville J. *The Myth of the Negro Past.* New York: Harper and Bros., 1941.

Herskovits, Melville J. "The Negro in Bahia, Brazil: A Problem in Method." *American Sociological Review* 8, no. 4 (1943): 394–404.

Heywood, Linda M., ed. *Central Africans and Cultural Transformations in the American Diaspora.* New York: Cambridge University Press, 2002.

Heywood, Linda M. *Njinga of Angola: Africa's Warrior Queen.* Cambridge, MA: Harvard University Press, 2017.

Hine, Darlene Clark. "Rape and the Inner Lives of Black Women in the Middle West." *Signs: Journal of Women in Culture and Society* 14, no. 4 (1989): 912–20.

Højbjerg, Christian K. "The 'Mandingo Question': Transnational Ethnic Identity and Violent Conflict in an Upper Guinea Coast Border Area." In *The Upper Guinea Coast in Global Perspective*, edited by Jacqueline Knörr and Christoph Kohl, 255–79. New York: Berghahn Books, 2016.

Hucks, Tracey E. *Obeah, Orisa, and Religious Identity in Trinidad*, vol. 1: *Obeah: Africans in the White Colonial Imagination*. Durham, NC: Duke University Press, 2022.

Hucks, Tracey E. "Perspectives in Lived History: Religion, Ethnography, and the Study of African Diasporic Religions." *Practical Matters Journal* 3 (2010): 1–17.

Hughes-Watkins, Lae'l. "Moving Toward a Reparative Archive: A Roadmap for a Holistic Approach to Disrupting Homogenous Histories in Academic Repositories and Creating Inclusive Spaces for Marginalized Voices." *Journal of Contemporary Archival Studies* 5, no. 1 (2018). https://elischolar.library.yale.edu/jcas/vol5/iss1/6.

Hunte, Keith. "Protestantism and Slavery in the British Caribbean." In *Christianity in the Caribbean: Essays on Church History*, edited by Armando Lampe, 86–125. Mona, Jamaica: University of the West Indies Press, 2000.

Hunter, Tera W. *Bound in Wedlock: Slave and Free Black Marriage in the Nineteenth Century*. Cambridge, MA: Belknap Press, 2019.

Hurd, Elizabeth Shakman. *Beyond Religious Freedom: The New Global Politics of Religion*. Princeton, NJ: Princeton University Press, 2015.

Hurston, Zora Neale. *Tell My Horse: Voodoo and Life in Haiti and Jamaica*. New York: Harper Classics, 2008.

Hüsgen, Jan. *Mission und Sklaverei: Die Herrnhuter Brüdergemeine und die Sklavenemanzipation in Britisch- und Dänisch-Westindien*. Stuttgart: Franz Steiner Verlag, 2016.

Ilogu, Edmund. *Christianity and Igbo Culture: A Study of the Interaction of Christianity and Igbo Culture*. New York: NOK, 1974.

"Irrupt (v.)," *Oxford English Dictionary*. Oxford: Oxford University Press, 2023. https://doi.org/10.1093/OED/2847251598.

James, C. L. R. *Black Jacobins: Toussaint L'Ouverture and the San Domingo Revolution*. New York: Vintage, 1989.

Jaudon, Toni Wall. "Obeah's Sensations: Rethinking Religion at the Transnational Turn." *American Literature* 84, no. 4 (December 2012): 715–41.

Johnson, Amy M. "Gradations of Freedom: The Maroons of Jamaica, 1798–1821." *Journal of Caribbean History* 49, no. 2 (2015): 160–88.

Johnson, Jessica Marie. *Wicked Flesh: Black Women, Intimacy, and Freedom in the Atlantic World*. Philadelphia: University of Pennsylvania Press, 2020.

Johnson, Paul Christopher. "On Leaving and Joining Africanness Through Religion: The 'Black Caribs' Across Multiple Diasporic Horizons." In Palmié, *Africas of the Americas*.

Johnson, Paul Christopher, ed. *Spirited Things: The Work of "Possession" in Afro-Atlantic Religions*. Chicago: University of Chicago Press, 2014.

Johnson, Paul Christopher, Pamela E. Klassen, and Winnifred Fallers Sullivan. *Ekklesia: Three Inquiries in Church and State*. Chicago: University of Chicago Press, 2018.

Johnson, Sylvester A. *African American Religions, 1500–2000*. New York: Cambridge University Press, 2015.

Jones, Adam. "Oldendorps Beitrag zur Afrika-Forschung des Radikalen Pietismus." In Meier et al. *Christian Georg Andreas Oldendorp*, 181–190.

Jones, Jacqueline. *Labor of Love, Labor of Sorrow: Black Women, Work, and the Family, from Slavery to the Present*. New York: Basic Books, 2009.

Jones-Rogers, Stephanie E. *They Were Her Property: White Women as Slave Owners in the American South*. New Haven, CT: Yale University Press, 2019.

Kaelin, Kelly. "To Be Proposed as Useful: Women, Missionaries, and the Moravian Church in the Eighteenth-Century Caribbean." PhD diss., Pennsylvania State University, 2022.

Kaelin, Kelly. *Women, Race, and the Moravian Church in the Early Modern Atlantic World: Convert, Migrant Missionary*. Cham, Switzerland: Palgrave Macmillan Cham, 2025.

Karras, Ruth Mazo. *Slavery and Society in Medieval Scandinavia*. New Haven, CT: Yale University Press, 1988.

Kars, Marjoleine. *Blood on the River: A Chronicle of Mutiny and Freedom on the Wild Coast*. New York: New Press, 2020.

Kars, Marjoleine. "Dodging Rebellion: Politics and Gender in the Berbice Slave Uprising of 1763." *American Historical Review* 121, no. 1 (2016): 39–69.

Kea, Ray A. "Akwamu-Anlo Relations, c. 1750–1813." *Transactions of the Historical Society of Ghana* 10 (1969): 29–63.

Kea, Ray A. "Crossroads and Exchanges in the Scandinavian Atlantic and Atlantic West Africa: Framing Texts of Eighteenth-Century African Christians." *Itinerario* 43, no. 2 (2019): 262–82. https://doi.org/10.1017/S0165115319000263.

Kea, Ray A. "From Catholicism to Moravian Pietism: The World of Marotta/Magdalena, Woman of Popo and St. Thomas." In *The Creation of the British Atlantic World*, edited by Elizabeth Mancke and Carole Shammas, 115–36. Baltimore, Baltimore: Johns Hopkins University Press, 2005.

Kea, Ray A. *Settlements, Trade, and Polities in the Seventeenth-Century Gold Coast*. Baltimore, Baltimore: Johns Hopkins University Press, 1982.

Kea, Ray A. "'When I Die, I Shall Return to My Own Land': An 'Amina' Slave Rebellion in the Danish West Indies, 1733–1734." In *The Cloth of Many Colored Silks: Papers on History and Society, Ghanaian and Islamic in Honor of Ivor Wilks*, edited by John Hunwick and Nancy Lawler, 159–93. Evanston, IL: Northwestern University Press, 1996.

Keel, Terence. *Divine Variations: How Christian Thought Became Racial Science*. Stanford, CA: Stanford University Press, 2019.

Kelley, Sean M., and Paul E. Lovejoy. "Oldendorp's 'Amina': Ethnonyms, History, and Identity in the African Diaspora." *Journal of Global Slavery* 8, nos. 2–3 (2023): 303–30.

Khan, Aisha. *The Deepest Dye: Obeah, Hosay, and Race in the Atlantic World*. Cambridge, MA: Harvard University Press, 2021.

Klassen, Pamela E. "Medals, Memory, and Findspots." *MAVCOR Journal* 6, no. 3 (2022). https://doi.org/10.22332/mav.ess.2022.9.

Klassen, Pamela E. "Spiritual Jurisdictions: Treaty People and the Queen of Canada." In Johnson et al. *Ekklesia: Three Inquiries in Church and State*.

Kolapo, Femi J. "The Igbo and Their Neighbours During the Era of the Atlantic Slave-Trade." *Slavery & Abolition* 25, no. 1 (2004): 114–33.

Konadu, Kwasi. *The Akan Diaspora in the Americas*. New York: Oxford University Press, 2010.

Kopelson, Heather Miyano. *Faithful Bodies: Performing Religion and Race in the Puritan Atlantic*. New York: NYU Press, 2014.

Kopytoff, Barbara K. "Religious Change Among the Jamaican Maroons: The Ascendance of the Christian God Within a Traditional Cosmology." *Journal of Social History* 20, no. 3 (1987): 463–84.

Kopytoff, Barbara Klamon. "Colonial Treaty as Sacred Charter of the Jamaican Maroons." *Ethnohistory* 26, no. 1 (1979): 45–64.

Kopytoff, Barbara Klamon. "The Early Political Development of Jamaican Maroon Societies." *William & Mary Quarterly* 35, no. 2 (1978): 287–307.

Kopytoff, Barbara Klamon. "Jamaican Maroon Political Organization: The Effects of the Treaties." *Social and Economic Studies* 25, no. 2 (1976): 87–105.

Kopytoff, Barbara Klamon. "The Maroons of Jamaica: an Ethnohistorical Study of Incomplete Polities, 1655–1905." PhD diss., University of Pennsylvania, 1973.

Krug, Jessica A. "Social Dismemberment, Social (Re)Membering: Obeah Idioms, Kromanti Identities and the Trans-Atlantic Politics of Memory, c. 1675–Present." *Slavery & Abolition* 35, no. 4 (2014): 537–58.

Landers, Jane. "Maroon Women in Colonial Spanish America: Case Studies in the Circum-Caribbean from the Sixteenth Through the Eighteenth Centuries." In *Beyond Bondage*, edited by David Barry Gaspar and Darlene Clark Hine, 3–18. Free Women of Color in the Americas. Urbana: University of Illinois Press, 2004.

Landry, Timothy. "Vodún, Spirited Forests, and the African Atlantic Forest Complex." *Journal of Africana Religions* 8, no. 2 (2020): 173–201.

Law, Robin. "Ethnicities of Enslaved Africans in the Diaspora: On the Meanings of 'Mina' (Again)." *History in Africa* 32 (2005): 247–67.

Law, Robin. "Ethnicity and the Slave Trade: 'Lucumi' and 'Nago' as Ethnonyms in West Africa." *History in Africa* 24 (1997): 205–19.

Law, Robin. "Problems of Plagiarism, Harmonization and Misunderstanding in Contemporary European Sources: Early (pre-1680s) Sources for the 'Slave Coast' of West Africa." *Paideuma* 33 (1987): 337–58.

Law, Robin. "Religion, Trade and Politics on the 'Slave Coast': Roman Catholic Missions in Allada and Whydah in the Seventeenth Century." *Journal of Religion in Africa* 21, no. 1 (1991): 42–77.

Law, Robin. *The Slave Coast of West Africa, 1550–1750: The Impact of the Atlantic Slave Trade on an African Society*. Oxford: Clarendon Press, 1991.

Lindsay, Lisa A., and John Wood Sweet. *Biography and the Black Atlantic*. Philadelphia: University of Pennsylvania Press, 2013.

Livesay, Daniel. *Children of Uncertain Fortune: Mixed-Race Jamaicans in Britain and the Atlantic Family, 1733–1833*. Chapel Hill: University of North Carolina Press, 2018.

Lofton, Kathryn. *Consuming Religion*. Chicago: University of Chicago Press, 2017.

Lofton, Kathryn. "Religious History as Religious Studies." *Religion* 42, no. 3 (2012): 383–94.

Lovejoy, Paul E. "Autobiography and Memory: Gustavus Vassa, Alias Olaudah Equiano, the African." *Slavery & Abolition* 27, no. 3 (2006): 317–47.

Lovejoy, Paul E. "Olaudah Equiano or Gustavus Vassa—What's in a Name?" *Atlantic Studies* 9, no. 2 (2012): 165–84.

Lovejoy, Paul E. *Slavery in the Global Diaspora of Africa*. New York: Routledge, 2019.

Lowry, James. "'Displaced Archives': Proposing a Research Agenda." *Archival Science* 19, no. 4 (2019): 349–58. https://doi.org/10.1007/s10502-019-09326-8.

Lowry, James, ed. *Disputed Archival Heritage*. London: Routledge, 2022.

Lum, Kathryn Gin. *Heathen: Religion and Race in American History*. Cambridge, MA: Harvard University Press, 2022.

Lum, Kathryn Gin. "The Historyless Heathen and the Stagnating Pagan: History as Non-Native Category?" *Religion and American Culture: A Journal of Interpretation* 28, no. 1 (2018): 52–91.

MacGaffey, Wyatt. "A Central African Kingdom: Kongo in 1480." In Bostoen and Brinkman, *The Kongo Kingdom: The Origins, Dynamics and Cosmopolitan Culture of an African Polity*, 42–59.

MacGaffey, Wyatt. *Religion and Society in Central Africa: The BaKongo of Lower Zaire*. Chicago: University of Chicago Press, 1986.

Mann, Kristin. "Shifting Paradigms in the Study of the African Diaspora and of Atlantic History and Culture." *Slavery & Abolition* 22, no. 1 (2001): 1–21.

Martínez, María Elena. *Genealogical Fictions: Limpieza de Sangre, Religion, and Gender in Colonial Mexico*. Stanford, CA: Stanford University Press, 2011.

Masuzawa, Tomoko. *The Invention of World Religions: Or, How European Universalism Was Preserved in the Language of Pluralism*. Chicago: University of Chicago Press, 2005.

Masuzawa, Tomoko. "Troubles with Materiality: The Ghost of Fetishism in the Nineteenth Century." *Comparative Studies in Society and History* 42, no. 2 (2000): 242–67.

Matory, J. Lorand. *Black Atlantic Religion: Tradition, Transnationalism, and Matriarchy in the Afro-Brazilian Candomblé*. Princeton, NJ: Princeton University Press, 2005.

Matory, J. Lorand. *The Fetish Revisited: Marx, Freud, and the Gods Black People Make*. Durham, NC: Duke University Press, 2018.

Matory, J. Lorand. "From 'Survival' to 'Dialogue': Analytic Tropes in the Study of African-Diaspora Cultural History." In *Transatlantic Caribbean: Dialogues of People, Practices, Ideas*, edited by I. Kummels, C. Rauhut, S. Rinke, and B. Timm. Bielefeld, Germany: Transcript Verlag, 2014.

Matory, J. Lorand. *Sex and the Empire That Is No More: Gender and the Politics of Metaphor in Oyo Yoruba Religion*. Minneapolis: University of Minnesota Press, 1994.

May, Nicholas. "Holy Rebellion: Religious Assembly Laws in Antebellum South Carolina and Virginia." *American Journal of Legal History* 49, no. 3 (2007): 237–56.

McCrary, Charles. "Fortune Telling and American Religious Freedom." *Religion and American Culture* 28, no. 2 (2018): 269–306.

McCrary, Charles. *Sincerely Held: American Secularism and Its Believers*. Chicago: University of Chicago Press, 2022.

McCrary, Charles, and Jeffrey Wheatley. "The Protestant Secular in the Study of American Religion: Reappraisal and Suggestions." *Religion* 47, no. 2 (2017): 256–76.

McGeary, Stephen A. "On Fanaticism and Funding: Obeah Acts in Jamaican Moravian Missionary Communities." *Journal of Moravian History* 22, no. 1 (2022): 1–19.

McKee, Helen. "From Violence to Alliance: Maroons and White Settlers in Jamaica, 1739–1795." *Slavery & Abolition* 39, no. 1 (2017): 1–26.

McKittrick, Katherine. *Demonic Grounds: Black Women and the Cartographies of Struggle*. Minneapolis: University of Minnesota Press, 2006.

McKnight, Kathryn Joy. "Gendered Declarations: Testimonies of Three Captured Maroon Women, Cartagena de Indias, 1634." *Colonial Latin American Historical Review* 12, no. 4 (2003): 499–527.

McNally, Michael D. *Defend the Sacred: Native American Religious Freedom Beyond the First Amendment*. Princeton, NJ: Princeton University Press, 2020.

McTighe, Laura, and Women With A Vision. *Fire Dreams: Making Black Feminist Liberation in the South*. Durham, NC: Duke University Press, 2024.

Meier, Gudrun, Peter Stein, Stephan Palmié, and Horst Ulbricht, eds. *Christian Georg Andreas Oldendorp: Historie der caribischen Inseln Sanct Thomas, Sanct Crux und Sanct Jan: Kommentarband*. Herrnhut: Herrnhuter Verlag, 2010.

Meyer, Dietrich. "Zinzendorf und Herrnhut." In *Geschichte des Pietismus. Vol. 2, Der Pietismus im Achtzehnten Jahrhundert*, edited by Klaus Deppermann and Ulrich Gäbler, 5–106. Göttingen, Germany: Vandenhoeck & Ruprecht, 1995.

Merritt, Jane T. "Dreaming of the Savior's Blood: Moravians and the Indian Great Awakening in Pennsylvania." *William & Mary Quarterly* 54, no. 4 (1997): 723–46.

Mettele, Gisela. *Weltbürgertum oder Gottesreich: Die Herrnhuter Bruedergemeine als Globalgemeinschaft, 1727–1852*. Göttingen, Germany: Vandenhoeck & Ruprecht, 2009.

Miller, Joseph Calder. *Way of Death: Merchant Capitalism and the Angolan Slave Trade, 1730–1830*. Madison: University of Wisconsin Press, 1988.

Mintz, Sidney W. *Caribbean Transformations*. Chicago: Aldine, 1974.

Mintz, Sidney W. *Sweetness and Power: The Place of Sugar in Modern History*. New York: Penguin Books, 1986.

Mintz, Sidney W. and Richard Price. *The Birth of African-American Culture: An Anthropological Perspective*. Boston: Beacon Press, 1992.

Monroe, Alicia L. "Black Brotherhoods in the Portuguese Atlantic." In *Oxford Research Encyclopedia of Latin American History*. Oxford: Oxford University Press, 2023.

Morgan, Jennifer L. *Laboring Women: Reproduction and Gender in New World Slavery*. Philadelphia: University of Pennsylvania Press, 2004.

Morgan, Jennifer L. "Partus Sequitur Ventrem: Law, Race, and Reproduction in Colonial Slavery." *Small Axe: A Caribbean Journal of Criticism* 22, no. 1 (2018): 1–17.

Morgan, Jennifer L. *Reckoning with Slavery: Gender, Kinship, and Capitalism in the Early Black Atlantic*. Durham, NC: Duke University Press, 2021.

Morgan, Philip D. "Slaves and Livestock in Eighteenth-Century Jamaica: Vineyard Pen, 1750–1751." *William & Mary Quarterly* 52, no. 1 (1995): 47–76.

Moulton, Alex A. "Towards the Arboreal Side-Effectsof Marronage: Black Geographies and Ecologies of the Jamaican Forest." *Environment and Planning E: Nature and Space* 6, no. 1 (2023): 3–23.

Mt. Pleasant, Alyssa, Caroline Wigginton, and Kelly Wisecup. "Materials and Methods in Native American and Indigenous Studies: Completing the Turn." *William & Mary Quarterly* 75, no. 2 (2018): 207–36.

Murphy, Joseph M. "Yoruba Religions in Diaspora." *Religion Compass* 4, no. 7 (2010): 400–409.

Newman, Brooke N. *A Dark Inheritance: Blood, Race, and Sex in Colonial Jamaica*. New Haven, CT: Yale University Press, 2018.

Newman, Simon P. *A New World of Labor: The Development of Plantation Slavery in the British Atlantic*. Philadelphia: University of Pennsylvania Press, 2013.

Nongbri, Brent. *Before Religion: A History of a Modern Concept*. New Haven, CT: Yale University Press, 2013.

Northrup, David. "Igbo and Myth Igbo: Culture and Ethnicity in the Atlantic World, 1600–1850." *Slavery & Abolition* 21, no. 3 (2000): 1–20.

Nwokeji, G. Ugo. *The Slave Trade and Culture in the Bight of Biafra: An African Society in the Atlantic World*. Cambridge: Cambridge University Press, 2010.

Ogborn, Miles. "The Power of Speech: Orality, Oaths and Evidence in the British Atlantic World, 1650–1800." *Transactions of the Institute of British Geographers* 36, no. 1 (2010): 109–25.

Ogundiran, Akinwumi, and Paula Saunders. "On the Materiality of Black Atlantic Rituals." In *Materialities of Ritual in the Black Atlantic*, edited by Akinwumi Ogundiran and Paula Saunders, 1–27. Bloomington: Indiana University Press, 2014.

Olupona, Jacob K. *City of 201 Gods: Ilé-Ifè in Time, Space, and the Imagination*. Berkeley: University of California Press, 2011.

Owens, Emily A. "Consent." *Differences* 30, no. 1 (2019): 148–56.

Owens, Emily A. *Consent in the Presence of Force: Sexual Violence and Black Women's Survival in Antebellum New Orleans*. Chapel Hill: University of North Carolina Press, 2023.

Palmié, Stephan, ed. *Africas of the Americas: Beyond the Search for Origins in the Study of Afro-Atlantic Religions*. Leiden: Brill, 2008.

Palmié, Stephan. "Oldendorps Bedeutung für die Afroamerikanistik." In Meier et al., *Christian Georg Andreas Oldendorp*, 191–206.

Palmié, Stephan, ed. *Slave Cultures and the Cultures of Slavery*. Knoxville: University of Tennessee Press, 1995.

Palmié, Stephan. *Wizards and Scientists: Explorations in Afro-Cuban Modernity and Tradition*. Durham, NC: Duke University Press, 2002.

Parés, Luis. "The Hula 'Problem': Ethnicity on the Pre-Colonial Slave Coast." In *The Changing Worlds of Atlantic Africa: Essays in Honor of Robin Law*, edited by Toyin Falola and Matt D. Childs. Durham, NC: Carolina Academic Press, 2009.

Paton, Diana. *The Cultural Politics of Obeah: Religion, Colonialism and Modernity in the Caribbean World*. Cambridge: Cambridge University Press, 2015.

Paton, Diana. "Mary Williamson's Letter, or, Seeing Women and Sisters in the Archives of Atlantic Slavery." *Transactions of the Royal Historical Society* 29 (2019): 163–65.

Paton, Diana. "Obeah Acts: Producing and Policing the Boundaries of Religion in the Caribbean." *Small Axe: A Caribbean Journal of Criticism* 13, no. 1 (2009): 1–18.

Paton, Diana. "The Racist History of Jamaica's Obeah Act." *The Gleaner*, June 16, 2019.

Paton, Diana. "The Trials of Inspector Thomas: Policing and Ethnography in Jamaica." In Paton and Forde, *Obeah and Other Powers*.

Paton, Diana. "Witchcraft, Poison, Law, and Atlantic Slavery." *William & Mary Quarterly* 69, no. 2 (2012): 235–64.

Paton, Diana, and Maarit Forde. *Obeah and Other Powers: The Politics of Caribbean Religion and Healing*. Durham, NC: Duke University Press, 2012.

Patterson, Orlando. "Slavery and Slave Revolts: A Socio-Historical Analysis of the First Maroon War Jamaica, 1655–1740." *Social and Economic Studies* 19, no. 3 (1970): 289–325.

Patterson, Orlando. *The Sociology of Slavery: An Analysis of the Origins, Development, and Structure of Negro Slave Society in Jamaica*. Rutherford, NJ: Fairleigh Dickinson University Press, 1969.

Paugh, Katherine. *The Politics of Reproduction: Race, Medicine, and Fertility in the Age of Abolition*. Oxford: Oxford University Press, 2022.

Paugh, Katherine. "Yaws, Syphilis, Sexuality, and the Circulation of Medical Knowledge in the British Caribbean and the Atlantic World." *Bulletin of the History of Medicine* 88, no. 2 (2014): 225–52.

Pearsall, Sarah M. S. "'Having Many Wives' in Two American Rebellions: The Politics of Households and the Radically Conservative." *American Historical Review* 118, no. 4 (2013): 1001–28.

Perry, Imani. *Vexy Thing: On Gender and Liberation*. Durham, NC: Duke University Press, 2018.

Pestana, Carla Gardina. *The English Conquest of Jamaica: Oliver Cromwell's Bid for Empire*. Cambridge, MA: Belknap Press, 2017.

Peucker, Paul. "Aus allen Nationen: Nichteuropäer in den deutschen Brüdergemeinden des 18. Jahrhunderts." *Unitas Fratrum: Zeitschrift für Geschichte und Gegenwartsfragen der Brüdergemeine* 59–60 (2007): 1–35.

Peucker, Paul. *Herrnhut: The Formation of a Moravian Community, 1722–1732*. University Park: Pennsylvania State University Press, 2022.

Peucker, Paul. "Pink, White, and Blue: Function and Meaning of the Colored Choir Ribbons with the Moravians." In *Pietism and Community in Europe and North America*, edited by Jonathan Strom, 179–98. Leiden: Brill, 2010.

Peucker, Paul. *A Time of Sifting: Mystical Marriage and the Crisis of Moravian Piety in the Eighteenth Century*. University Park: Pennsylvania State University Press, 2015.

Pietz, William. "The Problem of the Fetish, I." *RES: Anthropology and Aesthetics* 9 (1985): 5–17.

Pietz, William. "The Problem of the Fetish, II: The Origin of the Fetish." *RES: Anthropology and Aesthetics* 13 (1987): 23–45.

Pietz, William. "The Problem of the Fetish, IIIa: Bosman's Guinea and the Enlightenment Theory of Fetishism." *RES: Anthropology and Aesthetics* 16 (1988): 105–24.

Podmore, Colin. *The Moravian Church in England, 1728–1760*. Oxford: Oxford University Press, 1998.

Price, Richard. *Alabi's World*. Baltimore: Johns Hopkins University Press, 1990.

Price, Richard, ed. *Maroon Societies: Rebel Slave Communities in the Americas*. Baltimore: Johns Hopkins University Press, 1996.

Price, Sally. *Co-Wives and Calabashes*. Ann Arbor: University of Michigan Press, 1993.

Price, Sally. "Sexism and the Construction of Reality: An Afro-American Example." *American Ethnologist* 10, no. 3 (1983): 460–76.

Promey, Sally M., ed. *Sensational Religion: Sensory Cultures in Material Practice*. New Haven, CT: Yale University Press, 2014.

Raboteau, Albert J. *Slave Religion: The "Invisible Institution" in the Antebellum South*. New York: Oxford University Press, 1978.

Ramsey, Kate. "Powers of Imagination and Legal Regimes Against 'Obeah' in the Late Eighteenth- and Early Nineteenth-Century British Caribbean." *Osiris* (Bruges) 36, no. 1 (2021): 46–63.

Ramsey, Kate. *The Spirits and the Law: Vodou and Power in Haiti*. Chicago: University of Chicago Press, 2011.

Raphael-Hernandez, Heike. "The Right to Freedom: Eighteenth-Century Slave Resistance and Early Moravian Missions in the Danish West Indies and Dutch Suriname." *Atlantic Studies* 14, no. 4 (2017): 457–75.

Reis, João José. *Death Is a Festival: Funeral Rites and Rebellion in Nineteenth-Century Brazil*. Chapel Hill: University of North Carolina Press, 2003.

Reis, João José. *Divining Slavery and Freedom*. New York: Cambridge University Press, 2015.

Reis, João José. *Slave Rebellion in Brazil: The Muslim Uprising of 1835 in Bahia*. Baltimore: Johns Hopkins University Press, 1993.

Robertson, James. "Architectures of Confidence? Spanish Town, Jamaica, 1655–1792." In *Articulating British Classicism: New Approaches to Eighteenth-Century Architecture*, edited by Barbara Arciszewska and Elizabeth McKellar, 227–58. New York: Routledge, 2004.

Robertson, James. "Giving Directions in Spanish Town, Jamaica: Comprehending a Tropical Townscape." *Journal of Urban History* 35, no. 5 (2009): 718–42.

Robertson, James. "Late Seventeenth-Century Spanish Town, Jamaica: Building an English City on Spanish Foundations." *Early American Studies* 6, no. 2 (2008): 346–90.

Robinson, Carey. *The Fighting Maroons of Jamaica*. Kingston, Jamaica: William Collins and Sangster, 1969.

Roeber, A. G. "The Waters of Rebirth: The Eighteenth Century and Transoceanic Protestant Christianity." *Church History* 79, no. 1 (2010): 40–76.

Rowe, Erin Kathleen. *Black Saints in Early Modern Global Catholicism*. Cambridge: Cambridge University Press, 2019.

Rucker, Walter C. "Conjure, Magic, and Power: The Influence of Afro-Atlantic Religious Practices on Slave Resistance and Rebellion." *Journal of Black Studies* 32, no. 1 (2001): 84–103.

Rucker, Walter C. "'Earth from a Dead Negro's Grave': Ritual Technologies and Mortuary Realms in the Eighteenth-Century Gold Coast Diaspora." In *Slavery and Its Legacy in Ghana and the Diaspora*, edited by Rebecca Shumway and Trevor Getz, 62–84. London: Bloomsbury Academic, 2017.

Rucker, Walter C. *Gold Coast Diasporas: Identity, Culture, and Power*. Blacks in the Diaspora. Bloomington: Indiana University Press, 2015.

Rugemer, Edward B. "The Development of Mastery and Race in the Comprehensive Slave Codes of the Greater Caribbean during the Seventeenth Century." *William & Mary Quarterly* 70, no. 3 (2013): 429–58.

Rugemer, Edward B. *Slave Law and the Politics of Resistance in the Early Atlantic World.* Cambridge, MA: Harvard University Press, 2018.

Sanneh, Lamin. "Christianity in Africa." In *The Cambridge History of Christianity*, edited by Stewart Brown and Timothy Tackett, 411–32. Cambridge: Cambridge University Press, 2006.

Sanneh, Lamin. *Whose Religion Is Christianity?: The Gospel Beyond the West.* Grand Rapids, MI: Wm. B. Eerdmans, 2003.

Schattschneider, David A. "The Missionary Theologies of Zinzendorf and Spangenberg." *Transactions of the Moravian Historical Society* 22, no. 3 (1975): 213–33.

Schiebinger, Londa. "Agnotology and Exotic Abortifacients: The Cultural Production of Ignorance in the Eighteenth-Century Atlantic World." *Proceedings of the American Philosophical Society* 149, no. 3 (2005): 316–43.

Schiebinger, Londa. *Plants and Empire: Colonial Bioprospecting in the Atlantic World.* Cambridge, MA: Harvard University Press, 2007.

Schipper, Jeremy. "'On Such Texts Comment Is Unnecessary': Biblical Interpretation in the Trial of Denmark Vesey." *Journal of the American Academy of Religion* 85, no. 4 (2017): 1032–49.

Schuler, Monica. *Alas, Alas, Kongo: A Social History of Indentured African Immigration into Jamaica, 1841–1865.* Baltimore: Johns Hopkins University Press, 1980.

Schwartz, Marie Jenkins. *Born in Bondage: Growing Up Enslaved in the Antebellum South.* Cambridge, MA: Harvard University Press, 2001.

Schwartz, Marie Jenkins. *Birthing a Slave: Motherhood and Medicine in the Antebellum South.* Cambridge, MA: Harvard University Press, 2010.

Scott, Shavagne. "Women on the Fringes: Reimagining Marronage Through the Gendered Landscape of Colonial Jamaica, Nova Scotia, and Sierra Leone." PhD diss., New York University, 2023.

Sebro, Louise. "Freedom, Autonomy, and Independence: Exceptional African Caribbean Life Experiences in St. Thomas, the Danish West Indies, in the Middle of the 18th Century." In *Ports of Globalisation, Places of Creolisation*, edited by Holger Weiss. Leiden: Brill, 2016.

Sebro, Louise, *Mellem afrikaner og kreol: Etnisk identitet og social navigation i Dansk Vestindien, 1730–1770.* Lund, Sweden: Historiska Institutionen ved Lunds Universitet, 2010.

Sedgwick, Eve Kosofsky. *Touching Feeling: Affect, Peogy, Performativity.* Durham, NC: Duke University Press, 2003.

Seeman, Erik R. *Death in the New World: Cross-Cultural Encounters, 1492–1800.* Philadelphia: University of Pennsylvania Press, 2010.

Seeman, Erik R. "'Justise Must Take Plase': Three African Americans Speak of Religion in Eighteenth-Century New England." *William & Mary Quarterly* 56, no. 2 (1999): 393–414.

Sensbach, Jon F. "'Don't Teach My Negroes to Be Pietists': Pietism and the Roots of the Black Protestant Church." In *Pietism in Germany and North America, 1680–1820*, edited by Jonathan Strom, Hartmut Lehmann, and James Van Horn Melton, 183–98. Burlington, VT: Ashgate, 2009.

Sensbach, Jon F. "Race and the Early Moravian Church: A Comparative Perspective." *Transactions of the Moravian Historical Society* 31 (2000): 1–10.

Sensbach, Jon F. "Religion and the Early South in an Age of Atlantic Empire." *Journal of Southern History* 73, no. 3 (2007): 631–42.

Sensbach, Jon F. *A Separate Canaan: The Making of an Afro-Moravian World in North Carolina, 1763–1840*. Chapel Hill: University of North Carolina Press, 1998.

Sensbach, Jon F. *Rebecca's Revival: Creating Black Christianity in the Atlantic World*. Cambridge, MA: Harvard University Press, 2006.

Settles, Joshua. "The Place of Christianity in the Critical Debates of Africana Religious Studies." *Journal of Africana Religions* 9, no. 1 (2021): 101–17.

Sharpe, Jenny. *Ghosts of Slavery: A Literary Archaeology of Black Women's Lives*. Minneapolis: University of Minnesota Press, 2002.

Sheldon, Myrna Perez, Ahmed Ragab, and Terence Keel, eds. *Critical Approaches to Science and Religion*. New York: Columbia University Press. 2023.

Sheridan, Richard B. "The Maroons of Jamaica, 1730–1830: Livelihood, Demography and Health." *Slavery & Abolition* 6, no. 3 (1985): 152–72.

Sheridan, Richard B. "Slave Medicine in Jamaica: Thomas Thistlewood's 'Receipts for a Physick,' 1750–1786." *Jamaican Historical Review* 17 (1991): 1.

Shumway, Rebecca. *The Fante and the Transatlantic Slave Trade*. Rochester Studies in African History and the Diaspora. Rochester, NY: University of Rochester Press, 2011.

Shumway, Rebecca. "The Fante Shrine of Nananom Mpow and the Atlantic Slave Trade in Southern Ghana." *International Journal of African Historical Studies* 44, no. 1 (2011): 27–44.

Sidbury, James. "From Igbo Israeli to African Christian: The Emergence of Racial Identity in Olaudah Equiano's Interesting Narrative." In *Africas of the Americas*, edited by Stephan Palmié.

Simonsen, Gunvor. "Belonging in Africa: Frederik Svane and Christian Protten on the Gold Coast in the Eighteenth Century." *Itinerario* 39, no. 1 (2015): 91–115.

Simonsen, Gunvor. "Magic, Obeah and Law in the Danish West Indies, 1750s–1840s." In Weiss, *Ports of Globalisation*, 245–79.

Sivapragasam, Michael. "After the Treaties: A Social, Economic and Demographic History of Maroon Society in Jamaica, 1739–1842." PhD diss., University of Southampton, 2018.

Smallwood, Stephanie E. *Saltwater Slavery: A Middle Passage from Africa to American Diaspora*. Cambridge, MA: Harvard University Press, 2008.

Smith, Jonathan Z. "Religion, Religions, Religious." In *Critical Terms for Religious Studies*, edited by Mark C. Taylor, 269–84. Chicago: University of Chicago Press, 1998.

Smith, Linda Tuhiwai. *Decolonizing Methodologies: Research and Indigenous Peoples*. London: Zed Books, 2021.

Sobel, Mechal. *Trabelin' On: The Slave Journey to an Afro-Baptist Faith*. Princeton, NJ: Princeton University Press, 1988.

Sommer, Elisabeth. "Fashion Passion: The Rhetoric of Dress Within the Eighteenth-Century Moravian Brethren." In Gillespie and Beachy, *Pious Pursuits*, 83–96.

Sparks, Randy J. *The Two Princes of Calabar: An Eighteenth-Century Atlantic Odyssey*. Cambridge, MA: Harvard University Press, 2004.

Sparks, Randy J. *Where the Negroes Are Masters: An African Port in the Era of the Slave Trade*. Cambridge, MA: Harvard University Press, 2014.

Spillers, Hortense J. "Mama's Baby, Papa's Maybe: An American Grammar Book." *Diacritics* 17, no. 2 (1987): 65–81.
Stewart, Dianne M. *Obeah, Orisa, and Religious Identity in Trinidad*. Vol 2, *Africana Nations and the Power of Black Sacred Imagination*. Vol 2: Orisa. Religious Cultures of African and African Diaspora People. Durham, NC: Duke University Press, 2022.
Stewart, Dianne M. *Three Eyes for the Journey: African Dimensions of the Jamaican Religious Experience*. Oxford: Oxford University Press, 2004.
Stewart Diakité, Dianne M., and Tracey E. Hucks. "Africana Religious Studies: Toward a Transdisciplinary Agenda in an Emerging Field." *Journal of Africana Religions* 1, no. 1 (2013): 28–77.
Stoler, Ann. *Along the Archival Grain: Epistemic Anxieties and Colonial Common Sense*. Princeton, NJ: Princeton University Press, 2008.
Strickrodt, Silke. *Afro-European Trade in the Atlantic World*. Martlesham, UK: Boydell and Brewer, 2015.
Strickrodt, Silke, and Thomas Miles. "A Neglected Source for the History of Little Popo: The Thomas Miles Papers, ca. 1789–1796." *History in Africa* 28 (2001): 293–330.
Strom, Jonathan. *Pietism and Community in Europe and North America 1650–1850*. Leiden: Brill, 2010.
Strom, Jonathan, Hartmut Lehmann, and James Van Horn Melton. *Pietism in Germany and North America, 1680–1820*. Burlington, VT: Ashgate, 2009.
Sullivan, Winnifred Fallers. *The Impossibility of Religious Freedom*. Princeton, NJ: Princeton University Press, 2018.
Sutherland, Tonia. "Disrupting Carceral Narratives: Race, Rape, and the Archives." *Open Information Science* 4, no. 1 (2020): 156–68.
Sweeney, Shauna J. "Market Marronage: Fugitive Women and the Internal Marketing System in Jamaica, 1781–1834." *William & Mary Quarterly* 76, no. 2 (2019): 197–222.
Sweet, James H. *Recreating Africa: Culture, Kinship, and Religion in the African-Portuguese World, 1441–1770*. Chapel Hill: University of North Carolina Press, 2003.
Thomas, Todne. *Kincraft: The Making of Black Evangelical Sociality*. Durham, NC: Duke University Press, 2021.
Thompson, Alvin O. "Gender and Marronage in the Caribbean." *Journal of Caribbean History* 39, no. 2 (2005): 262–89.
Thompson, Alvin O. *Flight to Freedom: African Runaways and Maroons in the Americas*. Kingston, Jamaica: University of the West Indies Press, 2006.
Thornton, John F. *Africa and Africans in the Making of the Atlantic World, 1400–1800*. Cambridge: Cambridge University Press, 1998.
Thornton, John K. "Afro-Christian Syncretism in the Kingdom of Kongo." *Journal of African History* 54, no. 1 (2013): 53–77.
Thornton, John K. "Cannibals, Witches, and Slave Traders in the Atlantic World." *William & Mary Quarterly* 60, no. 2 (2003): 273–94.
Thornton, John K. "Central African Names and African-American Naming Patterns." *William & Mary Quarterly* 50, no. 4 (1993): 727–42.
Thornton, John K. "The Coromantees: An African Cultural Group in Colonial North America and the Caribbean." *Journal of Caribbean History* 32, nos. 1–2 (1998): 161–78.

Thornton, John K. "The Development of an African Catholic Church in the Kingdom of Kongo, 1491–1750." *Journal of African History* 25, no. 2 (1984): 147–67.

Thornton, John K. *The Kingdom of Kongo: Civil War and Transition, 1641–1718.* Madison: University of Wisconsin Press, 1983.

Thornton, John K. *The Kongolese Saint Anthony: Dona Beatriz Kimpa Vita and the Antonian Movement, 1684–1706.* Cambridge: Cambridge University Press, 1998.

Thornton, John K. "On the Trail of Voodoo: African Christianity in Africa and the Americas." *The Americas* 44, no. 3 (1988): 261–78.

Thornton, John K. "The Origins of Kongo: A Revised Vision." In Bostoen and Brinkman, *The Kongo Kingdom*, 17–41.

Thornton, John K. "Religious and Ceremonial Life in the Kongo and Mbundu Areas, 1500–1700." In Heywood, *Central Africans and Cultural Transformations in the American Diaspora*, 71–90.

Thornton, John K. "Soyo and Kongo: The Undoing of the Kingdom's Centralization." In Bostoen and Brinkman, *The Kongo Kingdom*, 103–22.

Thorp, Daniel B. "New Wine in Old Bottles: Cultural Persistence Among Non-White Converts to the Moravian Church." *Transactions of the Moravian Historical Society* 30 (1998): 1–8.

Tomlins, Christopher. *In the Matter of Nat Turner: A Speculative History.* Princeton, NJ: Princeton University Press, 2020.

Tortorici, Zeb. *Sins Against Nature: Sex and Archives in Colonial New Spain.* Durham, NC: Duke University Press Books, 2018.

Tortorici, Zeb. "Visceral Archives of the Body: Consuming the Dead, Digesting the Divine." *GLQ: A Journal of Lesbian and Gay Studies* 20, no. 4 (2014): 407–37.

Trouillot, Michel-Rolph. *Silencing the Past: Power and the Production of History.* Boston: Beacon, 1995.

Turner, Mary. *Slaves and Missionaries: The Disintegration of Jamaican Slave Society, 1787–1834.* Urbana: University of Illinois Press, 1982.

Turner, Sasha. *Contested Bodies: Pregnancy, Childrearing, and Slavery in Jamaica.* Philadelphia: University of Pennsylvania Press, 2017.

Turner, Sasha. "The Nameless and the Forgotten: Maternal Grief, Sacred Protection, and the Archive of Slavery." *Slavery & Abolition* 38, no. 2 (2017): 232–50.

US Department of State. "2019 Report on International Religious Freedom: Jamaica." Washington, DC: US Department of State, 2019.

Vermeulen, Heather V. "Thomas Thistlewood's Libidinal Linnaean Project: Slavery, Ecology, and Knowledge Production." *Small Axe: A Caribbean Journal of Criticism* 22, no. 1 (55) (2018): 19.

Vogt, Peter. "Nicholas Ludwig von Zinzendorf." In *The Pietist Theologians: An Introduction to Theology in the Seventeenth and Eighteenth Centuries*, edited by Carter Lindberg, 207–23. Malden, MA: Wiley-Blackwell, 2004.

Vogt, Peter. "Zinzendorf und die Pennsylvanischen Synoden." *Unitas Fratrum: Zeitschrift für Geschichte und Gegenwartsfragen der Brudergemeine* 36 (1994): 5–62.

Ward, W. R. *The Protestant Evangelical Awakening.* Cambridge: Cambridge University Press, 1992.

Ward, W. R. "The Renewed Unity of the Brethren: Ancient Church, New Sect or Interconfessional Movement?" *Bulletin of the John Rylands University Library of Manchester* 70, no. 3 (1988): 77–92.

Warner-Lewis, Maureen. *Archibald Monteath: Igbo, Jamaican, Moravian*. Kingston, Jamaica: University of the West Indies Press, 2007.

Weisenfeld, Judith. "The House We Live In: Religio-Racial Theories and the Study of Religion." *Journal of the American Academy of Religion* 88, no. 2 (2020): 440–59.

Weisenfeld, Judith. *New World A-Coming: Black Religion and Racial Identity During the Great Migration*. New York: NYU Press, 2017.

Weiss, Holger, ed. *Ports of Globalisation, Places of Creolisation*. Leiden: Brill, 2015.

Wells-Oghoghomeh, Alexis. "'She Come Like a Nightmare': Hags, Witches and the Gendered Trans-Sense Among the Enslaved in the Lower South." *Journal of Africana Religions* 5, no. 2 (2017): 239–74.

Wells-Oghoghomeh, Alexis. *The Souls of Womenfolk: The Religious Cultures of Enslaved Women in the Lower South*. Chapel Hill: University of North Carolina Press, 2021.

Wenger, Tisa. *We Have a Religion: The 1920s Pueblo Indian Dance Controversy and American Religious Freedom*. Chapel Hill: University of North Carolina Press, 2009.

Wenger, Tisa. *Religious Freedom: The Contested History of an American Ideal*. Chapel Hill: University of North Carolina Press, 2017.

Wenger, Tisa, and Sylvester A. Johnson. *Religion and US Empire: Critical New Histories*. New York: NYU Press, 2022.

Wheeler, Rachel. *To Live upon Hope: Mohicans and Missionaries in the Eighteenth-Century Northeast*. Ithaca, NY: Cornell University Press, 2008.

Wheeler, Rachel, and Sarah Eyerly. "Singing Box 331: Re-Sounding Eighteenth-Century Mohican Hymns from the Moravian Archives." *William & Mary Quarterly* 76, no. 4 (2019): 649–96.

White, Deborah G. *Ar'n't I a Woman? Female Slaves in the Plantation South*. New York: W. W. Norton, 1999.

Wilson, Kathleen. "The Performance of Freedom: Maroons and the Colonial Order in Eighteenth-Century Jamaica and the Atlantic Sound." *William & Mary Quarterly* 66, no. 1 (2009): 45–86.

Wisecup, Kelly. "Knowing Obeah." *Atlantic Studies* 10, no. 3 (2013): 406–25.

Wisecup, Kelly. *Medical Encounters: Knowledge and Identity in Early American Literatures*. Amherst: University of Massachusetts Press, 2013.

Yeo, Geoffrey. "A Case Without Parallel: The Bishops of London and the Anglican Church Overseas, 1660–1748." *Journal of Ecclesiastical History* 44, no. 3 (1993): 450–75.

Young, Jason R. "All God's Children Had Wings: The Flying African in History, Literature, and Lore." *Journal of Africana Religions* 5, no. 1 (2017): 50–70.

Young, Jason R. *Rituals of Resistance: African Atlantic Religion in Kongo and the Lowcountry South in the Era of Slavery*. Baton Rouge: Louisiana State University Press, 2011.

Index

Note: page numbers followed by *f* refer to figures.

Accompong, 12, 63–70, 75, 77–78, 80–81, 104, 170n42, 170n45

Accompong Town, 13, 28, 62, 68–70, 72–74, 77, 79–80, 116

Accra, 42, 44–47, 58

Act to Remedy the Evils arising from irregular Assemblies of Slaves, 1, 21, 122, 130, 133, 135, 137

Africa, 37, 44, 55–57, 161n107; Christianity in, 54, 167n83; fetish and, 181n53; Francophone, 166n75; Islam and, 50; nations and, 39–40, 50; Poppo op, 48, 165n45; religious traditions of, 4, 50, 59; West Central, 42, 54, 167n83. *See also* West Africa

Africana religions, 1–2, 19, 132, 139, 144

Africana Religious Studies, 2, 8–9, 41

Africana traditions, 2, 6

African diaspora, 4–5, 39–41, 43, 47, 49–50, 56, 65, 165n50

Africans, 1, 10, 15, 22, 33–34, 38–40, 55–56, 138; baptism and, 29, 119; belonging and, 47; in Brazil, 40; Christianity and, 41; conversion of, 23–24; Coromantee and, 45; in the diaspora, 165n50; evangelization to, 11, 158n32; enslaved, 20, 23–24, 36, 106, 158n32; enslavement of, 7; from Gold Coast, 43, 163n31; Great Awakening and, 4; Moravian Christianity and, 27, 59, 87, 106; nations and, 41, 59; Protestant exclusion of, 7; religio-national identification and, 42, 48; religio-nations of, 39, 143; sin and, 111; West Africans, 50. *See also* Maroons

Afro-Caribbeans, 25, 30; Caries and, 18, 29, 36; Moravian Christianity and, 19; Moravian missions and, 13; Obeah and, 119, 157n5

Afro-Jamaicans, 2–3, 7, 19, 102; baptismal ceremonies and, 119; Caries and, 11, 15, 18, 25, 36, 62; Moravian Church and, 27, 31, 144

Afro-Moravian community, 5, 34

Afro-Moravians/Black Moravians, 11, 23, 27, 30–32, 34, 47, 50, 53–54, 58–59, 126–28, 142, 145; African religious heritage of, 45; baptism and, 16, 176n1; blood and wounds and, 28; at Bogue plantation, 62, 104, 107; Caries and, 12, 27, 30–31, 33, 35–36, 61, 103, 115; missionaries and, 13, 107, 118, 120, 126, 144; Oldendorp and, 39; Rauch and, 102, 106; sin and, 115

Aja (Ewe), 46–50, 164n38, 165n44

Akan, 43, 157n11; blood oaths, 28; language, 45, 53; political culture, 69; traditions, 30

Akkim language, 112, 114

Akripon language, 112, 114

Akwamu, 42, 45–46, 58, 164n38, 167n98

Americas, 163n29; Africans in, 58–59; Bambara in, 52; Christianity in, 55; Cormantee and, 45; Maroon towns in, 74; Moravians' reputation in, 24; Nago/Yoruba and, 49–50; nations and, 40

Amina, 163n31; language, 112, 114

Amos, 92–93, 144–45

Anglican Church, 23, 25, 131–32; ministers, 20, 25
Anomabo, 43–44, 162n17
archives, 3, 5, 6, 8–9, 12–13, 35, 64, 81, 84, 153n4, 155n24; colonial, 2, 6, 11, 19, 41, 65, 143–44; dissimulation in, 62, 100, 143; legal, 124, 132, 135, 144; missionary, 2–3, 5–6, 12, 16, 19, 41, 69, 143; Moravian, 3, 8, 10, 16, 69, 85, 89, 96, 98, 110, 156n34; patriarchal, 143; of slavery, 1, 19, 85; Thistlewood's, 95; visceral, 9, 153n4
archival documents, 6, 20, 62, 103, 108, 124, 143, 156n38, 181n60
archival knowledge, 97, 100, 144
archival producer, 2, 9, 62, 88, 143–44
archival silence, 84, 91
Asante, 58; kingdom, 44, 162n16
assembling, 13, 122–24, 130, 133, 137–38
Atlantic World, 57; Afro-Christian communities in, 41; Anglophone, 44; Anomabo in, 162n17; anti-Moravian pamphlets in, 24; belonging in, 39, 45; British, 1, 13, 81, 121, 132; Luso-Atlantic world, 51; Protestantism in, 4; rebellion and religion in, 136–37, 139; sacred communities in, 37, 59, 143; slave rebellions in, 133 (*see also* Tacky's Revolt)
authority, 16, 66; of Black men, 175n56; Black women's parental, 173n19; colonial, 106–7, 115–16, 123; of enslavers, 129; imperial, 131; institutional, 115; of Maroon leaders, 67, 71; of Maroons, 72; over meaning of death, 33; of missionaries, 93; of Obeah, 63, 66; political, 123, 130; religion and, 3, 7; sacred, 3, 68, 72, 131; of treaties, 68, 72, 118; women and, 67

backsliding, 62, 102, 110–11
Bambara, 50, 52–53, 166n61, 166n75, 166n77
baptism, 26, 28–32, 38, 44, 50, 55, 58, 74*f*, 79, 89, 107–8, 119, 175n56; Afro-Moravians and, 16; Catholic, 54; Christian, 8, 29–30, 99; communal, 37; Moravian, 15, 18, 45, 59, 115, 136, 176n13; proper preparations for, 61; Quambo, 57; Rauch and, 101–4, 106, 109, 116–17, 136, 176n1; women and, 99; Zinzendorf and, 105, 177n14
baptismal registers, 10, 38–39, 44
baptismal rites, 19, 36, 104

Barbados, 15, 20, 122; conspiracy, 181n63; lawmakers in, 137; Obeah in, 158n28; St. Lucy Parish, 26
belonging, 7, 39, 45, 47, 56
Benin, 46, 49, 164n35; Bight of, 46, 50, 57. *See also* Dahomey
Benjamin, 89–90, 98
Bethlehem (Pennsylvania), 62, 87, 109, 155n33; Mohican Christians and, 177n17; Moravian church leaders in, 12; Saint Thomas and, 177n18; Spangenberg in, 108. *See also* Moravian Archives
Bilby, Kenneth, 26, 68–69, 157n5, 158n27, 169n21, 169n25, 170n27, 170n34, 179n3
binding, 13, 21, 122–23, 137–38, 158n20
Black leadership, 19, 26, 32, 36
Black people, 34, 41, 117, 128, 137–38
blood, 16, 18, 28, 68, 75–76, 134–35, 144; Jesus Christ's, 16, 26–28, 35, 106, 111–14, 117, 124, 144; rituals, 71
blood and wounds theology, 18, 27, 31–32, 36, 115, 119, 134
blood oaths, 6, 12, 16, 18–20, 24, 26–29, 31, 32, 35, 61, 63–65, 67–69, 71, 75–79, 81, 105, 106, 111–15, 117, 119, 134, 135, 144, 154, 168, 170, 172, 180; Akan, 28, 170n27, 170n34; Maroons and, 69, 71
Bogue plantation, 11–12, 26–27, 39, 56, 62, 64, 73*f*, 74–75, 80, 89–90, 96, 114–16, 118–20, 172n72; Caries and, 15, 23, 25, 28–32, 102, 111; cemetery, 141–42; diary, 86*f*; Maroons and, 77–79; Moravians' library at, 52; Powell and, 173n25; Rauch and, 99, 101, 104, 107, 111; Tacky's Revolt and, 127–28; worship practices at, 123
Bollettino, Maria Allessandra, 135, 179n2
Brazil, 40, 49, 156n37
British West Indies, 21
Brooks, Lisa, 2, 8, 11, 142, 153n4
Brown, Vincent, 21, 33, 45, 135, 163n29, 179n2
Browne, Patrick, 73*f*, 94*f*–95*f*
Burnard, Trevor, 94, 97, 158n18
Byrd, Alexander X., 39, 56, 167n92

Camba language, 111, 114
Camilla, 83–84, 86–92, 96–101, 143, 172n1
Camp, Stephanie, 74, 171n63
Candomblé, 40, 156n37

Caribbean, the, 17, 37, 143, 156n34; African diasporic religions in, 179n3; Akwamu elites in, 58; blood oaths in, 69; evangelization in, 24; missions in, 15, 23, 105; ribbon wearing in, 159n48; slavery in, 132, 158n32

Caries, Zacharias George, 11–13, 15–16, 18–20, 22–37, 43, 45, 61, 92–93, 109, 118–20, 143–44; Accompong and, 63–65, 72, 80–81, 104; baptism and, 54, 156n3, 159n60, 160n71, 161n90, 176n3; Carmel and, 141; Coromantee and, 163n24; diaries of, 62, 64–65, 68, 87–88, 142, 157n3, 176n4; English and, 158n33; Margery and, 65, 72, 74–81; Maroons and, 65, 116; Obeah and, 2–3, 35–36; Rauch and, 62, 101–3, 107–11, 115–16, 176n1; Seidel and, 116–17; Sampson's burial and, 33–35, 142; Spangenberg and, 108–10; Titus and, 74–76, 78–79

Carmel, 11, 87, 141, 172n5, 180n21

Cennick, John, 23, 158n34

censorship, 10, 62, 87, 143–44

children, 180n16; adult, 99; baptism and, 29; Maroon, 65, 80; slavery and, 50, 98; Yoruba, 50

Christianity, 2–3, 10–11, 16, 18, 22–25, 41, 62, 115, 118–20, 122, 134; in Africa, 4, 54, 59; African religious practices and, 102; Black, 137; history of, 5; Kongo, 27, 55, 167n83; missionary, 123; Moravian, 2, 11, 13, 19, 26–27, 29, 47, 55, 75, 119, 144–45; Protestant, 7; white, 40, 91

churches, 131–32; Protestant, 7, 24; Reformed, 25

Coal, 28, 54–56, 59, 114

Coastal Coalition, 43–44, 163n21

colonial authorities, 67, 115; British, 71, 80; Rauch and, 103, 106–7; religion and, 13, 133; Tacky's Revolt and, 21, 123

colonial government, 135, 177n19; Jamaican, 131; Maroons and, 65–67, 69–71, 76, 81, 116; Rauch and, 13, 104, 116, 118

colonial law, 129; African diasporic religions and, 132–33; Rauch and, 13, 102–3, 118–20

colonial lawbooks, 6, 135

colonial lawmakers, 1, 6, 13, 134–35, 137; Maroons and, 71; Moravians and, 120

colonial militia, 121, 124, 127

colonialism, 4, 8, 19, 22; missions and, 104; religion and, 2, 154n16; settler, 104, 122; slavery and, 122

community, 10, 31–33, 36, 43, 110, 115, 119; Afro-Caribbean, 10; Afro-Moravian, 5, 34; bonds, 16, 63, 69; Christian, 22; enslaved, 33, 91, 93; linguistic, 56; local, 141; Maroon, 67, 116; microhistories, 53; Mohican Christian, 105; Moravian, 39, 55, 104, 158n32, 177nn17–18; Obeah and, 21; plural, 46; religio-national, 77; religio-political, 28, 139; sacred, 32, 36, 55, 80, 98

Congo, 30, 54, 59, 111, 114–15

congregating, 13, 122–23, 130, 137–38

Connecticut, 116

conversion, 8, 18, 47, 55, 59, 61; baptismal rites and, 29–30; Rauch and, 102–3, 106; of slaves, 23, 178n43; Zinzendorf and, 105, 177n4

Coromantee, 30, 38, 43–46, 53–54, 57, 66, 71, 163n24; nation, 45

crime, 5, 62, 84, 99–100, 145; Black religion as, 138; Obeah as, 1, 22, 137, 144, 158n28; religion and, 6, 122; witchcraft as, 21, 134

criminalization, 6, 9; of Obeah, 1–3, 11, 13, 18, 22, 100, 122, 144–45, 179n3

Critical Archival Studies, 2, 153n4

critical fabulation, 88, 100, 129, 143

Crosson, J. Brent, 22

Cuffy, 17–18, 27–28, 31–32, 34, 141, 145

culture, 46, 50; Akan, 158n20; Akan political, 69, 170n27, 170n34; British, 20; of dismemberment, 97–99; European, 22; of sexual dismemberment, 62, 86, 93, 102, 118; of southern Ghana, 43; visual, 55; white, 93

Currie, Richard, 69, 170n33

Cyrus (Zebedi), 31, 46–47, 114

Dahomey, 46, 49–50

Damma (aka Madlena or Marotta), 47–49, 165nn44–46

Danish West Indies, 23, 29, 34, 39, 51, 106, 117, 156n34

death rituals, 19, 32

Devil, 1, 134–35

dissimulation, 12, 62, 100, 103, 110–11, 143

Dumbarton, 43–44, 53–54, 163n20

Dunn, Richard, 179n10, 181n60

Edwards, Bryan, 21, 131

Elizabeth (Coco), 32, 83–84, 86, 88–91, 98–101, 141, 143, 145

INDEX 213

empire: Akwamu, 46; British, 71, 123, 130; Mali, 51, 166n66; Oyo, 49–50
epistemology, 19; Africana, 4–5, 18, 38, 142–43; of Obeah, 11, 102; of separation, 60
Equiano, Olaudah, 56, 57f, 167n92, 167n94
eschatology, 19; Christian, 161n108
ethnicity, 41, 52, 162n
ethnogenesis, 45
Etsi language, 43–44
Europe, 33, 47, 52; Caries in, 62, 87, 102, 116; Moravians in, 24
evangelism, 4, 25
evil spirits, 1, 134–35

fact assembly, 9, 86
faith, 105, 177n14; Catholic, 55
Fante, 42–47, 53, 59, 162n18, 163n21; language, 43–44, 47
fetish, 5, 166n68, 181n53
First Maroon War, 20, 65–67, 169n13, 169n24
Foster, William, 23–24, 27, 75, 126, 159n60. *See also* Bogue plantation
freedom, 7, 21, 117, 143; of mobility, 75, 77; religious, 179n3; spatial, 65, 80
Fromont, Cécile, 18, 27, 51, 55, 154n9, 160n64, 167nn82–83, 176n5
fugitivity, 171n63
Fuentes, Marisa, 84–85, 88, 153n4, 155n24

Ga, 45–47; language, 45, 47
Gandrup, Nicholas, 125, 127, 129
gender, 32, 62, 156n3, 158n32, 173n6, 175n54. *See also* irruptions: gendered
geographies: Black, 74; black women's, 65; rival, 74, 76–78, 171n63
German language, 12, 23, 62, 89, 111, 156n34; Caries and, 157n3, 158n33; handwritten, 3, 10; modern, 10, 110, 164n31; Oldendorp and, 160n75; Rauch and, 173n25
Germany: Bernburg, 104; eastern, 4. *See also* Herrnhut
Ghana, 43–44, 58, 162n18, 163n21
Gien language, 112, 114
Gold Coast, 43–47, 50, 53, 58, 66, 68
Gospel, 105, 128; of Luke, 136
governance: colonial, 102, 131; decentralized, 44, 163n21; Maroon, 66; postcolonial, 6

Grand Popo, 42, 46–47, 164n35, 164n38
grave dirt, 6, 134–35, 137
Great Awakening, 4, 154n12. *See also* Moravian Church
Guan language, 43–44
Guthrie, John, 67, 71

Haberecht, Gottlieb, 11, 23, 29
Handler, Jerome, 26, 157n5, 158n27, 179n3
Hartman, Saidiya, 84, 88, 95–97, 143
Herrnhut, 2, 12, 33, 62, 87, 143, 155n33, 157n3, 158n32
Heuchelei, 12, 62, 103, 110. *See also* dissimulation; hypocrisy
Hucks, Tracey, 8–9, 22, 39–40, 123, 154n14, 162n5
Hughes, Griffith, 20, 26
Hula, 46, 164n37
hypocrisy, 12, 62, 103

Ibo, 30, 38, 54, 56–57, 59, 113–15, 157n11
identity, 41, 55, 59; Christian, 40; Damma (Madlena) and, 165n44; Equiano's, 167n92; ethnic, 45, 49, 52, 162n6; Fante, 53; Mandingo, 53; religio-national, 45, 47
Igbo, 56, 160
indigenous leadership, 105–6, 109
indigenous people, 7, 63, 69, 122
Islam, 4, 41–42, 50–53, 59, 166n59
intellectual histories, 7, 9
irruptions, 2–3, 8–10, 16, 19; Africana, 3, 5, 11, 19, 22, 38–39, 69, 84, 86, 103, 135, 138, 143–45; censorship as, 144; gendered, 64–65, 72, 74, 143; reading for, 2–6, 9–10, 13, 18, 39, 80–81, 88, 122, 124, 132, 135, 138, 142, 144

Jacobs, Harriet, 90–91, 174n31
Jalunkan, 112, 114
Jamaica mission, 102, 116
Jamaican Assembly, 21, 123, 130, 135
Johnson, Paul, 123, 131

Kanga language, 111–12 114–15
Karabari language, 111, 113–15
Kassenti: language, 113–14; nation, 34
Kea, Ray A., 58, 165n44

Khan, Aisha, 7, 22, 155n22
Kimpa Vita, Dona Beatriz, 54–55
kinship, 32, 66; bonds, 10, 97–98, 119; networks, 26, 30, 36, 39, 64, 80
Klassen, Pamela, 122–23, 131
Kojo (Cudjoe), 66–68, 72, 169n22
Kongo, 27–28, 30, 34, 42, 54–55, 59, 167n83; founding of, 167n82; salt and, 161n107; South Carolina and, 167n88
Kromanti language, 66, 68
Kurrent (German Script), 3, 9–10, 94, 154n7, 156n34

labor, 65, 76; reproductive, 74
land tenure, 67, 69
language, 10, 45, 47, 53, 56, 110, 114, 133; African, 103, 111, 114–15; Gbe, 165n46; Gur, 58; of the heart, 27; Kromanti, 66, 68; Mande, 51; metalanguage, 8; of nation, 40; Portuguese, 43, 166n68; primers, 52; West African, 103, 111, 115
Latin, 94–95, 97, 123
law, 7, 76, 123–24, 130–31, 134–35, 137, 178n43; colonial, 13, 102–3, 118–20, 129, 132–33; Islamic, 52; Obeah and, 1–2; religion and, 126; rituals of, 71; slave, 6, 135; vagrancy, 21
Law, Robin, 46, 48, 165n50
lawmakers, 7, 131–35, 137, 144; British, 104, 122; Euro-Jamaican, 4; slave-owning, 6, 123, 138. *See also* colonial lawmakers
lawmaking, 4, 71, 123, 130–31, 138
literacy, 51, 117
Little Popo, 42, 46–47, 164n35, 164n38
lived religion, 13, 22, 123, 179n8
Loango language, 111, 113–14
Long, Edward, 21, 131, 136

Manatie, 34–35
Mandinga, 51, 166n62, 166n69
Mandingos, 51–52, 166n66
Margery, 12, 31–32, 64–65, 72, 74–81, 116, 143, 145, 172n76
Maroon communities, 26, 63, 65–67, 116, 171n48
Maroon raids, 66
Maroons, 12–13, 28, 62–72, 74–81, 102–4, 108, 168n5, 168n7, 170n44; 1739 Treaty, 65, 68–72, 77, 170n33, 170n36; baptism and, 176n1; Leeward, 66–67, 69, 168n7; Moravians and, 115–16, 120–21; Obeah and, 20, 182n68; polygyny and, 172n76; Windward, 66–67, 74, 77, 168n7, 169nn22–23. *See also* Accompong; First Maroon War
Maroon sovereignty, 12, 64, 69–72, 76, 78, 80
Maroon towns, 71, 73f, 74, 77–79, 150, 169n23
marronage, 74, 171n63
Mathew, 25, 126–28
Matory, J. Lorand, 39–40, 156n37
Mesopotamia plantation, 25, 61, 94f–95f, 99, 115, 121, 124, 126, 128; archives at, 181n60; baptism at, 136; missionaries at, 135–36, 179n10
metaphor, 8, 142, 155n24, 172n4
Middle Passage, 4, 37, 40, 55–56, 60
missions: Caribbean, 105; Christian, 19; colonialism and, 104; global, 87, 154n11; Moravian, 32, 102, 105–6, 154n11, 177n13
missionaries, 2, 6, 8, 10–13, 33, 38, 41, 61–62, 97, 165n53, 180n16; Camilla and, 88–89, 91; Dumbarton and, 163n20; Elizabeth and, 88–91; European Christian, 55; on marriage, 175n55; Moravian, 3–4, 7–8, 22–25, 39, 79–80, 96, 99–105, 107–11, 115–21, 123–29, 135–36, 141–44, 158n32, 173n11, 177n19; Protestant, 30; sexual violence and, 86–87, 93, 96; Titus and, 75; white, 10, 32, 93, 106; Yoruba and, 49
Mohicans, 177n17; baptism of, 176n13; missions and, 102, 104; Rauch and, 103–4, 104–6, 109
Mokko language, 111, 113–14
Morgan, Jennifer, 173n6, 173n19
Moravian archives, 3, 8, 10, 85, 89, 96, 98, 110, 155–56nn33–34; Caries's diaries and, 157n3; German script and, 154n7
Moravian Church, 4, 10, 18, 30, 64; Renewed, 154n10; synods, 176–77n13
Moravian communities, 33, 39, 55, 104, 177nn17–18. *See also* Afro-Moravian community

Moravians, 4, 24–26, 29, 87, 92, 99, 104–7, 117, 120, 124–26, 130, 136, 154n10; blood and wounds theology of, 27, 134; in Danish West Indies, 39; enslaved, 80, 141; evangelism of, 4, 25; library of, 51; Maroons and, 65, 116; at Mesopotamia plantation, 61, 115; Mohicans and, 176–77n13; as Obeah men, 12, 101; political position of, 109; sexual assault and, 84; sexual morality and, 99, 175n54, 175n56. *See also* Afro-Moravians/Black Moravians

Nago (Naga/ Lucumí), 46, 49–50, 53, 57, 165n50, 165n53. *See also* Yoruba
Nananom Mpow, 43–45, 53–54, 59
Nanny, 20, 65–67, 74, 169nn16–17, 169n23
Nanny Town, 66, 169n15
narrative fields, 2, 8–9, 11–12, 18–19, 135, 143
nation(s), 5, 38–42, 45–46, 56–57, 59–60, 143, 167n94; African, 11, 40, 44, 50, 53, 59, 66, 111, 162n6; Africana, 4, 39–41, 53; conversion of, 105, 177n14; indigenous, 170n36, 170n42; poor black, 23. *See also* religio-nations
Native American and Indigenous studies (NAIS), 2, 8, 155n26
Native Americans, 87, 106
New Eden, 142
New York, 102, 104, 106, 116, 137, 182n64
Niger River, 51, 56

oaths, 21, 63, 68, 131; in Akan culture, 158n20; Obeah, 64, 131. *See also* blood oaths
Obeah men, 12–13, 20–21, 26, 30, 62–63, 66; Moravian missionaries as, 93, 101–2, 104, 115, 119, 124
Obeah women, 20–21, 30, 63, 66. *See also* Nanny
Oldendorp, Christian G. A., 29–30, 34, 39, 51, 111–12, 114–15, 160n75, 166n69; Jankombum and, 163–64n31
oral histories, 164n38, 169n25; Maroon, 64, 68–69, 168n7, 169nn21–22; sacred, 44
Oroonoko: or, The Royal Slave (Behn), 44
overseers, 20, 75, 80, 85, 89, 94, 95f, 104, 132; abuse of, 120; white, 72, 93, 117–19, 121
Oyo, 49–50

Papaa, 38; language, 111, 113–15
Paton, Diana, 20–21, 31, 134, 157n6, 157nn10–11, 158n25, 179n3
Peace Cave (Ambush Cave), 68–69, 169n24
Pennsylvania, 101, 108–9. *See also* Bethlehem
Peucker, Paul, 159n48, 175n54
plantations, 65, 76, 121, 127, 132, 133. *See also* Bogue plantation; Mesopotamia plantation; slavery
policing, 3–4, 13, 102–3, 120; of boundaries of religion, 6, 62, 115, 119; of enslaved population, 122; of Maroon movements, 78; within Moravian congregation, 100; Obeah and, 179n3
Political Theology, 6, 122
politics, 19, 43, 56, 163n29; African, 49; of authenticity, 16; coastal, 44; colonial, 131; Gold Coast, 68; Jamaican, 64, 131; Maroon, 71, 80; of plantations, 90; religion and, 6, 123; the sacred and, 122
polyandry, 78, 172n73
polygyny, 78, 117, 172n73, 172n76
Popo, 42, 46–50, 114, 164n35
Portuguese, 46, 54. *See also* language: Portuguese
Powell, Joseph, 89–90, 99, 100, 127–29, 173n25
prayer, 75–76, 87, 164n31; meetings, 88
prophecy, 35–36
prophetic practice, 3, 19, 35
Protestant churches, 7, 24
Protestantism, 4, 7; Black, 4, 154n13
Protestant Supremacy, 7, 132
Protten, Christian, 47, 48f, 165n41

Quakers, 125, 137
Quambo nation, 37–38

race, 7; religion and, 5, 22, 39–41, 155n20, 155n22, 162n9
racism, 35; epistemic, 9
rape, 12, 83, 87–90, 93–98, 175n55; child, 84, 100
Rauch, Anna, 12, 32, 61–62, 87, 91, 93, 106–8, 129, 136, 173n13; baptizing women and, 156n3, 160n71, 176n3; Camilla and, 83–84, 88–89, 96, 98

Rauch, Christian Heinrich, 11–13, 61–62, 87–89, 92–93, 97, 99, 101, 104, 106, 117–21, 129, 136, 177n18; burial site of, 141; Caries and, 62, 101–3, 107–11, 115–16, 142, 176n1; diaries of, 62, 83–84, 100, 172n1, 173n25, 176n4; Spangenberg and, 178n43

re/formations, 4–5, 13, 37, 42, 45, 55–56, 59, 108

religio-nation(s), 3, 26, 36, 41–46, 53–54, 57, 63, 80, 176n3; Africana, 5–6, 10, 59; Afro-Moravians and, 11; formation, 39, 59–60, 66; Moravian, 19, 31; re/formation, 42, 56

religio-racial, 4, 39, 41, 162n12

religious practices, 3, 36, 45–46, 50, 123, 133; Africana/African, 5–6, 102; African diasporic, 134; of southern Ghana, 43

religious traditions, 30; African, 4–6, 55, 59, 76, 105, 119; Africana, 68, 76, 122, 134; anticolonial, 6; European, 6, 105; West African, 27, 50

re/membrance, 4, 13, 97–100, 143; reading for, 86

Rucker, Walter, 28, 32, 45, 68, 158n20, 162n15

St. Elizabeth Parish, 11, 23–24, 121, 127–28
St. Jago de la Vega (Spanish Town), 123, 130
St. Mary Parish, 121, 181n51
Saint Thomas, 15, 23, 51; Moravian church in, 47, 159n38; Moravian missionaries in, 99, 117, 175n56, 177n19; Oldendorp and, 111; Rauch and, 106–7, 116, 177n18; ribbons and, 159n48

Sampson, 33–34, 142
Schiebinger, Londa, 5
Schulz, Charles, 12, 61–62, 87, 108–9
Schulz, Maria, 12, 61, 109, 173n13
science, 1, 119, 182n68
Sebro, Louise, 165n44, 165n46
Seidel, Nathanael, 102, 116–20
Senegambia, 50–52, 54, 59, 166n59, 166n62
Sensbach, Jon, 156n34, 158n32, 159n38, 165n41, 177n19
sex, 86, 94, 97, 175n54; nonprocreative, 98
sexual dismemberment, 97–98, 100; culture of, 62, 86, 93, 102, 118
sexual ethics, 97–99
sexual violence, 5, 12–13, 62, 83–86, 91, 93–94; erasure of, 12, 96, 100, 143; threat of, 174n31

Shallecross, Thomas, 11, 23–24, 156n38
Sharper, 46, 49–50
Shekomeko (New York), 102–7, 109, 116, 120, 177n17
Sherry, 43–45, 54
Shumway, Rebecca, 43, 163n21
silence(s), 3, 84–87, 91, 96, 100, 153n4, 155n25, 172n4; of missionaries, 12, 93
Simeon, 107, 114, 135–36
sin (*Sünde*), 8, 13, 27, 78, 99, 103, 109–15
Slave Codes, 132, 137
slave owners, 7; absentee, 23, 93, 126; English; 44–45, 169n21; Jamaican, 44; Protestant, 132
slavery, 2, 4–7, 22, 35, 93–95, 97–98, 126, 132–33; archives of, 1, 19, 85, 135, 144; Atlantic, 78, 84, 86, 97; Bible and, 117; Black women and, 143, 173n14, 173n19; Caribbean, 10, 99, 119; colonial, 122, 124, 129, 137–38; colonialism and, 122; gender and, 173n6; hierarchies of, 35; laws about, 132; legacies of, 3, 13; love and courtship under, 174n31; Maroons and, 63, 65; marriage and, 174n28; plantation, 55, 65, 79, 174n29; religion and, 86, 178n43; Slavs and, 52; transatlantic, 46, 50. *See also* trade: slave

Smith, Jonathan Z., 154n16, 179n4, 179n6
Sokko language, 111, 113–14
spaces of correlation, 18–19, 26, 33, 36, 55, 62, 102, 115, 119, 144, 154n9, 176n5
Spangenberg, Joseph, 33, 101, 108–10, 178n43
Spanish Town, 123, 130
spirits, 33, 161n107; ancestral, 30; evil, 1, 134–35
Stewart, Dianne, 8–9, 39–40, 154n14; on ethnicity, 162n5; on Obeah, 19, 22, 30, 123, 157n6, 157n11
Stoler, Ann, 9, 153n4, 155n24
Stono rebellion, 133, 137
Strickrodt, Silke, 46, 164n40
sugar, 107, 109; boilers, 26, 52; cultivation, 65; fields, 84, 107; harvest, 109
Sullivan, Winnifred, 123, 131
superstition, 2, 5, 20, 26, 122, 144, 181n53
surveillance, 21, 103, 110

Tacky, 135–36
Tacky's Revolt, 1, 13, 21, 65, 81, 121–24, 132–33, 135–37, 179n2; church attendance during, 128. *See also* criminalization of Obeah

Tado, 42, 46–47, 49
Tambi language, 111–12, 114
Tembu language, 112, 114
theology: Africana, 4; blood and wounds, 18, 24, 27, 31–32, 36, 115, 134; Caries's, 35; Christian, 30, 119; Moravian, 26, 42, 45, 55, 60, 105, 124; political, 6, 122; Protestant, 7, 30, 134; Zinzendorf's, 154n10
Thicknesse, Philip, 67, 169n23
Thistlewood, Thomas, 12, 20, 72, 85, 93–97, 158n18, 170n45, 175n40
Titus, 27, 31, 64, 72, 74–79, 116, 141, 170n47, 171n52
Tortorici, Zeb, 9, 153n4, 155n24
trade: European, 164n35; routes, 50; slave, 10, 56, 162n18
tradition, 2, 3, 68, 71–72
translation, 111–14, 156n35, 164n31, 165n44, 165n46
treaties, 12, 44, 64–65, 67–72, 163n21; sacred, 170n42. *See also* Maroons: 1739 treaty
Trouillot, Michel-Rolph, 9, 41, 84, 86, 144, 153n4, 155n25
Turner, Nat, 137, 182n65
Turner, Sasha, 85, 161n108

uncleanness, 111–14
uprisings, 1, 21, 58, 81, 121, 135

Vermeulen, Heather, 93, 95
Vesey, Denmark, 137, 182n65
violence, 97, 99, 118; epistemic, 6, 13, 88, 138. *See also* sexual violence

Walduck, Thomas, 20
Watteville, Johannes von, 2, 28–29
Wawu language, 113–14
weeds, 2, 8, 11, 142
Weisenfeld, Judith, 39, 41, 162n9, 162n12

Wells-Oghoghomeh, Alexis, 12, 62, 78, 85–86, 97–99, 143, 174n31. *See also* re/membrance
West Africa, 34, 44–47, 50–51, 58, 156n37, 181n60; Gold Coast of, 66; Gold Coast politics in, 68; Yoruba speakers in, 49, 165n50
West Indies. *See* British West Indies; Danish West Indies
Westmoreland Parish, 20, 93, 99, 115, 121, 124, 126, 128
White (Christian) Supremacy, 7, 22, 132
white people, 24–25, 92, 106, 121, 125, 144, 176n1
whiteness, 7, 40
Whydah, 49–50, 164n38
Wisecup, Kelly, 21
witchcraft, 2, 5, 7, 18, 20, 21, 26, 51, 134–35; language of, 122; pen-and-ink, 71
women, 9, 39, 72, 83, 99; authority of, 67; baptism of, 32, 75, 101–2, 156n3, 160n71, 176n3; Black, 10, 25–26, 29, 32, 38, 41, 65, 102–3, 119, 127, 143, 173n14, 173n19; enslaved, 13, 26–27, 29, 53, 60, 62, 84, 86–88, 90, 93–100, 124, 127–29, 131–32, 143, 162n16, 163n29, 172nn4–5; Maroon, 65, 74, 170–71n48, 172n76; missionaries, 107; Moravian, 25; role of, 80; Yoruba, 50. *See also* Obeah women
worship, 15, 123–24, 137; Christian, 133; criminal practices of, 6; meetings, 13, 75, 87, 92–93, 99–100, 102, 124, 126, 138; Moravian practices of, 26, 32, 55, 76, 117, 158n32, 173n11; services, 25–26, 28, 32, 77, 93, 173n11
wounds, 18, 26–27, 35, 124. *See also* blood and wounds theology

Yoruba, 40, 42, 46, 49–50, 53, 165n50

Zinzendorf, Ludwig von, 25, 28–29, 105–6, 117, 154n10, 176–77nn13–14

www.ingramcontent.com/pod-product-compliance
Lightning Source LLC
Chambersburg PA
CBHW021855230426
43671CB00006B/393